DOCTOR UNTOUCHABLE

J. SAMAN

Cover Design: Lori Jackson

Photographer: Rafa Catala

Editing: My Brother's Editor

Editing: Emily Lawrence

❀ Created with Vellum

1

I knew when this day started that it was going to be a fucking shit show. Nothing good ever starts with a wake-up call from your mother asking you to meet her for lunch. Especially when you already know the reason for the lunch and have been dreading it, well, practically since the day you were born.

Then there's this call...

"All I'm asking is if you think she'll say yes?"

I clench my jaw and run a hand through my hair, my other gripping the steering wheel so tight the leather creaks. "Luca, how should I know?"

"Because you somehow know Raven better than anyone. You're like secret girlfriends. She tells you shit. Confides in you."

I'd smirk at that if my insides weren't being poked at with something hot and sharp. Honestly, I hope Luca proposes. I hope Raven says yes. I hope they live happily ever after and suck all the attention and limelight for themselves. Then maybe for once in my life I can stop having that pesky four-letter word thrown at me with the hope it'll finally stick to me.

Love.

The one thing everyone from my family to the press, to the

endless stream of money-hungry women lining up at the mention of my name, try to shove down my throat. But the worst part, the part that has me mashing my molars is what's coming for me in the absence of love.

"I think she'll think it's too soon. You've only been back together a couple of months."

He puffs out a breath. "Rina and Brecken just got married. Oliver popped the question to Amelia for real on New Year's. Carter just did the same to Grace on fucking Valentine's Day."

"Feeling left out when the rest of your siblings are getting married and engaged? Don't worry, Landon's still only dating Elle," I quip.

"I just want Raven as mine. Truly mine. Wearing my ring and my last name. Forever."

"She's not going anywhere, brother."

"I know that. That's not why I want to seal the deal. I love her, Kap. This is what you do when you love someone."

I grunt, so beyond not in the mood for this. I grip the wheel tighter, which I didn't even realize was possible. Soon my knuckles will split. "I'm ignoring you."

"You shouldn't. It's time, old man."

"I have enough on my plate without trying to deal with yet another gold digger or entitled fledgling celebrity after more fame and headlines or a socialite looking to sit around in her designer digs and do lunch while we spend decades ignoring each other."

"There's that side of it. Or. You know. You could find actual love."

I blow out a silent breath, my eyes closing as I reach a traffic light. I knew this day was coming too. It's what happens when all of your younger siblings are happily hitched up to wonderful people and your mother is obsessed with love, marriage, and grandchildren.

But they're not me. Their path was always easier.

"Not interested," I tell him, opening my eyes again and shoving any useless frustration at this conversation down as the light turns green and I start to drive again. "How about you focus on Raven and leave me to handle my life. Raven is young. Give her time before you put a ring on it."

"I know. Maybe for her birth—"

"What the fuck?" I practically yell, coming to a screeching halt as a barrage of white that is absolutely not the snow currently falling practically lands right on the hood of my car with a thud.

"Kap? Kap, you okay?!"

"Luca, I gotta go." I disconnect the call, throw the car into park, and then get out right into the middle of traffic. The white starts to move, sliding across the hood of my SUV until it's on the opposite side of me. I slam my door shut and repeat myself. "What the fuck?"

"Oh my God!" the woman shrieks. "You stopped! Thank God you stopped."

I blink at least a thousand times, trying to make sense of the mass of tulle and silk and lace and unruly dark hair before me. "You flew onto my car. Didn't exactly give me a choice. What was I supposed to do, run you over?"

She's standing in the street, hugging the side of the hood so she doesn't get hit by passing cars, but her wild, frantic gaze is over my shoulder, anxiously watching whatever is there. Reflexively I turn to look, cars honking and shooting around me, spraying slush and ice onto my slacks, and find a cluster of people dressed in tuxedos and gowns standing at the top of the church steps, glaring down at us as if they're about to give chase.

"They followed me? I can't believe they followed me out!"

I flip back around to find the woman opening the passenger side door of my car and jumping in, pulling her dress in along with her before slamming the door shut. "What the fuck?!" This time I bellow it at the top of my lungs. "What are you doing getting in my car?"

Opening my door, I nearly get sideswiped by a passing taxi, the driver yelling and cursing at me. Yanking my door shut, I throw on my hazards, then turn to the marshmallow that's taking up half the front of my car.

"Get out!"

"No! I can't. You have to drive. Please. I'll pay you. Just drive before they come after me." Large, slightly watery, heavily made-up brown eyes plead with me, her hands directed toward me in supplication.

My head whips back around, and sure enough, the guy, who I can only assume is the groom, is shooting down the stairs, his fists balled up, an incensed scowl perched on his face. A couple of women follow him, staring straight at me as if I'm the asshole, and I turn back to the bride in my car, just as miffed as the dude she ran out on.

"Seriously," she cries. "You have to go now. If he gets to me, I won't be responsible for what happens next. The blood of many could be on your hands."

I level her with my no-bullshit glare. The one that makes sane women cower. Not this one. She simply throws her hands up in the air, unnerved and at the end of her rope.

"Please, please, please drive us out of here. Clearly, I'm desperate. Who throws themselves into oncoming traffic to escape their wedding if they're not?"

"Are you in some kind of danger or just crazy?"

A humorless laugh. "I'm possibly crazy, but not in the psychopathic, I need locking up kind of way. And I guess if you consider being chased after by my mother, my maid of honor who is also my cousin, and my lying, cheating user of a now ex-fiancé who has been fucking said cousin being in danger, then yes, I'm in danger. So now that we've cleared up my morning from hell, can you drive, or do I have to hurl myself on another moving vehicle?"

I scrutinize her for a second. What I can see of her, that is. Round face. Those big brown eyes as dark as the piles of hair pinned up on her head guilelessly imploring me in a desperate, slightly unhinged way. Glossy, pink, pillowy lips. Curves for days. Large breasts with an ample amount of cleavage spilling over the top of the stiff bust of her dress. Skin the color of the falling snow. Pretty.

For a runaway bride with smeared makeup and more layers than anyone should be wearing.

The groom is now edging toward the street, trying to find a safe path toward us among the Boston North End traffic. He's shouting something I can only guess at along with a tall, willowy older-ish— she's had more work done on her face than the Ted Williams tunnel here in Boston—woman beside him.

"Please," she says again, this time as a strained whisper. "I can't face any of them right now."

"Screw it."

I throw my Range Rover into drive and skid on the slushy road as I start to peel out, back into traffic.

Curves for Days sags back into her seat. "Thank you. Thank you so much." The relief in her voice is palpable. "I don't even care if you're a psycho who is going to take me back to his underground basement and make clothes out of my skin."

"Basements, by definition, are underground, and I think flying into a stranger's car makes you the psycho here. Not me."

"It's been a morning, in case you missed that. I think I should be afforded a modicum of slack."

She rights herself, ripping a sparkly clip and attached veil from her hair, followed by pin after pin. They fall onto her lap and a wry, incredulous grin hits my lips. I just picked up a runaway bride who threw herself on top of my car to escape her fiancé and her mother, and now I'm driving her... "Where are you headed?"

"Not to Scotland, that's for sure."

Huh? Whatever. "Fine then. I'm dropping you off on the next corner."

She shakes her head. Her long, long silky hair tumbles all around her as her fingers massage her scalp. She moans, throwing her head back and closing her eyes in ecstasy. And hell in a handbasket, my cock twitches in my pants.

"Wow, that might be better than any sex I ever had with Tod. It's amazing how good that feels."

I throw her an impatient scowl, trying not to think about the sound of her moan or how good whatever she just did feels to her.

"Sorry. I'm staying at The Newbury. You can drop me off there if it's not too much trouble or anywhere somewhat close where I can walk since I don't have my purse or my phone or even a damn coat." She lets out a cackle. "I just ran out on my wedding. Did you see my mother?" She points past me with something close to a dumbstruck, self-satisfied smile on her lips and an incredulous sparkle in her eyes. "She was furious. She didn't even care when I told her I over-heard Jackass McJackass and perfect McBackstabbing Bitch Face fighting about their love." She frowns now, her face falling toward her hands.

"Did you love him?" I don't know why I'm bothering to ask questions if for no other reason than I'm curious. And oddly, I want her to keep talking. Her voice... it's sweet and smooth and rich and warm—like caramel on a sundae.

She shrugs, her gaze going to the window, staring out at the passing landscape. "I thought I did. Or maybe more like I told myself I did?" She shrugs again. "I don't know. One of my stepfathers, Mitchell, told me love is for pansy asses and suckers, and my mother for once agreed with him."

Can't argue that.

"But I chose not to listen," she continues. "Always optimistic, glass half-full, blind to what's actually in front of me, Bianca. That's me. Oddly I'm more furious and hurt than heartbroken. But maybe that comes later? What are the stages of grief again?"

"Denial, anger, bargaining, depression, and acceptance."

Her gaze slingshots over to mine. "Wow. You just pulled that right off the top of your head. Are you a shrink? Because likely, I could use one of you right now. Or maybe a vat of vodka and fried food I could pretend is a shrink. Alcohol and carbs are medicinal, right?"

"No. I'm a different type of doctor."

"Hence the nice ride. One of my other stepfathers, Duke—he's the one who's currently married to my mother—has a car like this though his smells more like the ranch and less like sexy man cologne."

"Huh?"

She ignores me as she continues to orate and fidget in her seat. "Incidentally, thank you for stopping and not running me over. I figured it was a fifty-fifty chance I could die when I flew at your car but was willing to risk it given the alternative. I hope I didn't dent your hood."

"You didn't."

"Well. Thank you. Again." Her fingers toy nervously with her dress.

"You're welcome. You can relax. I'm not a psycho. I'll drive you to the hotel because as luck would have it, that's where I'm headed too."

"No way."

I nod in concession. "Way."

She smiles a crooked, shaky smile and something about that sparks something in me. A familiarity or a memory I can't place.

"It's like fate knew I was gonna need to run out on an asshole today or something."

I crack a hint of a smirk as I change lanes. "Or something. He cheated? That's why you ran?"

"Yep. The entire time he and I were together apparently, which was about two years. I had no clue. None. I don't know if that makes them exceptionally brilliant at hiding it or me insanely stupid for missing it."

I glance quickly in her direction before turning back to the slippery roads. "Them good at hiding it. You don't strike me as the stupid type."

"I launched myself into traffic and am now in a stranger's car after running out on my wedding," she deadpans.

Touché.

"Besides, it was two years. I mean, he and I were *living* together for the last six months I was finishing up grad school and yet somehow, I still missed it. I realize I was busy, but come on. That's just pathetic. I wish I could go back in time and smack myself upside the head with a healthy dose of sense."

I have nothing to say to that, but luckily I don't have to as she continues on without missing a beat.

"I thought he loved me. He gave me this whole dog and pony show about how he loved me all through college but was always too nervous to make a move or risk our friendship, which is why it took him until fucking graduate school to make a move. I was gullible, I guess. Hopeful. I didn't have a lot of guys pounding down my door and certainly not ones who looked like Tod. I never imagined when he proposed six months ago that he was actually in love with my cousin. Or that the only reason he did propose was because he has to marry me."

My eyebrows knit into a V, and I briefly catch her eye. "Why does he have to marry you if he's in love with her?"

She shifts, staring down at the white of her lap. "His last name is MacMillin as in MacMillin Investments. Only as it turns out, his father isn't much of an investor. His parents also have expensive vices. His dad's a gambler and his mom's a shopper. I don't know the details. I just heard him tell Ava, that's my cousin, that his family money is gone and the only way to save the company is to marry me." Another loud cackle, her hands flying all about, and I realize this woman is incapable of sitting still for a minute. "He genuinely thought that by marrying me, I'd fix his family's wealth. Fool clearly did not read the prenup my stepfathers made him sign."

"Stepfathers?"

"It's complicated." She hiccups out a sob, her moods swinging faster than a newborn's, and I glance over at her as I try not to kill us on the congested streets. "I should have known he never actually loved me. The signs were there all along." She shifts and then I hear a ripping noise as she tears apart her dress.

"What are you doing?"

"Removing some of this nonsense. I can't breathe." She starts yanking at the back of her dress and then tugs at the bustline, more of her full tits spilling out, and *Jesus*. If she doesn't stop doing that, I'll crash my car for sure from all the blood flow in my body rapidly shooting to my dick.

"Can you not do that?" I practically groan when she bounces in her seat and her tits do the same.

"There. Better." She sucks in a deep breath. "Do you have any clue how tight my mother cinched my corset? 'It'll make you look skinny, Bianca,'" she mocks, who I assume to be her mother. "'Come on and suck in. You couldn't lose weight for your own wedding?' Ugh. I didn't even want this dress. I wanted something sleeker. Something that accentuated my curves, not hid them. She's the one who made me look like Cinder-fucking-ella to hide my hips and thighs because she thinks the world has to be a size two or they're fat."

She starts to cry, and dear God, what have I gotten myself into?

"I'm such a fool. They turned me into such a fool. I must look so insane to you right now, but I'm not. I simply trusted the wrong people. I know I shouldn't be babbling on like this, and I'm positive you're likely annoyed with me, but I can't help it right now."

Shit. A strange woman in a wedding dress is having a breakdown in my car and I have no clue what to do other than drive and keep my mouth shut. But as insane—yes, that word again—as it seems, the idea of her crying like this, being this sad over a loser guy like that, hits me strangely. Almost... protectively? No. Maybe. I don't know. In a way that makes me want to right all her wrongs, which makes zero fucking sense given the situation.

She lets out a wet, mirthless laugh, her gaze casting over to me. "We were going to Scotland for our honeymoon." Her hands fly up in the air again, her voice rising with them. "Scotland! Can you believe it? Scotland in fucking February."

"I'm not following," I admit.

"You're a hot, sexy guy with money. In my experience, guys who look like you and drive cars like this only have sex with model-hot women. I bet you like looking at them naked any chance you get, right?"

I open my mouth to say something only to close it immediately. I can't decide what I'm supposed to focus on there. The fact that she thinks I'm hot and sexy or the way she just nailed my dating life down to a cliché. She's tall and young, but other than that, there is nothing about Curves for Days that even remotely resembles the women I typically date or, more aptly, fuck—not that I've been doing any of that recently.

Despite her observation, I have a very valid reason for that.

"Um..." I try again, still incapable of an adequate response because I'm not about to get into my personal life with this woman even if in the ten minutes she's been in my car, she's somehow managed the impossible. She intrigues me. If for no other reason than she has a nice rack and an interesting story.

Thankfully her question is rhetorical, and she continues blathering on without waiting on me.

"Most couples go to the Caribbean or Hawaii for their honeymoons. They go skinny dipping, snuggle on the beach together, and fuck in random public places like the ocean. We were going to Scotland in winter. You get me now?"

"Not exactly." I glance over at her, taking her in for a moment now that we're stopped at another light by The Commons. She's a mess. Her wild mane of hair is all over the place. Her face painted in dripping black makeup. Her huge dress is ripped and covers most of her and the front seat. I still don't know what to make of her while she spills her life story to me as if I'm Dr. fucking Phil and give a shit.

"Sweaters and parkas and heavy coats," she tells me, staring straight into my eyes as if the answer should be obvious. "He didn't want to see me in a bathing suit because he's disgusted by the way I look. I'm not a size two or a four or even a six or eight. I don't look like my perfect cousin or my perfect mother. He said something to her about it today. 'You think I like having to fuck her? It's all I can do to get hard. I close my eyes and picture you.' That's what he told my cousin." Her face falls to her hands once more, and she sobs into them. "He was always commenting on what I was eating. What I was wearing. How often I was exercising. He was going to marry me, and I disgust him."

She shakes her head, her hair flying, and I catch a hint of vanilla and brown sugar, sweet and richly warm, enticing like a cookie straight out of the oven. Falling back against the seat, she wipes at her face, all the while, I'm gripping the steering wheel again, enraged. I don't even know this chick, but what kind of man says things like that about a woman? Uses a woman like that and to such an extreme? It's taking everything inside me not to turn this car around, find that small-dicked asshole and bludgeon him to death with one of the golf clubs I have sitting in my trunk.

"If I were a stronger woman, I would have done more than chuck my engagement ring at him and dump the bottle of water I was holding on his head and run. I should have kicked his ass and then plotted his death. Hers too, for that matter. There were so many signs that I ignored over and over again," she effuses, oblivious to my fury. "My mother pushed me on him. 'He has a good last name. Family money. He's interested in you. Marry him, Bianca,'" she mocks again, gesticulating all over the place as she builds steam. "Now I'm in Boston and not Texas or California or Colorado and it's like... shit. What am I going to do now? We moved here last week so he could head up the Boston branch of his father's failing company. We don't even have an apartment yet, which now I see as a blessing. We're staying in the hotel." She snorts. "On me, of course. He had me book the room, and it's on my credit card. God, I'm so stupid. So blind and stupid."

"To me, it sounds like you dodged a bullet. You can do anything now, right? No apartment. Doesn't sound like you have a job here either. You obviously have money since that's what he was after. You're free. He's the one who's fucked. You're not marrying the loser. You should be out celebrating."

She doesn't say anything and that just pisses me off. I pull over into an open parking spot on the side of the road, throw the car in park, and turn to her. I give her a big once-over. I still can't see much. She's not small, I get that. But fuck all to hell if her curves for days aren't sexy. She edges back toward the door, because yeah, we don't know each other.

And I'm visibly angry.

And I have zero business doing anything that I'm doing right now.

She blinks at me, those milk-chocolate doe eyes wide as tears drip from them.

"You are beautiful, and he is a loser. You hear me? Any man who treats a woman like that is a fucking loser. A waste of space and life. And your mother and that asshole should shut their mouths about your body. Nothing hot or sexy about bone-thin, sweetheart. Nothing."

She tilts her head, studying me for a moment, her eyebrows knitting together and crap. Here we go. She's two seconds from recognizing me, and I'm not in the mood. I have enough of my own madness to deal with. My own family shit.

The last thing I should be doing right now is getting involved in her mess.

Without another word, I throw the car back into drive and head toward the damn hotel. I don't even know why I said all that to her other than I can't stand seeing a woman cry. Or hurt. A personal flaw I've been working on overcoming over the years. That's all that was.

But truly, she should know she's better off without him.

I pull up in front of the hotel and immediately the valet comes to open her door, icy wind and snow spilling inside and she shudders. But those big brown eyes are back on mine, a soft, sweet smile too, and something foreign inside of me shifts a little with it.

"Thank you again for rescuing me," she says tenderly. "I think you're right. I've been looking at this all wrong. I dodged a bullet today. And if I decide to stay in Boston, maybe fate will step back in, and I'll see you somewhere again. Then I can buy you a drink to thank you properly."

With that, she launches herself across the console, drops a kiss on my cheek, and then flees my car, racing into the hotel, a flutter of white trailing her.

I stare after her, a bemused smile curling up my lips as my fingers find the slightly wet, sticky spot on my cheek she just kissed. A chuckle hits the air and I shake my head. I step out of the car, handing the valet my keys and accepting the ticket in exchange.

That was the strangest half hour of my life. As I head toward the entrance of the hotel, the same one she just fled into, I can't decide if I'd mind running into her again or not. And if I did, would I let her buy me that drink?

2

I've done walks of shame. Sneaking out of frat houses or dorm rooms in the wee hours of the morning. Still dressed in my same skimpy dress and fuck-me heels. This has nothing on that. This is me sweeping into a posh hotel in the middle of Boston looking like a fabulous cocktail between a drag queen and a zombie bride. It's hot stuff. Let me tell you.

And the horrified looks from other patrons and staff are telling me I'm far more zombie than queen.

All I want right now is to go up to my room. But I don't have a key card on me. Nor do I have an ID or money or anything. I mean, I was getting married today. No purse required for that event. Then I had to listen to Tod my name is fucking Tod McDicklicker tell my cousin—my COUSIN!—that he loves her and he's so sorry, but he has to marry me for my money.

Yep. Oh, and I'm fat. He said that too.

So did she. So did my mother, in not as cruel of words as they used while she lamented squeezing me into a dress she insisted on ordering two sizes too small. A dress I never picked out or even tried on until this morning, mind you. They might as well have taken a baseball bat to my self-esteem and bashed its brains in.

I never had a problem with my curves until this morning. Fuckers.

I race toward the ladies' room off the lobby, needing to clean up before I beg for a new key card to my room. My room. All of Tod's things are still in his suitcases, and I'll ensure they end up with the bellhop so he's able to retrieve them. Because he will not step foot in that suite again. Ha! I guess he's stuck with my broke cousin now. She graduated college with a degree in sociology last May and has been working at Starbucks since. Her mom has zero money.

My mother was Miss Mississippi and earned herself a scholarship to college. She caught the eye of my Heisman Trophy–winning, football-playing father, and subsequently married up in the world since he was born to a very wealthy family—her life's aspirations.

But my broke cousin and broke Tod deserve each other.

No wonder she always wanted to spend time with us. Be my bestie.

"Ugh, I hate everyone!" I cry, running the water and catching my reflection only to wince. I pump some soap into my hands, lather it up, and then scrub vigorously at my face. Water pools in my hands and even as I wash the soap off, I can already tell that a lot of the makeup isn't coming along with it. "What did she use on me? India ink?"

The door to the bathroom opens and a second later, a woman enters. Oops. This is when privacy would have been nice. I blush the same deep crimson as the walls as I reluctantly meet the woman's eyes in the mirror, giving her a sheepish grin before dropping back to the sink.

She takes note of my dress and face dripping with water and black sludge and then sets her camel-colored ostrich Birkin down on the counter. "Here, dear." Opening her bag, she reaches in and retrieves a pack of makeup-removing wipes, handing them over to me. "These should do the trick for you."

I could cry. Again. And I do, sniffling and making horribly unladylike sounds. "Thank you. I'm sorry. I don't normally have breakdowns in a wedding dress in public restrooms."

She waves me away as she goes about washing her hands and adjusting her makeup. She's tall with a blonde bob and perfect designer clothes. But there is something else about her. Something in her eyes or her regal bone structure that I can't quite place. A familiarity possibly. No. Can't be. I've never been to Boston before. Maybe it's her hair? I think it might be a wig. That's it.

No matter, I attack my face with the wipes, and they do the trick. The makeup dissolves straight into them. "You're a lifesaver," I moan in relief. "Thank you again. I was not relishing the idea of going to the counter looking like this." I fluff up my already fluffed monstrosity of a ripped gown.

The hot hunk of man candy with the growly voice I hijacked was bad enough. A hotel full of people...

"Did you run out on him, or did he run out on you? I apologize if I'm being rude or intrusive," she adds politely but doesn't retract the question either as she dries her hand on a cloth napkin.

"Both. And I don't mind. I kind of need intrusive right about now and you're the furthest thing from rude. My fiancé cheated and I overheard him discussing his abhorrence over marrying me with my cousin, who was the woman he was cheating on me with. Then I ran out."

"Good for you." The sparkle of admiration in her eyes tells me she means it. "I imagine that was not an easy thing to do. You should be proud of yourself."

I pause, thinking about that. Hot hunk of man candy in the car said something similar, and you know what? I think both of them are right. "Honestly, it's what I should have done months ago. I wasn't... excited when he proposed. I didn't cry or squeal. Come to think of it, he didn't even propose, so much as slide a ring on my finger one day and told me we had to get married. I was fine with that. I never expected much from love or wanted anything real out of it."

"Why's that?"

"Looooong story. Bad role models. Innocence stolen. Crushing heartache blanketing my world."

"Hmm." She twists to face me, folding her arms and pursing her lips as she peruses me. "But you're not against love, correct?"

"Against love? How can anyone be against love? I'm being dramatic. I realize this. Love is beautiful. I just haven't seen or experienced enough of it. Obviously."

"If you were my daughter, I'd press on that. Something I wish I had done sooner with her. But you seem strong. Unflappable in your own right. I hope you hang on to that. Were you getting married here in the hotel?"

I shake my head, a strange sort of warmth spreading through me at this stranger's assurance in me. "No. At a church and the reception was in some chic warehouse-type place across town my mother insisted was the 'it' place to party. I'm staying here in the hotel." My gaze casts down to the stone countertop, my vision growing fuzzy. "Honestly, I'm not sure what I'm going to do now. I only just moved to Boston a week ago."

Turning back to the mirror, she reapplies her lipstick, which was already pristine. I'm not sure why she's continuing to talk to me or even why she came into the bathroom to start with, but I'm grateful. I always wanted a relationship like this with my own mother, but as fucked up as it is, I feel more comfortable confiding in this stranger than I do her.

Not to mention, I know my mother's six thousand shades of furious she's not able to attend the reception and socialize and network with Tod's side the way she was looking forward to.

I'm seriously dreading walking out there. Of what will come next for me.

"Where did you move here from?"

Her voice snaps me away from my dark thoughts and when I catch her reflection in the mirror, I can tell that was her intent. "I just got my master's degree from UCLA in business and finance. My bachelor's is in fine arts from the same school. It's how I met my jerk of a fiancé. He was a finance major. But I'm really an artist. I work with metal, but my third stepdad, Duke, insisted I earn a secondary degree in business if I wanted to know how to run one."

And I just dropped a pretty penny on a lease for six months of studio space that has a forge. Places like that are nearly impossible to find, especially in a city. I was so excited when I found it. I've been using a blowtorch since I began working with metal as my medium, but I've been desperate to try out forge welding and finding that studio felt like a sign that Boston wouldn't be so bad.

She nods, smiling in that polite way rich women do, not showing too many teeth and not wide enough to crinkle and make their faces show wrinkles. "That's impressive to have graduated with a master's in both business and finance as well as managing a bachelor's in fine arts. Are you currently looking for employment in those fields, or do you plan on making a living from your art?"

I shift my stance, leaning a hip against the counter. "Well, I don't *need* to work. Not for money at least. But I'd like to. I don't enjoy living off my trust funds unless absolutely necessary. I'd love to do something part time that uses my degrees. I'm not a sit still and do nothing type of person. Doesn't work well with me. Ideally, I'd love a job that helps others while affording me flexibility to still be able to work on my art."

Plus, I'm not one of those artists who can work for ten hours straight on a piece. I tend to go a little stir-crazy when I do that. I'm also far more creative at night than I am during the day.

"I see." She puts her lipstick back in her purse, and I hand her the package of wipes she gave me.

This poor woman has very kindly indulged me when she likely just wants to get the hell out of here. Who can blame her? We're in a ladies' room and I can't seem to shut off my verbal diarrhea about my disaster of a personal life. Seems to be the thing I'm doing today with unsuspecting strangers. I'm shocked she hasn't run out of here screaming yet, but she seems a bit too polished and refined for that. A lady of money and breeding.

I should know. I've spent my entire life surrounded by rich people.

Three stepfathers, each one wealthier than the last will do that.

"I'm sorry. I don't know why I'm blathering on this way." I cover my face with my hands. "I think I just need to go up to my room, take a shower, and forget that today ever happened." Along with the help of copious amounts of fried food and alcohol. My therapy. I wasn't kidding about that.

"Oh no, dear. You're absolutely fine. I was just thinking. What did you say your name is again?"

"I didn't. It's Bianca..." I hesitate, wondering which last name I should give her since I've had four since I was born, but decide to go with the one that's on my license even if it's not the one I've gone by most of my life. "Barlow."

"Bianca Barlow," she reiterates as if testing the flavor of my name on her tongue. "Pretty name. Unique. I haven't met too many Biancas before."

"I don't always go by that name, and I've had my share of last names, but I prefer being called Bianca now."

"I can understand why. It's lovely." Her eyes are all over me. So green, they're like summer grass. "Back to what we were discussing with your situation. Would it be completely out of line if I told you I happen to have a job that requires filling? Almost immediately. And it sounds to me as if this might just be the thing for you with your degrees."

I stare incredulously at the woman. "I'm sorry. It's like eleven thirty in the morning and I've already had the longest day of my life. So, I'm not exactly sure I heard you correctly. Did you just offer me a *job*?"

She grins at me, those green eyes glittering in amusement. "I believe I did."

"But... you don't know me. I must look and sound insane." I gesticulate to my scrubbed red face and puffy eyes down to what's left of my dress.

"Insane? No. Smart, brave, tender, honest? Yes." She steps into me, placing her hand on my shoulder. "Bianca, I'm going to level with you a bit. One of my many talents is reading people. And believe it or not, you just divulged a great deal of information that I find quite useful given the circumstances. My instinct tells me you'd be perfect for the role I have in mind, and my instincts have never led me astray."

My eyebrows pinch in. "I think you lost me a bit."

"I happen to run a rather large charitable foundation that could use an executive assistant with a strong business and finance background to help with some transitions we're going through." She reaches back into her purse and pulls out a cream-colored business card, handing it to me.

"Octavia Abbot-Fritz, Abbot Foundation CEO," I read. Fritz. Suddenly I start breaking out in hives, heat swarming my face while my heart races in my chest. I blink at the card and then up to her. "Fritz. As in Kaplan Fritz?" I whisper, the name flying from my lips without restraint, my voice shaky.

Oh my god. Things start churning through my head. Memories I haven't allowed myself to indulge in for years. Correspondences.

Green eyes...

She's not even slightly fazed by me mentioning her son's name. Likely because everyone on the planet knows of Kaplan Fritz. Even if I haven't allowed myself to look him up in years. I forced myself to ignore everything and anything published about the Fritz family.

"You know Kaplan?"

I shake my head because I'm absolutely, positively freaking out of my mind. He looked familiar. Her too. I just couldn't place it. I told myself I was imagining things. "He and I met a long time ago when I was very young. He knew one of my stepsiblings." I can't say anything more. Not about how I know Kaplan or the fact that I'm nearly positive now that it was him I hijacked and forced to drive me here.

He mentioned he was coming here to this hotel too. Was he coming to meet his mother? That must mean he's here somewhere, and oh my god, I'm going to throw up.

"How lovely. What a funny coincidence."

If only she knew just how big that not-so-funny coincidence might be.

She smiles softly down at me. "Well, I believe this was fate meeting you here."

The door to the bathroom flings open a second time and a very pregnant woman comes racing in only to stop short when she spots us. Her eyes round with shock and possibly a touch of embarrassment. "Sorry. I..." She points to the stall and then her belly as if that explains it all. It does. I mean, come on. She goes flying into the stall, locking it. "Lovely dress," she calls out and I'd roll my eyes or say thank you or whatever bullshit I should say, but I can't. I'm too stuck in this silent moment of hysteria.

"I must be going, otherwise I'll be later than I already am," Mrs. Fritz says. "But please consider the opportunity I spoke about. It is a very real offer, Bianca. I'd love for you to come work with us. Email or call me anytime and we'll work out the logistics."

With my thoughts scattered and my hands shaking, I offer an awkward smile. "Thank you, Mrs. Fritz. For everything." I wave my hand around the bathroom.

"It's Octavia, dear. And we'll be talking again very soon. I just know it." She squeezes my arm. "It was a delight meeting you. Best of luck." With that, she waltzes out of the bathroom, leaving me here reeling.

"Holy fuck!" Was that actually Kaplan? Could it have been? Sucking in a deep breath, I meet my reflection in the mirror. "Holy fuck," I mouth this time to myself only to hear the toilet flush and hightail it out of the bathroom. Nervously, I glance around the lobby, but there is no sign of Octavia or Kaplan.

Heading straight for the registration desk and thanking a merciful Jesus that there isn't a line I have to wait in, I explain my situation to the woman. Luckily, she remembers seeing me this morning when I first came downstairs to leave for the ceremony. She gives me a new key, which automatically shuts off Tod's key, and promises that someone will be up shortly to retrieve his bags and that he will not be given a new key to the room.

I can't get in the elevator fast enough. I can't get into the suite fast enough. Every second feels like an eternity as I scroll through all I remember about what Kaplan Fritz looks like. I'll be honest, I only saw him a couple of times and that was a child and then a teenager. I avoided him since. My already fragile, wounded heart simply couldn't take it.

Entering the suite, I can't decide if I want to laugh or cry at what's waiting for me. There is a trail of pink rose petals leading into the bedroom where there are more rose petals, these in the shape of a heart on the bed. There's also a bottle of champagne on ice and a plate of chocolate-covered strawberries.

Clearly housekeeping believed this was going to be the honeymoon suite of love.

I snort derisively, shoving all the petals onto the floor and letting out a shrill slew of curses I'd never dare say in front of someone like Octavia Abbot-Fritz. Stalking over to the phone, I pick up the receiver and hit the button for room service. I order up a bacon cheeseburger, fries, and a piece of chocolate cake. Once that's done, I gather up anything left of Tod's. All of his products and things from the bathroom and any remaining clothes. Then I shove them all into his suitcases and wheel them out the door of the suite, slamming it shut behind me with far more oomph than necessary.

Then I strip down out of this godforsaken wedding dress, throw it into the closet along with the bathrobes and slippers and shut the door. I shower quickly, doing my best not to think or analyze or anything else. I'm a robot. A woman on a mission.

I apply face moisturizer, run a brush through my long hair, throw on a pair of shorts and a tank top, and then climb on the bed. My phone is riddled with missed calls and texts. I don't dare look. I can already imagine what's waiting for me there.

Instead, I power it down, plugging it in on the nightstand.

That's when I open my laptop, staring at the home page—a picture of my latest creation—while I mentally pep talk myself a bit. *If it's him, it's not a big deal. If it's him, he obviously didn't remember you— not that you remembered him.* That stupidly makes me frown and I pop open the champagne, pouring myself a glass because I think the hot piece of man candy who is likely Kaplan Fritz was right.

I should be celebrating my newfound freedom.

The potential of a job that was just handed to me.

Fate. It's the word Octavia used and it's the same one I used in the car. It's not something I've considered all that often. In fact, most times, I'm more inclined to give fate double middle fingers while mooning it. But after today...

Maybe this *is* all fate? Or simply one hell of a fucked-up coincidence.

Let's find out for sure...

Taking a sip of my champagne, I type Kaplan Fritz into my search engine and hold my breath. In under a second, there are tens of thousands of articles and posts and magazine covers populating the page. All saying some variation of the same thing. Brilliant doctor. Billionaire. Most eligible and sought-after bachelor. Heir to the Abbot Foundation. Boston's favorite prince.

But it's his picture. His handsome face.

A deranged sort of laugh flees my lungs and I down the rest of my glass only to refill it.

Ho-lee-shitballs. I was in the car today with Kaplan Fritz and I didn't even realize it.

3

"I'm so sorry I'm late, sweetheart," my mother says, planting a kiss on my cheek and then wiping away the lipstick stain she left behind. Taking the seat across from me, her gaze catches on the amazing view of Boston through the glass of the walls of the restaurant. Snow continues to fall, blanketing The Public Garden and the Commons beyond in a glorious sea of white. It's majestic. Peaceful.

And yet my insides are a fucking mess.

"Not a problem. I was late arriving," I tell her, signaling the waiter so my mother can order something to drink, and I can focus on menial tasks instead of thinking about the reason for this lunch or the woman I rescued this morning who is somewhere in this hotel at this very moment.

My mother orders her usual chamomile tea and tells the waiter we need a few more minutes with the menu. I inwardly grimace. As much as I love my mother and love spending time with her, this is not just any casual lunch we're having.

"How has your morning been?"

I nearly snicker at that. As it is, I'm having a hell of a time hiding my smirk. Bianca, the crazy, intriguing runaway bride certainly made my morning interesting. "Uneventful," I go with, because anything else will lead to questions I don't want to answer.

"How's the hospital? Your patients?"

"Good. Fine. Busy."

"Are you seeing anyone?"

I raise a warning eyebrow. "Mother..."

She laughs, lifting her water glass and taking a sip. "You can't blame me for trying."

"No. I suppose not. Even when you know better than to ask."

"There is no such thing as knowing better when you're a mother. We throw darts and hope one eventually hits a bull's-eye. But I will always ask that question because I will always hope your answer changes."

A grunt and now it's my turn to stare out the window.

"Would you rather get the business side of this done? I don't want to ruin lunch alone with my son over it. We don't have many of these, just you and me."

My shoulders hunch forward, a frown curling down the corners of my lips, and I peel myself away from the snow and back to her. "I'm sorry," I tell her, feeling a touch bad for being so short. "I didn't mean to be curt. But you know this is not a conversation I've been looking forward to."

She sets her glass down and leans against the table, pinning me with her sweet, motherly stare. "I know and for that *I'm* sorry. I've held on as long as I can, but after the scare we had over Thanksgiving, your father is adamant that I retire and pass on the reins of the foundation on."

"It's not just him. We all think it's time you step down." Last summer, my mother was diagnosed with recurrent breast cancer. She underwent a double mastectomy and two rounds of chemo. Then over Thanksgiving, she collapsed in the shower, and it was discovered she had a bowel perforation that caused an abscess and a massive infection. She had surgery but was lucky to survive it all.

Now here she sits with me, looking healthy again. So far none of her tests and scans haven't shown any more cancer. We're keeping our fingers crossed on that. But she doesn't need the stress of running our family foundation and since her great-great-grandfather founded it, it's always been run by the eldest member of the Abbot family.

That's me. Whether I like it or not.

"I'll do what I have to do, but Mom, I honestly don't know when I'll have the time. My days are spent at the hospital. My hours there are long." Being a pediatric cardiothoracic surgeon is just about the hardest specialty there is. It requires perfection at all times. Every ounce of my focus and concentration.

And it's where my heart and passion lie. Not in the foundation. I love the foundation and I'm grateful for the work it does, but running it is not what I want. It never has been. I'd be a happy man if I could spend fifty percent of my time on the water and the other fifty percent in the OR.

The waiter comes over, delivers my mother's tea, and we order our food.

She takes a sip from her cup and then sets it back down. "The foundation requires a full-time person to run it and your job is already more than full time. I'm not asking you to choose one over the other or leave your work at the hospital. I would never do that. I understand the importance of what you do, Kaplan. Which is why I have a plan in place to help. You're going to need someone to work directly with you. Someone to help take over the extra burden I'm placing on you."

"I agree with that. Wholeheartedly."

"Wonderful." Her expression brightens. "As luck would have it, I believe I might have found you the perfect person for that."

I take a large pull of my coffee, holding on to the warm mug as I study my mother. Octavia Abbot-Fritz is no fool and is something of an evil genius when it comes to scheming and plotting her children's lives. Whoever this person is, I don't know them otherwise, she would have mentioned them by name. This is someone new she's bringing in and that's what gives me pause.

She's also impossible to read when she chooses to be.

"Do you now?" I question skeptically, setting my coffee down and folding my arms across my chest as I shoot her a disbelieving look she readily ignores.

"Yes. I'm waiting to hear back from her on the position I offered her, but she'll be excellent. She has a master's degree in both business and finance."

"Hmmm. I thought the foundation already had staff. Assistants."

She waves me away, knowing precisely what my tone is suggesting. "Of course they do, but this person would be assigned directly to you and not part of the admin pool. You require more than just an administrative assistant for you and the foundation to be successful. This person's sole purpose will be to keep you organized and on top of things. Attend meetings in your place when you're unable. Make decisions if need be. That sort of thing. Everyone else who works there is already so busy with all the important work the foundation does."

Impossible to argue that.

"Truly, dear, I know the position I'm putting you in with the foundation," she continues. "I know the demands of your work in the hospital. This person, should she accept the position, and I think she shall"—a glimmer of something hits her eyes when she says that—"will make your life so much easier."

I blow out a sigh just as our food arrives. My mother may be cunning when it comes to our love lives, but she'd never hire anyone to work for the foundation who isn't qualified. The foundation has always been her pride and joy, a job she takes as seriously as being a mother.

"Okay." I suck in a breath, ready to get this over and done with. "Yes, I officially accept the role as the new CEO of the Abbot Foundation and when you step down from the board, I'll take over as chairman. And yes, I will need someone who works solely for me to help with that because as you said, I'm not leaving the hospital or my work there and dividing time between the two feels impossible. If you believe this woman is right for the job, I will trust you on that." *For now*, I don't add. But I will secretly retain the right to fire her if needed.

"Wonderful." A warm, satisfied smile spreads across her face and the chill I have been wearing around my shoulders like an icy blanket since I woke up this morning starts to thaw. "Now, on to other topics."

We start to chat about my siblings, both of us digging into our meals when my phone vibrates in my pocket with a notification. Sliding it out, I see I have a text from my friend Ellis.

Unable to meet up for brunch tomorrow. Leaving town earlier than anticipated, but I'll be back for work in a couple of months, so let's plan something for then.

Disappointment coupled with an ancient sadness swims through me. I haven't seen or even talked to Ellis in a couple of years now and I was eager to catching up with him. While that's the reason for the disappointment, it's not the reason for the sadness. Ellis's younger brother, Forest, was my high school and college best friend. We were inseparable. Then he died in a horrifically awful way and even now, ten years later, I still can't shake the guilt and pain.

But it's more than that. Because every time I think of Forest or Ellis, I also can't help but think of Bunny. Their younger stepsister.

Sorry to miss you this time. Get in touch when you're back around and we'll make something work.

My finger hovers over the send button, my mind wandering, tempted to ask about her. About Bunny. Even though I know I shouldn't. She was one of the main reasons I had been looking forward to seeing him and now I feel robbed.

No one knows about the strange friendship I had with her. Not Ellis. No one.

It didn't start under the best of situations. Forest died, and I was wrecked over it. She was worse than I was, understandably so. I had met her once when she'd come out to Dartmouth to visit Forest. She was a child then and when he died ten years ago, she was barely a teenager. Fifteen at the most.

I didn't anticipate a connection like the one I had with Bunny.

I felt responsible for some of what happened and so did she. My heart broke for her. Such a young girl to live through something like that and out of love for my friend, I looked after her. Checked up on her frequently. But our calls and texts and emails were more...

I told her things I've never told another living soul. Real things. Not bullshit about school or work or my siblings or my life. Things about me. And she did the same. I trusted her in a way I don't trust easily or often. Maybe it's because she was so young and didn't pose a romantic threat—more like my baby sister Rina is to me than anything else—or because she has money of her own and never cared about mine. Maybe it's because we both loved and missed Forest.

Whatever it was, our friendship continued until I couldn't continue it anymore.

But that didn't mean I stopped caring or wondering.

Now, I know next to nothing about her. Nothing of her life. Where she is or what she's doing. I've never asked Ellis and since we don't talk often, when we do, we catch up on each other's things and he doesn't bring her up much. There is nothing on the internet about a Bunny Parker and I know that's because Bunny isn't her real first name. Her mom divorced Ellis's dad, so I can only assume her last name has changed as well since I don't believe Parker was her original last name since that's Ellis's and Forest's last name.

It's as if she exists but doesn't at the same time.

I hit send on my text to Ellis and finish up lunch with my mother. And the second as I feel like I've gotten away with murder, just as I walk her out of the elevator and into the lobby toward her waiting car, she grabs my arm, pulling me close, off to the side and into a quiet alcove. "You know what taking over the foundation means."

My heart starts to ricochet in my chest. This is what I was dreading. More than agreeing to be CEO. "Don't start."

She slips her hand into my elbow, her discomfort showing despite her cool Abbot-Fritz exterior. "It means it's time you find love. Settle down."

"And if I don't?"

"My boy, you've all but sworn off love. It's not a healthy way to live. But it's more than that now and I know you're aware of it. You're the eldest. You're taking over the foundation. That makes you the future of the Abbot-Fritz name, which is why it's important for you to marry."

"No thanks."

A deep sigh escapes as she shifts her stance, checking over her shoulder to make sure no one is nearby before turning back to me. "By the time I was your age, your father and I were already married and had the six of you."

"That was you and Dad."

"Your father and I were arranged, and we fell in love. It does happen, you know." She laughs lightly, but there isn't much humor to it. "An arrangement is certainly not the worst idea in the world, especially if you continue to refuse to meet or date or get involved with anyone."

I throw her a look that demands she stop this line of discussion now, but all she does is parry back at me with a smile that's meant to disarm me.

"After what that woman did to you by breaking into your home, I understand why you're not interested in trying to meet someone. But marriage *is* the next step. It's the safest way to secure our family's future holdings and name. The wealth and stability of generations. So what do we do if you're unwilling?"

I fold my arms and glare down at my mother. "We get over the fact that I have no intention of marrying anyone. Especially not some debutante princess."

She all but rolls her eyes at me. "I was a debutante princess, Kaplan. We're not all evil, and the right woman could be a partner. Not an adversary. Who knows, maybe you'll fall in love with her too."

Fat fucking chance. I lean back against the wall, running my hands through my hair. "It's antiquated."

"It's more modern than you think. Especially for people like us. We would find you someone agreeable. Someone smart and lovely who comes from a comparable family."

Agreeable. Comparable family. I just threw up in my mouth.

"Yes, it's important for you to find someone, darling, but I'm also worried." Her hand grips my forearm as she stares up at me with troubled green eyes. "I'm a mother, it's what we do. But your brothers and sister have all found love and happiness, and while I want that so desperately for you, I worry that the press are going to be all over you with this new position you're taking. Women too. The *wrong* women. If you're successfully matched that will take some of the pressure off you."

She has a point on that. I know she does. Being the new CEO of the Abbot Foundation will come with a barrage of attention from the press and from women. Likely the wrong women as she said. I'm the last billionaire bachelor of my family and we're Boston royalty. Sought after the way no others in this city are.

My eyes scan the lobby, shifting from person to person as I think. Suddenly curious about my runaway bride since I know she's staying here. Which in having this conversation feels absurd. I turn back to my mother.

"I'm not getting into an arranged marriage."

"Then tell me you've found someone," she quickly interjects, hope twinkling in her eyes. Seeing her children happily coupled up is Octavia Abbot-Fritz's greatest wish and happiest joy. And I'm the last one standing. The romantic holdout. And I've made it clear, I have no plans on changing that. Not now. Not ever.

I'm not anti-love or even anti-relationships. I just don't want that for myself. I like being alone. I like living my life how I choose to live it. Not to mention, I have some well-earned trust issues. Sweat is forming on the back of my neck just having this conversation.

I've seen what my siblings have gone through. The misery and pain love has caused them. If that isn't enough of a deterrent, I've had a plethora of women come after me, desperate to haul me in like a prize fucking tuna. They want my name. They want my money. They want to be Kaplan Fritz's wife.

And they're ruthless in their attempts.

Time and time again, my instincts have been proven correct with that. It's been getting to the point where I've stopped sleeping with anyone. Stopped dating altogether. I don't even care if that makes me grouchy and a miserable prick to be around.

The risk is just too high.

I'm a famous checkbook these women are anxious to get their greedy, conniving hands on.

Begrudgingly, I say, "I haven't met anyone."

She squeezes my arm, her eyes bleeding into mine. "Please think about this then. Marriage is not a death sentence."

My breath quickens, and I don't answer.

"How's about this? You promise to think about this conversation with an open mind. We'll give it a little time and see how things go with the foundation. Then we'll readdress and if you still haven't met anyone you're interested in being with, we'll investigate alternatives."

"Let me walk you out to your car," is my only response as I place her hand back in the crook of my elbow and lead her through the lobby. But just before we reach the hotel entrance, the overhead heater just outside the door hitting us and making my already over-heated skin itchy, I say, "I love you and I'll think about what you said but thinking about it won't change my mind."

"As long as you promise to think about it, for now, that's all I ask."

I kiss my mother's cheek and say goodbye. Her driver helps her into the car, and then they pull away. My hand grips the valet ticket in my pocket, but instead of handing it over to the man, I head back inside the hotel, straight into the lounge on the first floor.

I need a minute after all that.

My hands run through my hair and across my face as I replay our conversation. The idea makes me sick. Marrying someone, especially like that. I understand her concern. I'd be a fool not to. But I just... argh. No. No way. Settled on that, I push thoughts of it away. It's not difficult when a flurry of white passes me, heading up the stairs toward one of the event spaces. A bride, laughing, smiling, happy.

But it's not my bride from this morning and I hate that I wish it were.

I don't know what I'm doing here, looking for her, thinking about her. Clearly, I'm the one insane. An incredulous grin hits my face.

Bianca is here in this hotel and I'm grateful as much as I'm frustrated, I don't know her last name. What would I even do with that? Would I ask the front desk to call her room? For what purpose? To make sure she's okay... or to see her again?

After that conversation with my mother, what would be the point in that?

But... what does she look like when she's not done up like some Stephen King version of a bride? Her large, full breasts. The paleness of her skin. Soft bee-stung lips. Her long, long glossy hair and dark eyes.

Jesus. What is wrong with me?

It's clearly been too long since I've gotten laid. I should not be sitting in a hotel bar hoping for a glimpse of some woman who not only just ran from her wedding but also wouldn't shut up for two seconds simply because she managed to stir something inside me that has been dull and flat.

I just have too much on my mind. Too many things I'm juggling. That's all this is.

I pull out my phone and text my brothers Luca, Landon, Carter, and Oliver, as well as our little sister Rina, informing them that I am now the new CEO of the Abbot Foundation. That Mom is asking me to consider an arranged marriage. If that doesn't require a night out, I don't know what does.

Standing up, I slip my phone back into my pocket and head straight for the exit of the hotel. I'll never see that woman again and I'm better off for it.

4

I tell myself I'm not going to think about Kaplan Fritz again. That I don't care if he's in the hotel or that I met his mother or that he called me beautiful and said that there was nothing hot or sexy about bone-thin. After all, he had wordlessly tossed me and our friendship aside seven years ago. Therefore, he doesn't get to live rent-free in my mind.

Not anymore.

And I'm doing decently well with that too. I mean, sixty-eight percent of my thoughts are on fucking Tod and my bitch-face cousin and about twenty-five percent are stuck on the job offer and what I want for my future. That doesn't leave a lot of room for Kaplan.

Honestly, I hope I never see him again and I'm relieved we didn't recognize each other in the car. Most likely, I'll never run into Kaplan Fritz again. Or Tod McMillin. High-fives to that.

I just have to keep reminding myself that it's the bad experiences in life that make us strong. That build our character. That show us all we're made of. That help us to see the beauty at the end of the tunnel when we reach it. The champagne is helping my confidence with all of this. That's for sure. It's also been stopping me from second-guessing the major life-changing, rash decision I made this morning.

That confidence only slips marginally when I open the door to my suite and find four handsome men wearing matching frowns and tuxedos.

"Are you the four horsemen of the apocalypse sent to carry me to hell, otherwise known as my mother? Because if you are, I can already tell you, I plan to put up a fight."

"Bunny, honey, we're so sorry." That's my second stepdad, Elijah. He's the vet and the most tender of the bunch.

Bunny. I've been Bunny since the day I was born.

It's what my father called me the moment he saw me, and it stuck. Not just as a nickname either. I only shed it as my first name when I went to college, but it's still what my entire family calls me. I don't think any of them have ever referred to me as Bianca. My mother included.

I shrug, stepping back so they can enter the suite. They head into the sitting area, and I quickly run and throw on a sweatshirt since I'm wearing a tank top and no bra. When I join them again, my stepbrother, Ellis, who is Elijah's son, is picking at the leftovers of my burger and fries while the others hover around the room, refusing to sit.

Great. This should be fun.

"Good burger," Ellis garbles around a bite.

"I know. Help yourself," I deadpan. I guess I'm done with my lunch.

"Bunny—"

I hold up my hand, stopping Duke before he can start. He's stepdad number three, my current stepdad since my mom is still married to him. It's also his last name I'm currently carrying since my mother made me change it with each new husband. I know if he's starting, he's here doing her bidding.

"You can tell her I think it's crappy she didn't come herself."

His blue eyes cast down to the gold carpet. "She's dealing with your aunt and cousin. It's not pretty."

"Good," I snap, growing angry again at just the mention of my cousin. "Did Mom know?"

He shakes his head. "No sweetheart. She didn't."

Well that's a relief at least. Duke may be foolishly in love with my mother, eternally on her side, but I also know he'd never lie to me.

"She's in full-blown Mariana mode and your aunt and cousin are suffering her wrath."

I cringe but then think better of it because, again, my cousin deserves it all. Even full-blown Mariana mode, which is something akin to when Mount St. Helens erupted. My mother is no joke.

"I'm just glad you didn't marry the cocksucker," Mitchell, my first stepdad, growls, his hands on his hips as he starts pacing an agitated circle about the room. "And I'm even more relieved we talked you into that prenup despite Tod's protests that real love doesn't require a financial contract."

"Lying piece-of-shit, greedy-ass motherfucker."

Mitchell points at Ellis like he just summed it up. "Fucker wasn't going to get a dime anyway." He turns that pointed finger at me, and I nod because I'm grateful for it too even though I didn't marry Tod. Because, yeah, lesson learned. Four trust funds—including one from my birth father—worth somewhere in the neighborhood of fifty-five million and growing every day with a lot of interest. Mitchell is a big Los Angeles attorney and the person who drafted the ironclad prenup.

He was my birth father's attorney. It's how my mother latched onto him after my father's death when I wasn't even a year old. They lasted about seven years together before my mother divorced him and married Elijah. That's when we left LA and moved to Colorado, and I was Bunny Parker. We lived there until I was about sixteen or so. Then Mom divorced Elijah and married Duke and I became Bunny Barlow. We moved to his ranch in Texas before I went off to college back in LA.

My mother, for all her faults, married wonderful men. Caring men. Men who not only befriended each other for my sake, but still love me as their daughter. All these years and despite the divorces and name changes, we've all stayed close. Each one set up a trust fund for me when I became their daughter, and I can't help but understand that part of them never wanted my mother to be able to get her hands on them. I never lacked for positive male role models in my life.

Just anything resembling a positive, healthy relationship or a solid sense of self-worth.

My mother can be a toxic bitch even with herself.

"You don't have to worry about Tod," Ellis states, now going for my chocolate cake. I raise a don't even think about it pal eyebrow at him and he wisely drops the fork. "We kicked his ass for you."

My eyes pop out of my head. "You didn't?"

A mischievous grin curls up the corners of his mouth. "He might be sporting a couple of black eyes, a broken nose, and some sore balls."

A cackle burst from my lungs.

"No one fucks with our girl," Mitchell grunts, still pacing because he doesn't own a Zen bone in his body, only now his fingers are flexing and extending like he wants another go at Tod.

"I'm sure his father loved that," I quip.

"His father isn't speaking to him," Duke notes. "He stormed out just after you did. Fired him from the firm too. Right in front of all the guests, many of them clients. Told him any son stupid enough to get caught with his mistress on his wedding day is no son of his. Tod said he was going back to LA first chance he got."

"Wow." I collapse to the floor in front of the coffee table where the remains of my lunch and champagne are. Pouring myself my fourth glass, I hold it up to him in a toast. "That's the stuff of legends. Part of me wants to feel bad for Tod, but that's the old Bunny talking, and the old Bunny can't come to the phone right now because she's dead."

They stare at me like I'm not making sense, but I am. In my champagne-muddled mind, I'm making a lot of sense. I don't want to be that old Bunny anymore. The sweet, innocent Bunny who gets trampled on and used. Eating shit because I'm too polite to open a mouth about it.

Running out of that wedding was the best thing I've ever done for myself. This is my awakening. The kick in the ass I sorely needed. At least that's what I keep telling myself and I'll continue to do so until I make it my bitch and my reality.

"Bunny, honey, are you okay?" Elijah sits down, knees spread, hands intertwined between them, giving me the stare. He's been through so much. We have together. Forest's death bonded me even tighter with Ellis and Elijah and I know he's worried for me now. "You can tell us. You can tell us anything. This is a safe, protected circle and everyone here loves you."

"I know you guys do and I wouldn't be sitting here with my head up if I didn't have you on my side," I tell him as I take a sip. "I'll be okay. I promise. I just have to figure out what's next, but I was going to have to do that anyway. Tod or no Tod. I'm hurt and embarrassed," I admit. "My self-esteem and pride are wounded. People who I thought loved me don't and it sucks. It seriously sucks and saying anything else would be a lie. I thought I was going to be dancing and eating cake at my reception, not sitting here on the floor of our hotel suite drinking champagne by myself and eating room service cake."

"You can come home with your mom and me, sweetheart," Duke offers, taking the seat in the chair closest to me. "She wanted me to tell you that. That she wants you to come home with us."

"You can come home with any of us," Mitchell throws out. "Your home is with any of us. You've always been our daughter and you always will be."

That's when the tears start again. I made it a whole hour without them, and here they are. "Thank you," I murmur, sniffling way too many times for it not to be gross and everyone to know snot is trying to escape my nostrils. I'm tempted to follow after the only dads I've ever known as the lost puppy I could totally get away with being. I could crawl home, whether that's Texas or Colorado or California. Hide out for a while. Put this nightmare and embarrassment behind me.

But then I wouldn't be doing this whole self-exploration, Dr. Phil's couch awakening thing any justice. It's tempting to rely on others the way I always have. But at some point, I need to learn how to start relying on myself.

I could tell them I was offered a job, but the truth is, even though the lovely and gracious Octavia Abbot-Fritz told me it was legit, I'm not sure it truly was. I have to investigate first. Then there's the whole Kaplan side of that coin. Would I see him again if I took this job with Octavia? Would I eventually grow a set of lady lips and tell him who I am if I did? Tell him how badly his ghosting me hurt?

Inquiring minds want to know.

I think I've officially had too much champagne.

But at the very least... "I've already rented forge and studio space here in Boston to work on my metal pieces. Now that I know Tod won't be staying in the area, I have nothing to lose by doing just that. Besides, I like the snow. I'm a total ski bunny." I cheekily wink at that, annoying myself and dragging a new round of frowns from the rest.

Duke looks adorably confused. "Bunny, are you telling us you're planning on *staying* in Boston?"

"There's nothing for me anywhere else," I admit.

"Your family," Mitchell grunts.

"I'm twenty-five. I have two degrees. It's time I use them."

"You're sure about this?" Ellis asks, coming over and sitting beside me on the floor, his blue eyes boring straight into mine. "I get that the three members of Motley Crue are rough, but I'm your brother. If you want to come and stay with Amira and me, you're more than welcome. Frankly, we could use a good babysitter."

My adorable nieces were set to be my flower girls this morning. "Can I plan a spring break out your way to do that? I just don't want that to be my life. No offense."

A satisfied grin hits his lips. "I think she's going to be just fine," he declares. "Anyone who can turn down my monster angels isn't letting the champagne run their thinking. I have a friend here, you know. He was best friends with Forest. I was supposed to have brunch with him tomorrow, but we're leaving early now. I could get in touch with him again. Have him look out for you."

I blanch. He's obviously referring to Kaplan. And I could tell him I ran into him just this morning. That he's the one who gave me a lift back here. I know they kept in touch for a while after Forest died, though I didn't know they still do.

"No thanks. I don't need a babysitter."

The thought of him calling Kaplan to watch out for me makes me stupidly scowl at an inopportune moment.

"See, she's having second thoughts," Duke jumps in.

"No!" I hold up my hand, reluctantly setting my glass down. "I'm not. I want to stay," I tell him. "Tell Mom I'm staying. And that she owes me about six thousand apologies and that I will not speak to her until she's ready to deliver them. And I love you. All of you. So much. Thank you for coming. A girl could seriously not want for better dads or a brother."

"Aw, Bunny, you're our only girl."

Sadly true with the exception of my nieces, but I'll take it. I stand up, hugging and kissing and making promises for weekend trips and holidays and updates and yada yada yada. Who knew having three dads would require so much hand-holding? Not that I'm complaining. I'm not.

Instead of feeling heartbroken and despondent and self-loathing and venomous, I'm feeling light. Loved. Free.

I feel totally free and ready for my next obstacle.

I'd go check out my art space or do some work, but welding, fire, and champagne don't mix so that will have to wait until tomorrow. Flopping down on the bed, I close my eyes and blow out a breath. If I'm staying then I have some things I need to do. Like find an apartment. Furnish it. Maybe buy a car since the studio isn't in an area accessible by public transportation.

I should also find a job. Something to keep me occupied when I'm not working on my art.

Sitting up, I grab the business card Octavia gave me and stare at it for a solid five minutes, debating my next course of action. Do I want to do this? Risk opening a wound I should know better than to open? It's not just Kaplan. It's Forest too since he was so closely tied to him. I roll my eyes. If I'm working for Octavia, I'll never have to see Kaplan and a job this good just fell in my lap. I'd be a fool to pass it up.

Call or email?

Email, I decide. I email her, telling her that if she was serious this morning, I'd love the opportunity to be the Abbot Foundation's next executive assistant. I attach a copy of my résumé for good measure and hit send.

And with a huge, slightly deranged smile on my face, still ignoring my phone and the lingering messages I know are there waiting for me, I finish off my champagne and that piece of cake and wait for what's to come next.

That's when the pounding comes at the suite door. Again. And I don't even have to check the peephole to know who it is. "How did you get up here?" I bark through the door, wishing my fathers and brother were still here.

Speaking of, now I do look through the peephole, anxious for a glimpse of his face.

"I snuck on the elevator with someone since you had reception cancel the original room key. I'm not allowed a key to my own goddamn suite, Bianca?"

Oh. He's drunker than I am. "Your face looks fantastic. Is that a fist imprint on your cheek or are you just happy to see me?"

"Let me in, Bianca. We need to talk."

I press my hands to the wood, glaring at him through the small hole. "The hell we do, Tod. Your stuff is packed and down with the bellhop."

He collapses against the door. "I love you. I mean it. I love you so much. I was ending it with her, Bianca."

I squint into the peephole, my fists balled up. "Uh-huh. Nothing says I love you like fucking my cousin and best friend for *two years*."

"She's been obsessed with me. I swear. Back in grad school she got me drunk at a party just after you and I got together, and I don't know what happened. I woke up and she was naked and on top of me and it was somehow morning. She told me if I didn't continue to see her, she'd tell you everything. What you heard today was me trying to let her off easy. Come back to LA with me. We'll start over."

I shake my head, so tired and miserable. "Like you weren't after my money?"

"My dad is, okay? That part was all him. I never cared about your trust funds. It's why I signed the prenup, knowing I wouldn't get anything from you."

My hands press into the door, and I push myself back away from it. "Whatever. It's over. It's done. We're not married, hooray for me. Now please leave and never come back."

"Bianca—"

"I said leave and never come back!" I scream, smacking my hand against the thick wood of the door. "I don't want your excuses. I don't care about them. It's over."

Without waiting on him to say anything else, I run back through the suite and into the bedroom, throwing myself under the blankets, willing, pleading with myself not to cry. I just have to get through today. Because after today, it'll get better. All of it will. I'll make damn sure of it.

5

"Bunny, you have to know how upset I am about this decision of yours," my mother spews into the phone as I briskly jog up the steps from the T station. I've been avoiding her phone calls and texts all weekend. It's Monday morning, eight thirty, seven thirty Texas time and she's already called ten times.

"Mom, it's done. I have a job. A studio space. I went and saw some apartments yesterday and I think I might have one lined up near work. This is where I'm choosing to stay. I don't want to be in Texas and there is no way I'm moving back to LA with Tod and Ava there."

She huffs, but other than making her displeasure at my life choices abundantly clear, she can't do or say anything about it. I'm an adult with my own resources. And truth be told, yeah, I'm still a little pissed at her.

That notwithstanding, Octavia emailed me back almost immediately on Saturday, telling me I was hired with what I believe to be a competitive salary and full benefits even though I'm only set for thirty-five hours a week. The caveat? I start first thing today.

I told her I was in.

Why? I don't even know. I have no experience with this. I've never been an executive assistant. I've never worked for a charitable foundation. It has close ties to Kaplan and after a lot of soul searching, I decided I definitely don't want to open that can of worms again.

But I still said yes.

Truth, I figure Octavia has to be as crazy as I am. The woman offered me a job in a ladies' room while I had makeup smeared down my face wearing a ruined wedding dress. I'm trying to take the gifts I'm being handed and roll with them.

"I wish you could be happy for me."

"Happy?" she shoots back. "I would have been happy if you had come back home to Texas with me. I don't like you there in Boston. It's far and it's cold and you don't know anyone." She pauses. Clears her throat. "I'm worried about you. After what happened this weekend, I'm worried your emotions are getting the best of you and you're not thinking rationally."

"I'm thinking rationally," I quasi lie. I'm honestly not sure if I am. "I'm excited about this, Mom. This could be the start of something incredible for me. I'm on my own for the first time ever. Never in my life have I been more than half an hour from one of my parents. This will be good for me."

Another huff, but I ignore it, trying to get my bearings as the icy Boston wind whips all around me. I looked everything up on a map and I know where to go but talking with my mother is messing with my focus.

"Mom, I have to go. I don't want to be late on my first day and I can't talk to you and find my way in a strange city."

"Just promise me one thing, Bunny?"

"What's that?"

"If it gets to be too much or you're unhappy, you'll come home to me. Or if you need me, for anything, you'll call, and I'll fly in."

A smile hits my lips. My mother isn't always the easiest person to be around or talk to, but I never doubted her love for me. Even if I'll never be the person she wishes I were.

"I promise."

"Okay. Call me tonight so I know how your first day went."

"Will do."

"Love you, Bunny."

"Love you too, Mom."

I slip my phone back into my purse, wrap my arms around myself, duck my head against the wind and barrel through the streets until I come upon what appears to be a restored warehouse in the North End. The trendy burnished copper plaque affixed to the brick facade says The Abbot Foundation.

Opening the door, I practically moan out a hallelujah at the welcome blast of warm air. This isn't what I expected for a nonprofit charitable foundation, but then again, it's run by a family of billionaires. Instead of old, worn furnishings from two decades ago, everything is new, modern, and brightly colored. The walls are exposed brick adorned with expensive art, the floors a sleek gray concrete, the stairs metal.

"May I help you?" a young, impeccably dressed woman with a tighter than tight bun on top of her head asks with a professionally polite smile affixed to her ruby lips.

A flash of nerves has my insides flip-flopping as I step toward the main desk. "Hi. I'm Bianca Barlow. I'm here to meet with Octavia Fritz."

"Oh. You're Bianca." The girl practically leaps out of her chair, zooming around the large metal-and-glass desk. "Hi! I'm Charlie. I'm one of the other admins." She shakes my hand. "I'm just covering the front desk until Juan Carlo comes in." She sighs dramatically, fanning her face. "Wait till you meet him. Anyway, come with me. I'll take you upstairs. Octavia isn't here yet, but she asked that I show you around. I expect her by nine. She's never late. That's something you should know. The Fritzes are never late for anything."

"Okay." That's as far as I get before she continues.

"I still can't believe all this is happening. I mean, we knew it was going to eventually. Just not this soon." She pauses halfway up the stairs, turning back to me. "Not that I'm complaining. I'm totally not. It's just sad, right? The end of an era."

My eyebrows scrunch together.

"The admin pool is the best. Most of the girls are supercool and nice. Some of us go out for drinks a couple times a month." Her head swivels until her eyes meet mine over her shoulder. "With the exception of one, and I am warning you about her now. She's not happy you're here. I have no doubt you'll meet her later." She grimaces theatrically. "Anyway, even though you're not technically part of the pool, you're still invited out with us. Man. I'm just super jealous of you, you know?"

My head spins as I try to take in all that information, landing on the last thing she said and feeling no less confused. "You are? Why?" My mystified expression causes her to laugh.

"If you have to ask, you're either gay or haven't met him yet."

She gives me a conspiratorial wink and I have no clue who she's talking about, but again, I don't get the chance to ask because in her next breath, she's opening a glass door that leads to a large open-concept room. There are dozens of desks arranged throughout the space, along with walking treadmills, yoga balls, a couple of lounge areas with couches and coffee tables as well as an open kitchen along the far wall.

"This is the admin floor. There are about twelve of us down here plus the grant reviewers, social marketing team, and event planners, though we lost two of them the other day. They were a married couple and decided to retire to be with their grandkids in Arizona or something. Anyway, the floor above us is the main floor that includes basically everyone else from HR to the executives. It's also where all of our conference rooms are located. Your space will be up there since you'll be working directly for the CEO."

I pause midstep. "I'm working for the CEO?"

She blinks at me. "Yes. You didn't know?"

"I... um... I mean, Octavia mentioned something about being an executive assistant. She just didn't get into specifics about it."

She tilts her head quizzically. "Oh. Well, that's surprising. But yes, that's what I was told. I'm to show you the floor and then bring you up to HR and Octavia before the big announcement."

"Big announce—"

"Is this her?" An insanely tall, thin Black woman with the most strikingly beautiful features I've ever seen comes prancing up to us.

"This is her." Charlie beams, waving a hand in my direction.

"Wow. Yes, I saw the company-wide email this morning. Did you tell her we're all insanely jealous of her?"

Charlie laughs. "I told her, but I don't think she quite gets the punch line yet."

The new woman waves me away. "Oh, honey. You will. Just wait. I promise, you won't be sad about it either. I'm Greta."

"Bianca."

"Bianca, wow. Pretty name. And I love your outfit. Your boots are epic."

I glance down at my knee-high studded suede boots with red soles. "Thank you. I have a small thing for clothes and shoes."

Charlie and Greta exchange glances. "Us too," they say in unison and all of us start laughing. And with it, some of the knot that's been sitting in my stomach since Saturday unwinds itself. Friends. I could have friends here. I haven't had friends other than Ava in so long.

"This is where we sit," Greta informs me, pointing to two desks along the far wall. "Come visit us anytime, but you have to have lunch with us today. We're going to need all the gossip."

"Gossip?"

"I'm getting the impression she doesn't know yet," Charlie stage-whispers to Greta, cupping her hand over her mouth.

"You're kidding me." Greta's dark eyes go comically wide before they give me a big once-over.

"I know!" Charlie squeals, grabbing Greta's arm and shaking it excitedly. "Isn't that just the best? I can't get over it."

"Well, that has to be why Octavia hired her, right? Because she doesn't know?"

Charlie nods enthusiastically, leaning against the edge of a random desk. "Totally what I was thinking too."

"You realize you've completely lost me, right? Or more aptly, you never had me." More people start filing in, walking past us while staring at me. The moment they see me, they start whispering to each other in that obvious way people do when they don't exactly care they're being obvious while blatantly talking about you. This feels like that dream where you show up to high school naked and you didn't know you had an exam.

"This must be her," a nasal voice snidely remarks seconds before yet another tall, thin, stunning woman appears on my side. She's a lot of blonde hair and blue eyes with incredible lashes I'm tempted to touch just to make sure they're fake. She takes me in from head to toe, the disdain on her face clear as a bell before she smugly grins. "One look at you and I know why they hired you instead of promoting me."

"Excuse me?" I practically choke on the words.

"You heard me," she snaps. "They were afraid I'd be too distracting. Too much of a temptation. Could potentially cause a scandal. But you..." She shrugs with that fake pity look bitchy girls perfected when they were toddlers. She pretends to examine her nails. "I have to imagine there wasn't a concern of that in hiring you."

"Bianca, this is Mean Jenny." Greta's voice is utterly monotone. "We call her Mean Jenny for a reason. She never realized that graduating high school and college meant she no longer needs to be a bitch."

"I can see that," I mutter dryly.

Mean Jenny's eyes narrow into tiny slits. "Just don't get your hopes up. That's all I'm saying." She folds her arms across her chest and straightens her spine. "I've been here five years. That job was supposed to be mine. I guess it's lucky for you I'm not fat and ugly, otherwise you wouldn't have a job." With that Mean Jenny flips her hair and saunters off and all I can think is, what the hell have I gotten myself into?

"Um..." I stare after her.

Maybe my mother was right. Or maybe this is exactly why Octavia hired me in a bathroom instead of promoting Mean Jenny, though I have no clue what exactly I've been hired for. Evidently, I meet the fat and ugly quota and they're trying to avoid a scandal? What the absolute fuck?

"That was fun," I mumble, feeling like I've been railroaded yet again. "Like something out of *Mean Girls* or a soap opera. I wouldn't have believed girls like that existed in real life, except hard truths seem to be my thing lately."

Part of me is tempted to turn and flee. To run for my life. I've had enough embarrassment and scandal over the past few days. Enough hard hits to my ego. I don't need this job anyway.

"Come with me." Charlie grabs my arm, hauling me back toward the stairs without giving me the option to object. "Don't let Mean Jenny get to you. Seriously, don't. She's, well, mean and obviously insecure enough that she feels the need to degrade others. She wanted the job you have and has no issues springing out her claws."

"Right," I murmur.

"It's true," Greta agrees, giving my other arm a reassuring squeeze. "Please don't quit because of Mean Jenny. She's a sad person and I don't mean that emotionally. I'd feel bad for her if she wasn't such an awful human being. But hey, it was nice meeting you."

"You too," I manage, still staring after that girl and trying to wrap my head around things I have no clue how to wrap my head around. Maybe I should have worked in a professional environment before today. My required business and finance internships were always done with artists. I've never been in the corporate world.

I throw Greta a half wave a bit too late, my head spinning as Charlie drags me up another flight of stairs to the third and top floor of the building.

"I feel like I'm in a movie, only this isn't a movie I want to be the star of or even the sidekick in. So tell me, what the hell is going on here?"

Charlie throws me a nervous side-eye, her lips in a flat line. "It's not that big of a deal. There is just some organizational transition stuff going on."

"Uh-huh. Go on."

"Octavia has been sick. Breast cancer, and her family wants her to step down as CEO. So she is. Though I believe, for now, she's staying on as chairperson of the board."

"And who exactly is replacing her that I'm supposed to be working directly for?"

We reach the top of the stairs, and she pulls open yet another glass door. "Him." Charlie points across the room and my eyes naturally follow.

That's when they lock on him. The man standing beside Octavia.

Tall. Broad. Gray three-piece suit with no tie. Dark-blond hair brushed back from his face. Smooth, square jawline that could sharpen a knife. Intense green eyes. Stony presence.

"Kaplan Fritz," I whisper, my gut falling along with my blood pressure.

As if the nonexistent winds carried my voice across the room, his head snaps in my direction. His eyes do a slow perusal of my body, starting at my shoes and sliding up before they land on my face. It takes him a second or two or even three before he figures out I'm the woman who ran into his car Saturday morning. But the second he does, everything about him changes. Our eyes hold. Mine shocked. Slightly panicked. His angry. Bitter cold.

And that reaction throws me completely.

Does he know I'm Bunny or just think I'm the girl from the car? I don't know which I want, or even which scenario would be worse.

If he knew or didn't.

My throat constricts and any second I'm going to pass out. I rasp out in a hoarse whisper, "You're telling me Kaplan Fritz is my new boss?"

Charlie, oblivious to my crisis, gives me a small hip bump. "Now you know why we're all jealous. He's so hot it's like staring into the sun, right? So beautiful it hurts. But yes, that's exactly what I'm telling you. It's why Mean Jenny was ready to rip your eyeballs out of their sockets and wear them as earrings. You stole her direct shot at him. Octavia is stepping down and Kaplan Fritz is the new CEO. And your boss."

Oh. Shit.

6

Kaplan ♥

I stare across the room, directly at her, unable to stop. I don't even know the woman and yet I want to destroy her with my bare hands. She shouldn't be here. Not even close. This feels like a setup. Like a ploy.

Too beautiful to ignore, my eyes scour every delicious inch of her, and that only fuels my ire more.

Even as she appears just as horrified as I am. A fact she proves when she mumbles something to the assistant on her right, whose name I can't quite remember in this moment, and then attempts to bolt for the exit.

The girl stops her. I wish she had just let her flee.

More words and she's shaking her head. Her long as fuck dark hair hanging loosely down her back snaps wildly around her waist. Images of wrapping it around my fist and commanding her gaze spring into my head and how on earth is this woman here? Her. Of all the fucking people my mother hired. *Her.* It doesn't even make sense if the crap the girl was spewing at me in the car that morning is accurate.

She was supposed to be on her honeymoon. She just moved here.

There is no feasible way she could have applied and gotten the job as my new assistant when my mother never actually posted the job online. Hell, my mother told me she had the perfect person lined up that day at lunch, not even a half an hour after Bianca got out of my car.

Her brown eyes hit mine again only to immediately drop to the floor, her hands on her hips, and I find myself frowning along with her. There's something about her. Something I'm unable to put my finger on. A familiarity almost. No longer streaked in makeup, it's there in her perfect features.

I only spent thirty minutes of my life with her but somehow, I haven't been able to stop thinking about her in the two days since she ran into my car.

And I've had a lot of other shit to keep my mind occupied.

I've hated myself for my thoughts. For allowing them to form in the first place, but I told myself I'd never see her again so there was no harm in it.

Now she's here.

Storms of enmity thrash violently within me. A tumor needing to be excised, she has to go.

"A word, Mom," I demand because it's not a question. I don't give a fuck that she's chatting shit up with Harold from HR. Dweeb can hold off his ass-kissing ways and wait five minutes.

My mother's sharp gaze cuts over to me. Octavia Abbot-Fritz does not entertain poor manners or displays of rudeness, but the moment she registers my expression, she nods her head and excuses herself. She hasn't seen Curves for Days as I've been calling her in my head by the door yet and before she can, I gently grasp her arm and lead her into her office.

Soon to be my office.

I slam the door shut with a bit more force than I intend. "What did you do, Mom?"

She takes a seat on the cream silk sofa, crossing her legs in her pink St. John's suit. "Kaplan, if you're going to throw a temper tantrum in front of your staff before whisking me away for a closed-door meeting, at least have the decency to use your words a little clearer so I understand what you're asking."

"The new executive admin, Mom. The woman you hired."

She tilts her head, her eyebrows pinching in. "What about her?"

"She's here. How could you have hired *her*?"

"What do you mean by *her*? Do you know her?"

I shake my head. "No and that's the problem. Something isn't right with her. She shouldn't be here. How could you have hired her?" I repeat.

"Bianca Barlow. Twenty-five. Graduated from UCLA with a master's in business and finance. Just moved to Boston from LA. Comes from a very affluent family in Texas and has not one, but four trust funds."

I blink at her, unimpressed. "That's all you know about this woman you hired? How did you even meet her?"

She gives me the stern, motherly *don't give me that attitude young man* glare she's perfected over the years. "Kaplan Davis Abbot-Fritz, what is your problem here?"

"Her! That woman." I pace a small circle, my hands through my hair only to land on my hips. There is only so much I can say before Octavia runs away with herself. "She's crazy, Mom. I met her already, believe it or not. She ran into my car—*literally*—while fleeing her *wedding*. I gave her a ride to the hotel we ate lunch in."

A smile cracks clear across her face. "Well, I ran into her in the hotel prior to our lunch meeting and I thought she was lovely. Strong and brave for running out on a bad situation. Honest. And smart—she had a perfect GPA in graduate school and college."

Jesus. I think I'm having a stroke.

My hands scrub up and down my face and I start to pace again, only to stop and turn toward the glass door. Yep. People are watching us while pretending they're working. Fantastic. I flip one of the heavy wooden chairs sitting in front of the desk around and drop into it facing her, thighs parted, elbows digging into them, mind a fucking catastrophe.

"You're telling me you hired this woman right before coming up and meeting with me?"

"No. I'm telling you I offered her the position then. I officially hired her after she emailed me several hours later. I liked her instantly and you know I don't suffer fools or threats easily."

My jaw unhinges itself. "There is absolutely no possible way you can know she's neither of those. What experience does she have? Has she ever worked for a charitable foundation before?"

My mother shifts, leaning forward ever so subtly and holding my gaze. "Kaplan, I had to hire outside of the foundation for this. And it had to be someone very specific."

"I'm not following."

"The only person in this building with the right degree and experience to help you the way you need to be helped with this new role is Jenny."

"Jenny," I parrot because the name is familiar, but I'm drawing a blank on who exactly she is.

"The blonde pit bull who fawns all over you and your other brothers any time one of you enters the building. She was poised for this position, and she cannot have it. Short of firing her, which I will not do because she's not only very good at her job, we have no actual grounds, I had no choice but to take measures into my own hands with this. Jenny has been working here when I know she's had other, more lucrative offers waiting for the day that *you*"—she points at me —"would take over. I don't believe I need to go into further explanation with that. I told you this would happen with women. It's yet another reason why an arranged marriage is advantageous for you. Bianca has plenty of money of her own. Is recently out of a jilted relationship. Has the right degrees. And from my research into her social media accounts, only posts things about her art and her nieces. Everything she's said to me thus far has been one-hundred-percent truthful and her background check is pristine."

I fall back in the chair, running my hands through my hair before clasping them at the back of my head, my elbows butterflied out.

"You think I can't handle a woman like Jenny? A woman after a throne she'll never sit on?"

"I think thwarting her primary objective with you isn't the best use of your already limited time here. Not to mention, I'm not sure given her desires with our family that she would be able to assist you properly in your new position."

"Couldn't we do a proper search? Convince Henrietta to stay on instead of retiring?" My mother's assistant, who had been with her practically since my mother took over the foundation from my grandfather is officially retiring along with my mother. She was nearing seventy and only stayed on because she adamantly refused to leave Octavia Abbot-Fritz's side. But damn if I don't need her now more than ever.

"She moved to Florida last week. Into a lovely condo in a fifty-five-plus community with Lance."

"Let me guess, you bought it for her?"

"She deserved that and more. But back to your previous question. I had feelers out for weeks prior to Henrietta's retirement. Bianca is who I hired."

I squint. "Meaning what exactly?"

"Meaning you can't fire her without going through the board that I'm still chairperson of for at least the next two months. I know you, Kaplan. You clearly already don't like this girl for your own reasons that are eluding me, but do me a favor? Give her a chance. One month to prove herself. If she hasn't in that time or I've misread her intent with this position, then we'll see about replacing her."

One month working with Bianca. Then I can get rid of her. Or better yet, make her life a living hell before that and get her to quit. If she doesn't need the money, then why is she working here? How did she con my sharp-as-a-tack mother into this job?

She must have recognized me in the car.

She must have recognized my mother as well.

And somehow went in for the kill.

But why? It's not even as though the position was public knowledge, which means my mother brought it up to her. So why did she look like she was ready to throw up her breakfast and make a break for it when she saw me?

Something isn't adding up.

Regardless of whatever it is, I can't work with that woman. Not only do I not trust her or her intentions here, but my dick likes the way she looks far too much. If my mother thinks dealing with Jenny will be a waste of my limited time here, then attempting to corral my dick into some kind of intelligent submission is equally such.

Still, I can be a cruel, ruthless bastard when properly motivated.

"One month," I concede because I'll make sure she doesn't last a week.

"Excellent." The relieved smile on my mother's face is enough for me to hold my tongue on anything else. "I have a speech to make. After, let's go get ourselves better acquainted with her, shall we?"

Yes. Let's.

Standing, I help my mother up and open the door for her. Few children love and respect their mother as much as us Fritz children do, but that doesn't mean I'm going to flop over and take whatever bullshit she's handing me. That goes tenfold when I catch Bianca lingering at the edge of the office, laughing at something Harold in HR says to her.

I didn't catch much of her smile in the car. It was mostly tears and hysterics, but this smile... yeah. Chick has to go.

Black leggings tucked into fuck-me boots. Bright floral top that hugs her full tits without being inappropriate. Waist-length wavy hair that I want to wrap around my fist. Petite nose that is the ultimate contrast to her large, pillowy red lips and giant anime eyes. She's tall and curvy and definitely not the type someone would consider a classic beauty. But there is something striking about her that draws the eye. Makes it impossible for you to look away.

She's arresting even as her features twitch with nervous discomfort. Her lips part when she catches us approaching, my name a whisper that instantly has me thinking about her breathing it from beneath me. She holds my gaze with steadfast determination, but there is a visible undercurrent of something else running through her.

I like that, I decide. She's shit at hiding her feelings.

"How are we doing, Harold?" my mother asks. "Are we all set up for the announcement?"

"Just about. I'll go and rally the troops." He walks off, leaving the three of us lingering by his open office door.

"Bianca," my mother greets immediately, her smile warm and welcoming. "How lovely it is to see you again."

Bianca's almond-colored eyes shift away from me, and her expression instantly transforms back into that smile she was just giving Harold. Interesting. She's as unhappy to see me as I am to see her.

"Mrs. Fritz. It's lovely to see you as well."

They shake hands. "Octavia, dear. Mrs. Fritz was my mother-in-law." She gives Bianca a conspiratorial wink. "Now then, I'd like to introduce you to my eldest son, Kaplan."

"Yes," she says, her voice dropping. "We've actually met."

My eyes narrow when she leaves it at that.

"It's nice to see you again, Dr. Fritz, and under better circumstances than the last time. I'm Bianca... Barlow." She extends her hand to me, and I catch the hint of a tremor as she places it in mine, trying for firm, only I feel it too. Snap. Crackle. Pop. Her touch sends a strange burst of electricity through my palm and up my arm.

I grip her tighter, attempting to squash the odd sensation. Her eyes lock on mine, shockingly wide and deliciously innocent and something fuzzy niggles at the recesses of my mind, only for it to immediately disappear when she extricates her hand from my grip.

"I didn't realize I'd be working with you," she says, blushing slightly as if the words just spilled out.

I tilt my head, raising an eyebrow. "Is that going to be a problem for you?"

A smirk. "We'll see. Honestly, I'm disappointed I won't be working with you, Octavia."

Her attention casts back to my mother whose face is dancing with delight.

"Me too, dear. But I'm sure you'll enjoy your time working with Kaplan." I get a quick flash of the motherly warning again and I inwardly sigh. She likes Bianca. Why? Lord Jesus only knows.

"I have no doubt. Though I've been promised he won't be around often. Mostly working at the hospital?" She quirks her head in my direction.

"Are you being antagonistic to your new boss or is this how you treat all men who help you out in a moment of need?"

Her eyes sparkle and that smirk grows into a surefire grin. "I suppose that depends on the man and the boss."

The fuck? What on earth does she have to be pissy with me about? I was her goddamn savior. She gave me a kiss on the damn cheek and promised me a drink to properly thank me if we ever met again. And honestly, I would have preferred a quick, dirty fuck instead of a drink, but now I just want her gone.

Gone from my head. Gone from my skin. Gone from my existence.

My mother chimes in. "It seems this meeting is going better than expected."

My head whips over to her but she is not looking at me at all. She's entirely focused on Bianca, the two of them with matching beaming smiles.

"Bianca, dear. How about you and I take to my office after our official announcement to the staff about my retirement and Kaplan's succession? Kaplan was a love with showing up here this morning, but I know he's anxious to get to the hospital. He's taken all of next week off from there so my plan is to train you this week so you're ready to hit the ground running next week."

"That sounds perfect. Though I will admit, I was surprised when I came in and found out I'll be working not only directly for the CEO but for Kaplan instead of you."

"I have my reasons for that."

"I assumed you did. I might have even heard a bit about it downstairs."

"Ah. Well. Yes." My mother reaches out, takes her hand, and gives it a solid squeeze. "My reasons are valid and once you and I sit down to chat, I'm positive you'll understand that."

My brow crinkles in confusion. What is my mother up to?

"Octavia, you have taken an enormous chance on me. Of course, I will stay and talk with you."

"I appreciate that." She releases Bianca and grazes my shoulder. "I guess it's time." Sadness hits her eyes and I lean in, kissing her cheek. I know how difficult this is for her. Having to step down from the foundation she's worked at her entire life. A foundation she loves as if it's one of her children.

My mother turns, walking over to the head of the room and calling attention to the crowd I hadn't realized had assembled. She starts in on her speech about love and family and life and the importance of this foundation. I smile behind her only to angle to my right, my teeth clenched as I speak through them.

"What game are you playing?"

"No game," Bianca snaps quietly in response, edging in closer until her distantly alluring fragrance falls over me. "This is absolutely not how I saw my first day going."

"That makes two of us."

"Well, don't get used to us buddying up with stuff in common. I wanted to work with your mother. Not you."

"And why is that exactly?"

She huffs a breath, inching in ever closer until our arms are practically touching. Her feet inches from mine in those stupidly hot boots. "It could be your warm reception of my being here. Or maybe I've just taken an anti-men stance and that includes bosses."

"But what about saviors?"

"I didn't know who you were in the car. I only figured it out after when I met your mother and she handed me her card."

"Is that why you took this job? To get closer to me."

A burst of a laugh flees her lungs that she quickly stifles. "Don't flatter yourself. Your mother never mentioned a thing about you to me. I wouldn't have accepted the position had I known."

Instead of filling me with relief, that rubs me all kinds of wrong. I inch in, my head dropping so my lips hover closer to her ear. "Feel free to resign anytime now, Echidna."

A small shudder slips through her as my warm breath fans her skin. She smiles. "Don't get your hopes up, Typhon."

I grin like a fool before I can stop it. Not many would know that Echidna and Typhon were the mother and father of all monsters in Greek mythology.

"Your mother hired me, and I like and respect her," she continues. "I might be excited and a touch naive to see what this world has to offer me but being a sly fox and trying to get me to quit won't get you too far with a small bunny like me."

"What?" I give up pretenses and twist to glare at her. "What on earth are you talking about?"

She studies me, her eyes glued to my face. "You have no idea."

"Obviously not."

She frowns, blowing out a slow, even breath as her eyes cast to my chest while my mother goes on to her enamored room of patriots. "That's what I thought. Maybe that makes it easier for me." Her gaze meets mine again. "I like the idea of this job. Of doing something to help others. And maybe if you're at the hospital and I'm here, our paths will rarely cross. Or we could try to get along."

"Doubtful. Now that the drama is over and the gloves have come off, we seem to already dislike each other."

"And yet here we are. Together. Already agreeing on something."

I grunt, resisting the urge to squeeze the tension out of the back of my neck or pinch the bridge of my nose to stave off the headache this woman is giving me. "Look. I need someone who knows what they're doing to help me run this thing. I'm a pediatric cardiothoracic surgeon, not a CEO of a charitable foundation. My patients need me. The families of my patients need me. What I don't need is to hand hold and babysit some green newbie who knows even less than I do."

"Your mother hired me for a reason, and I like your mother too much to quit."

"I bet I can make you do it anyway."

Now she twists, her eyes a visceral snarl as they squint up into mine. My cock twitches in her direction. It likes this little standoff we have going. Clearly a challenge hasn't hit its radar before.

"Doubt it. But I'll enjoy watching you waste your time trying, Typhon." She gives me a coy smile, her voice matching as she says that.

I hate that smile.

"Wasting my time is not something I'm known for. Neither is failing at something."

This time she bats her eyelashes at me and *hell*. I hate that even more.

"Whatever you say, *boss*."

This woman is already driving me crazy while proving herself to be a tenacious pain in the ass. The sooner I convince her to quit, the better.

7

I'm angry. I'm frustrated. I'm annoyingly horny, which only seems to add to the angry and frustrated side of me. So when my mother finishes her speech and I deliver mine—I'm not good at speeches, I'm good at operating on tiny human hearts—and the room is left staring at me with owl eyes, all I can do is think about fleeing for the exit.

Hospital. Hospital. Hospital.

My brain is single-minded because if it wasn't, I'd be thinking about the troublesome woman I had some weird showdown with. My new assistant. The woman my mother is trying to usher into her office for a tête-à-tête. Bianca has questions. My mother has been skirting answers.

I need to leave them to it.

But as I cast a stupid glance back over my shoulder, my eyes snag straight on hers. *Why you?* I want to ask. Why did my mother hire you? And why do you have to be the one person I find fucking interesting?

Being the eldest in a family of billionaires is impossible. I'm inter-minably trying to be set up by EVERYONE! They think I need to be married. They think that will solve all the world's problems. Like a single billionaire is why there is still hunger and homelessness and smog. People cannot handle it. They couldn't handle it for my brothers either, but they're not me.

They're not the heir. The next in line. The one with the biggest bank account or largest yacht—thanks, Dad, for finding my one and only weakness in this world and hand delivering it if I agreed to this position and considered a betrothal or simply settling down and getting married.

Yeah, he got in on that too.

I am a surgeon of tiny humans. I fix their broken hearts.

So being here... having to deal with her...

"Kaplan, I'm so glad I caught you before you left."

My head whips back around, regretfully abandoning the dark antagonism of my new assistant. Blonde. Tall. Rail thin. Surgically redefined nose. Fake tits and lashes. Pretty, if you're into that sort of thing. Which I outwardly am but inwardly am not.

"Um. Yeah, I'm just leaving."

She juts in front of me, thwarting my escape as I attempt to make it. "I understand. But I wanted to let you know that when things with Bianca don't work out, I'm available."

I blink about fifty times too many. "I'm sorry. Who are you?"

She frowns in disappointment for a hot second before righting her features. "Jenny. I was supposed to be your new assistant, but now you're stuck with Chubby Brunette Rapunzel."

Did this woman honestly just call Bianca Chubby Brunette Rapunzel?

"And you think I want you as my assistant after you just openly degraded a fellow employee to my face and clearly show zero lack of appropriate workplace decorum?"

Her cheeks grow a blotchy red and she shifts her position.

"No. I mean, that's not how I meant it." She huffs when she sees I'm unamused. "She's underqualified for this job. I've been here five years. I know all the ins and outs of this foundation. The only reason your mother didn't promote me to the role I've earned is because I'm beautiful and she was afraid you'd fall for me, and we'd create a scandal."

I continue to stare, nonplussed. My mother wasn't kidding with this one.

"And this is what my mother told you?" I laugh mirthlessly, perplexed by how brazen she is about this.

"No. She didn't tell me anything, but it's not difficult to read between the lines."

"I'm sorry. You've completely lost me and I'm late." I shift to go around her when she sidesteps in front of me, intercepting me again.

"I'm your type," she practically demands, her tone growing urgent. "All the women you've been seen dating in the past look exactly as I do."

"And this was your design in looking this way?" I give her a quick, derisive once-over that she completely misreads as me checking her out.

She smiles suggestively at me, twirling a piece of hair directly over her breasts as if that will snag my eye and suddenly make me fall so stupidly, blindly in lust that I can no longer think straight. This shit. This shit right here. This is why I don't fucking date anymore. Why I've stopped spending time with people and women. Why alone is the way I like to be.

She reaches out with her other hand, touching my chest and her touch feels nothing like Bianca's did. Her touch feels like acid singeing through my suit and leaching into my flesh. I step back, causing her hand to fall and a frown to hit her too-pink lips. My gold-digger alarm is firing so loud I'm shocked the room isn't clearing out, thinking it's the fire alarm instead.

"Look," she says insistently, edging back into my personal space until her chest is now practically touching mine. "I'm very good at my job. And I was expecting to be promoted so I could do this job for you. If something else happened along the way between us, all the better. We both know it'd be amazing, and I'd never betray you. I'm a faithful employee and I'd be faithful to you. I promise. Your mother never liked me and certainly never liked me for you, which is why she hired *that other girl*."

Because my mother has excellent instincts, I'm about to say only to hold my tongue. She hired Bianca after all and as if I summoned her from my mind, she appears at my side.

"You forgot your coat, Doctor." Bianca hands me my black wool coat and I do my best not to look at her.

"Thank you," I begrudgingly murmur.

"Jenny, Harold also asked me to remind you that we have a no-fraternization policy here and that extends to unwanted advances. He said properly reading uncomfortable body language and taking the word no at face value was outlined in the sexual harassment video all employees are required to watch as part of compliance. So, if you're done trying to get fired for sexually harassing your new boss, you're needed downstairs."

"Jealous?" she snarls.

"That you're trying to get yourself fired by making your boss uncomfortable while sexually harassing him? No."

A shrill shriek hits my left eardrum, practically perforating it before Malibu Barbie storms off, muttering things I'm grateful I can't quite discern under her breath.

I turn back to Bianca. "What just happened?"

She shrugs smugly at me. "Jenny's after your dick and bank account, in case you missed that, and you looked like you were either suddenly constipated or a man in need of an escape. I supplied that for you. As a good assistant would. I think that also makes us even now."

"And you felt I couldn't do that on my own? Supply my own escape from Kelly."

She smirks at the obvious name blunder, dragging a fleshy piece of red lip between her teeth. It's not an attempt to be seductive, but hell if it's not that anyway. "Did you?"

"I was getting there."

She gives me a disbelieving look. "Uh-huh. Well, Harold didn't actually ask me to say any of those things and I don't even know if there is a no-fraternization policy here or not, but since she didn't call me out on it, I'm guessing she doesn't know either." Another shrug. "What she just did with you is the reason I was hired. She's thin and beautiful and again, after your dick and zeros. I'm fat and ugly and not."

"What?" My back snaps straight, my fists and jaw clenching. "Who the hell said that?"

Bianca rolls her eyes. "Read between the carbs, Kaplan Fritz. I was hired for a reason and keeping Jenny from you is one of them. Honestly, that just came spur of the moment and was likely not the best tactic. There might have also been a touch of cattiness left over from my interaction with her this morning, so for that, I apologize if I was unprofessional at all. But hopefully she'll mope and pout but leave you alone."

"I should hire you to be my fake fiancée to keep all the other women away, but that didn't work out so well for my baby brother, Oliver, when he tried it."

"Isn't he in love and engaged to someone now?"

"Exactly." I shudder. "Sounds horrible."

She sarcastically snorts. "Have a nice rest of your day, Doctor. See you next Monday."

"Not if I fire you before that." I slide on my coat.

"You won't."

"I wouldn't be so sure about that."

"No. Your mother informed me you can't fire me." I get a cheeky grin as she rolls up in my direction onto the balls of her feet. "Monday. I'll try to be polite next time we meet. This morning caught me a bit off guard. I was sort of hoping I wouldn't see you again after Saturday."

And then she's gone, skipping—shit, for real fucking skipping—across the office in her boots, back toward my mother's office. Jenny The Viper is nowhere to be seen and with any luck, gone for good, though I doubt that. Women like her with years-long plans don't just go away at the suggestion of some made-up policy.

Speaking of, I definitely need to find a way to get Bianca to quit. Before my dick and eyes start growing attached to the sight of her.

I make my way to the hospital, all the while ignoring calls from the press and business associates and charities looking for sound bites and to congratulate me. The official press release went out this morning around the same time my mother and I were making our speeches. Truth, I have no idea what to say because I have no idea how I'm going to make this work, assistant or no assistant.

All I know is I can't fuck it up when fucking it up feels inevitable.

By the time I reach my office in the hospital, I'm ready to put my morning behind me. Only my wish isn't entirely granted when I find my brothers Carter and Luca there waiting for me. I point at Carter. "I know why he's here, but why are you?"

Luca works here at Boston Children's Hospital with me two days a week as a pediatric neurosurgeon, but Carter is an OB-GYN across town at MGH.

"Grace has an OB appointment around the corner at the Brigham, so I thought I'd take the opportunity to come over and badger you along with this guy." Grace is our baby brother, Oliver's lifelong best friend. She ended up on Carter's doorstep by accident after she left her cheating fiancé and the two of them got together and ended up pregnant. Carter proposed on Valentine's Day just last week and is as anxious as Luca to seal the deal.

I shuck off my coat and hang it on the hook behind my door. "Badger away while I get organized for my day." Taking my chair, I glance quickly over the case files waiting for me on my desk.

"How did the announcement go?" Luca asks, sitting relaxed on my sofa, his hands behind his head, his eyes trained on the window overlooking the street.

"Fine. As expected. Mom was choked up and emotional in an Octavia Fritz I'm-in-public way. I had very little to say other than being sad about the circumstances for my taking over and lying about being excited that I am. Mom mentioned again this morning how an arranged marriage would be advantageous given the new climate of my life. Oh, and she hired the woman I nearly hit with my car on Saturday to be my new executive assistant."

"What?" That's Carter who is now staring at me as if I'm speaking Greek to him.

"The woman who ran into your car on Saturday?" Luca picks up when I don't respond. "You mean the runaway bride you told us about over drinks that night? Why the hell would Mom hire her?"

I fall back in my chair, bouncing a couple of times as I level my brothers with my annoyed scowl. "That's a seriously good question, Luca. Because other than having a master's degree in business and finance, the woman has zero experience with charitable foundations. So why our mother trusts her other than the fact that she claims she's not after my dick or wallet like the runner-up candidate for the position is, I cannot see the logic. She's also an impertinent little twit who seems to barf up whatever thoughts hit her brain the second they hit it."

Carter and Luca both spring matching smirks before exchanging looks that say a lot more than I'd like them to.

I glower. "Don't start."

"You like her."

I flip Luca off. "Not even a little. She's a supreme mouthy pain in my ass."

"You think she's hot then."

"Grow up, Carter. She's the exact opposite of the women I used to date."

Now they're both laughing. "Which is why we now know for a fact you not only like her but think she's hot. You can't stand any of the women you've dated, and we all know that's intentional. If you're not attracted to them or hate their personalities then you won't be tempted to be interested in them or risk trusting someone, or God forbid fall in love and end up married."

Wow. I had no clue I was that transparent.

"Where did you dig that psychobabble fluff up from? Since you became all in touch with your feelings about Grace you've been an insufferable sap with them."

Carter snickers, planting his hands on my desk. Right on the case files I'm pretending to look over.

"Why are your fists clenched, Kap? That baby-face jaw of yours too? If there is no merit behind what we're saying, why are you so tense over one woman?"

I glance up blandly. "Have you been listening or are your ears filled with placentas?"

I get a raised eyebrow, and Jesus, I am seriously not in the mood to go another round over this.

"Mom hired an unstable woman who literally threw herself onto my car to escape her wedding. Mom met her in the hotel right before our lunch. Other than a background check, she knows next to nothing about the woman she hired to help me *run* the foundation our *great-great-grandfather* started. Am I the only one who sees this as a problem?"

"Is she unstable because you like her and think she's hot or because you know she's genuinely unstable?" Luca questions. "And running out on a wedding from an asshole fiancé who you discover is cheating and using you does not make you unstable. It makes you smart."

"Fine. I don't know if she's legitimately unstable, but I don't trust her either. There is something about her I can't quite put my finger on, but I know it's there."

"For the record, you didn't deny you like her and think she's hot. Does Mom know you want to inappropriately touch your new assistant while making her scream your name?"

I glare at Carter, ready to reach out and strangle him.

"It is a bit weird," Luca concedes, saving his younger brother's life.

I toss my hands up in the air. "Thank you. Finally. Someone who isn't taking crazy pills with their morning coffee."

Carter sharply shakes his head, cutting me off. "Mom would never hire anyone for that position who she didn't feel could do the job not just well, but up to her impossibly high standards. If the runner-up is a gold digger, then obviously, she's out, but Mom doesn't do shit hastily or without the utmost consideration."

"Right," Luca agrees. "What he said. She must know something we don't. Or maybe she's just running on instinct, and you should trust her."

I fall back in my chair, scrubbing my hands up and down my face, my eyes closed. Why couldn't she have hired a fifty-year-old lesbian, mother of three, who has been happily and devotedly married for the last twenty-five years? Why did she have to hire the one person I allowed myself to find moderately attractive because I never thought I'd see her again?

"She can't stand me."

"Who?"

"Bianca. The new girl. I need her to quit because Mom set a moratorium on firing her for the next month. I want to hire someone who knows what they're doing. Someone who can literally run this for me because I can't."

Carter's phone pings with a notification, interrupting my miserable thoughts.

"Shit," he hisses.

My eyes snap open. "What? Is Grace okay?"

"She's fine. Finishing up. Baby Owen is growing like a champ. But she sent me this." He flips his phone around and suddenly Luca is behind my desk, right by my side as we read the headline.

"Kaplan Fritz, Boston's last billionaire bachelor, is now CEO of the Abbot Foundation, adding to his immense wealth and power in the city. Ladies, may the odds forever be in your favor."

"You've got to be fucking kidding me. The press had to put an even bigger target on my back? The assholes *Hunger Games*'d me."

"You should pull an Oliver," Luca muses in such a way I can't tell if he's kidding or not.

"Funny you say that. I mentioned something similar this morning to Echidna as I've affectionately taken to calling my monster of a new assistant."

"You didn't!"

"Call her that or say that?"

"Don't be a dick."

I roll my eyes at Carter. "Both? Yes. Will act on pulling an Oliver? No. Not a chance in hell. Evidently, as the Fritz heir, I have to marry a certain caliber of woman," I mock in an obnoxiously posh accent only with a growl. I hate this. I hate absolutely everything about this.

Why can't the damn world leave me alone?

Luca sits on the corner of my desk, his expression serious and solemn. "This is why Mom and Dad are pushing for the betrothal or for you to finally get off your ass and meet someone. Dude, I know you don't want to get married, and I know love isn't your favorite topic, but I'm starting to think it's not a bad way to go."

I sigh. "Being the eldest sucks balls."

"Better you than us," Carter quips.

"Thanks," I mutter dryly, picking up a pen and twirling it through my fingers.

"But this woman she hired? She's not interested in you?"

I shake my head, already knowing where Carter is going with this.

"No. I don't think she is. She's recently jilted in love and has plenty of money of her own, coming from an affluent family in Texas or something. She seems to hate me for reasons I can't quite figure out."

Carter points at me in an aha way. "*That's* why Mom hired her. She knew this would happen with the press the second the announcement was made. My advice? Give this new woman the month and see if this crap dies down so you can hire someone else if she still isn't what you need for the position."

Luca nods. "Carter is right. I think it's your only option."

Great. One month suffering through Bianca Barlow as my new assistant. If we don't kill each other first.

8

Bianca

Me: Good morning, Dr. Fritz. Your mother informed me that she has sent you my phone number and forced you to program it into your phone, so I'm assuming I don't have to explain who is texting you. I've taken the liberty of setting everything up for you in our system. Our calendars are synched, your office is in the process of undergoing redecoration, and everything should be set for you for Monday.

Kaplan: Echidna, we said Monday we'd start. Today is Wednesday and I'm stuck at a lunch that has me considering drowning myself in the bathroom sink. Now is really not the time. And what the hell do you mean you redecorated my office?

Me: If you're at lunch then why did you take the time to text me back? And your mother gave me carte blanche to make your office more you and less her. I've had it done in the style of Typhon's layer. I assumed you'd be most comfortable dwelling in the pit of a monster.

He doesn't respond and I can't help my laughter as it flees my lungs. Actually, his office is looking pretty great. I stare around his new space. Cool, sleek desk made of metal and glass and dark wood. Bookshelf, leather sofa, coffee table. It's nice in here.

I've spent the last two days getting myself acclimated to things here. Learning their computer systems and remembering names of people and memorizing every word out of Octavia's mouth. It's been fun. I won't lie and say it hasn't. What next week will bring is another issue.

He didn't recognize me. Even when I dropped the bunny Easter egg on him.

I've given up. I've moved past it. Our friendship ended seven years ago. I was a child, and he was an adult and clearly my childish mind that was grieving and feeling lost clung to something that wasn't as real as I thought it was.

I read through some of our texts and emails I saved on my computer. I couldn't bring myself to delete them after, but gah. One of our last exchanges was about the impermanence of life and the things in it. Maybe he was setting me up there. I'm trying not to let it hurt or bother me. I'm trying to put it behind me. Trying.

Exiting his office, I go back to mine which is right outside his door only to have Charlie and Greta there waiting for me. "Lunch," Greta demands. "You haven't had lunch with us yet and we need the gossip, remember?"

"I had lunch with Octavia the last two days."

"Right," Charlie says. "But not today since she's out. Come on, we eat in the kitchen on the first floor because no one ever goes down there, and we can talk without being bothered."

"Okay. Let me just go grab my food from the fridge."

I scoot across the room, grab the salad and soup I picked up this morning from a café on the way in, and follow Charlie and Greta down to the first floor. We take the elevator and the second the doors close, they start digging.

"So, what's he like? I mean, what's working for him like?"

"Yes. That. But did you really tell Jenny off by threatening her with a sexual harassment case if she continued to talk to Kaplan?"

I snicker under my breath at the memory of that. Jenny hasn't come near me since, but then again, Kaplan hasn't been here, and she's been working downstairs. "Yes. I did that because sexual harassment goes both ways. It's not just a female problem."

They give me a who are you kidding look just as the doors to the elevator open and I take that distraction and run with it. Only they're not having it. Both of them take the table by the window, the one that looks out onto the first floor while I go for the microwave to heat up my soup.

"Come on," Charlie chides. "Tell us what he's like. I heard he's kind of surly."

"He is. Honestly, my interactions with him have been minimal."

"He didn't hire you, right? That was Octavia?"

I nod at Greta, pulling the now steaming cup of soup out of the microwave and joining them at the table. Opening my salad, I debate how forthcoming I should be about things. "I met Octavia on Saturday at the hotel I'm temporarily staying in. That was after I met Kaplan."

"What?" both of them half shriek in unison, forks full of leafy greens poised in midair.

Blowing on my soup, I take a hesitant spoonful, not wanting to burn my tongue. "I was supposed to get married on Saturday, only I overheard my fiancé explaining to my cousin how awful marrying me is and that he loves her and yeah. Turns out they'd been having an affair the entire time he and I were together. Obviously I didn't take it well." I stir my soup around with my spoon, watching the noodles and vegetables shift around the yellow broth. "Anyway, I ran out and threw myself on a car. That car ironically belonged to Kaplan Fritz. He drove me to the hotel where he just so happened to be meeting his mother for lunch and I met her in the ladies' room without knowing it was his mother."

Silence.

Reluctantly, I peek up to find both of them impersonating a goldfish. Maybe I shouldn't have said anything.

Charlie is the first to blink. "You're telling us you met Kaplan by running into his car after you fled your wedding and then met Octavia after that in the hotel where she offered you a job?"

I nod, digging into my salad with gusto. "Crazy, right?" I garble around my food before chewing and swallowing it all down. "So yep, that's how I got here."

"Because they didn't want Jenny to be his assistant," Greta states.

I shrug up a miserable shoulder, still feeling not so great about that though Octavia swore it was because she liked me instantly and thinks I'll be perfect for the role. Whatever. I'm trying not to think about that either. The notion that I'm here because I'm the fat, ugly girl wrecks me. It's what I overheard both Tod and Ava talking about and my mother has never been shy about telling me I need to lose weight. And now I'm working for Kaplan instead of Jenny working for him.

My insides twist and my heart clenches painfully in my chest. I never saw myself that way. The way others seem to.

So I'm trying to put on a brave face and muster through when the desire to start a vicious self-loathing cycle is real. I don't need someone to validate that I'm beautiful because that's how I already see myself. I may not be what society and convention consider beautiful but fuck them. I've always been different, and I like that about myself. I just have to remember that when the words and actions of others try to get me down.

"Guess so," I mumble, staring down at my food and trying not to frown, or worse, cry.

"Huh. Wow." Charlie is flummoxed, her lunch all but forgotten.

"Right?" Greta nods. "Just wow. I mean, kinda cool. Fun story to tell and all. Still, I think Octavia was right in hiring you. Especially after what the papers and tabloids have been printing about him. Must be hard to have your life so open and public like that. Have women like Jenny all over you."

I go back to my soup, still frowning. "I'm sure it is."

"You know, I heard, oh, holy, look." Charlie points over my shoulder and both Greta and I swivel around to see what she's gawking at. "That's Kaplan. Right there. With Octavia and... Who is that?"

Greta flies out of her chair and races to the edge of the kitchen, half hiding behind the wall so she's not seen, as she watches Kaplan speaking with two other women plus his mother. One of them is older, the same age as Octavia is my guess, while the other appears somewhere closer to Kaplan's.

"It's Millie Van Der Heusen," she hisses, looking at Charlie with wide eyes.

"Who?" I squawk, but the name tickles my memory. "You mean as in Senator Van Der Heusen?"

"Yes," Charlie cries, getting to her feet and joining Greta for a better view. "Oh my god. I wonder if they're dating."

"I haven't heard anything about that anywhere."

"Me neither. But can you imagine? Talk about a power couple. Whoa."

"She's so pretty too. Like so pretty. And I hear she's the nicest person ever."

The two of them keep going back and forth and against my better judgment, I rise out of my chair and make a slow stroll over to the edge of the kitchen. And sure enough. There is Kaplan Fritz talking with a model-gorgeous woman who is every bit as tall and thin as Greta and Jenny are. She's wearing a pale-pink shift dress and a sparkling smile, her eyes fixed on his. He says something to her that makes her laugh, her hand slips to his arm, and so what?

Good for him.

Let all the beautiful, skinny people take over the world and marry and make babies. Blah. Boring. Maybe if they're together, I'll stop feeling this weird sensation in my stomach every time I look at him.

Millie Van Der Heusen gets up on her tippy-toes and places a kiss on Kaplan's cheek, and now that weird sensation is doing even weirder things inside me. Or maybe my salad was bad. You can get listeria or salmonella from spinach. Happens all the time. That's what this nausea is. Food poisoning.

"So cute. Look at them. Talk about being jealous." Greta laughs. "I wonder if his jaw is smooth or if it feels like the chiseled stone it looks to be made from."

More giggling from Charlie. "I hear they call him baby face. I mean, he does look young compared to his brothers, but damn, I think he's the hottest of them."

"Meh. He's not my type," I throw out just as he turns in our direction, looking in through the glass only to squint when he catches us standing here.

"Oh shit." Greta and Charlie flee the scene of the crime, but I can't manage to make myself move. He stares at me, into me with a burning intensity that has my knees weak and my breasts feeling heavy.

A smirk curls up his lips while the woman continues to prattle on to him, though now his focus is entirely on me. He pulls out his phone and types something into it. A second later, mine vibrates in my pocket. Unable to resist the urge, I slip it out and read the text he just sent me.

Kaplan: See something you like?

I smirk, shaking my head and coughing out a small laugh. I quickly reply.

Me: Not from where I'm standing. Then again, I haven't gotten a good look at your mother's dress yet.

I shoot the text and then shoot him a raised eyebrow. He reads it and smiles and that weird thing in my belly swoops at it. Just then his mother catches his attention, her gaze slingshotting over to me and then up to him questioningly. She says something to him and he nods, cutting his attention away from me and back over to the pretty senator's daughter.

Without a word, I go back to my lunch, listening without speaking as Greta and Charlie gossip about Kaplan and his lunch date.

∼

THURSDAY:

Kaplan: I need a large black coffee delivered to the hospital within the next ten minutes or you're fired.

Me: Call Uber Eats and get them to do it or better yet, get an intern to do your coffee bidding. You can't fire me. Frankly, you

need me too damn much. I'm sitting in a budget meeting with the event staff to discuss the spring events. Also, Jenny is glaring at me like she wants to siphon my blood, cook it down, and drink it. I'm naming her Draugr since we're all about mythological creatures instead of Mean Jenny—not enough punch to that. PS Your date was pretty.

Kaplan: I can't tell if you're jealous or fishing for information.

Me: Neither. I'm being honest.

Kaplan: She wasn't my date; she was an ambush. Since we're being honest. What's going on in the budget meeting?

Me: I'll email you my notes when it's over. Stop texting me. I have very important things to do.

Two hours later:

Kaplan: You never emailed me the budget stuff.

Me: I did. So either you know it's there but you wanted to text me or you haven't checked your email and are lazy. Which is it?

An hour later:

Me: Did you know the press has been lining the sidewalk, waiting for you? There is also a parade of women who walk back and forth in front of the building while pretending to casually stroll by. Your new girlfriend isn't among them. I know you're disappointed by that. Seriously though, Charlie had to call the cops on two who insisted they had appointments with you and wouldn't leave until they saw you. Did they not get the memo to stalk the hospital instead?

Kaplan: They've been here as well. Whatever you do, don't open that mouth of yours. Don't tell them who you are. Don't give them your name. And don't say anything about me.

Me: That's a lot of strong orders. Are you nervous they'll fall for me instead of you? And just who am I?

Kaplan: My soon to be unemployed pain in the ass assistant.

Me: Aw, you're cute when you baselessly threaten me. But did you ever consider I might be more than that? Check this out. Made it last night. *picture of metal monster with wings* I think that's a keeper for your bookshelf, Typhon.

Kaplan: You made that?

Me: I'm assuming you're shocked at my overwhelming talent since I can't determine over text if that was snarky or not. But yes. My second time using the forge. If you're nice, I'll make you some book ends to go with it.

Kaplan: I'm trying to think of something cruel to say to that, but for once, I'm coming up empty.

Me: Wow, that's practically a compliment.

Kaplan: It wasn't. My niece Stella could have done a better job and she's thirteen.

Me: That was lame. You're losing your touch.

Kaplan: What can I say to get you to quit?

Me: That you love me and want to marry me. That should do it. I'll run from Boston faster than you can say Bianca Fritz.

Kaplan: Ha. You wish. Speaking of, are you feeling threatened with all the women stalking the building? Do I need to set up security there?

Me: No. I'm fine. We're all fine. No one knows I'm your assistant. Shhh. I'm leaving for the day. See you, Monday, Typhon.

FRIDAY

Me: I have finally gained access to your hospital schedule and have tried to work important meetings here around those. I've also spoken with your IT department there and they have assured me you'll be able to access our meetings virtually if needed. Today was also your mother's last day and everyone here was in tears. You should know, if you don't already, she is very loved and will be greatly missed by her staff.

Kaplan: I already know this.

Me: Are you even planning on trying?

Kaplan: With you? No.

Me: Care to explain that? Or is it because you called me beautiful, and I kissed your cheek after spilling part of my life story to you? Or is it because I said if you tell me you love me, I'll quit?

Kaplan: It's Friday night, Bianca. Go home.

Me: I don't have a home yet, Kaplan. I move into my new place Sunday.

Kaplan: If you quit now, you can be back in Kansas by the morrow.

Me: No one says morrow unless they're Mr. Darcy and while you have his snobbish countenance and untouchable air, you're no Mr. Darcy. I was living in LA before this. Texas before that. And what is it with you trying to make me quit? Do you truly want a Jenny assisting you while you take over here or are you just being an ass because you don't like how we met, that I genuinely don't want to jump your bones, or that I am the only one brave enough not to take your crap?

Kaplan: Why were you going to marry him if you didn't love him?

Me: Why do you care?

Kaplan: Humor me.

Me: Family pressure. Poor role models. Lack of basic understanding of romantic love. Tragic past that might have broken me a little more than I like to admit. Self-esteem that needs a bit of polishing. I thought I loved him enough to marry him, but I didn't. Confession time: I'm glad I didn't marry him. I think I would have regretted it always.

Kaplan: Confession time: I'm glad you didn't marry him either.

Me: Are you dating that woman?

Kaplan: I don't date anyone. Not anymore. But I like that you're still jealous enough to ask.

Me: And I like that you care enough to tell me you're glad I didn't marry Tod. Why don't you date anymore?

Twenty minutes later.

Me: You can tell me, and I won't tell anyone. You're also not the totally cold, uncaring bastard you try to be. Why do you hide who you are from the world?

Kaplan: Good night, Bianca

Me: I told you mine.

Kaplan: Monday. Eight a.m. sharp. Don't be late. Or you're fired.

Me: Wait! Why do you get to ask all the questions and you answer none of mine?

9

"Infuriating, miserable man. Why am I even still here?" I set my phone down when he doesn't reply and peer around the now empty room, the lighting dim, the floor quiet. "To torture yourself of course." Ugh! I should have walked straight out of here when I discovered who I was going to be working for. Part of me wondered if I was that forgettable or if he'd eventually recognize me.

But when he didn't, when I even threw out the word bunny and he was more confused than ever, not even the slightest flicker of recognition in his eyes, *that's* when I should have left. My self-goddamn-respect demanded it and yet, Friday night, I'm still here. I like the job though. It's interesting. Most of the people—with the exception of Jenny—are really nice and I can even see becoming good friends with Greta and Charlie, who I've been having lunch with regularly.

But there are plenty of other jobs out there and they don't involve Kaplan Fritz.

Yet I'm still here. Texting him. Doing my job. Creating monstrous art in his name.

The problem is, I don't know if he hides from the world.

It was a guess. A wish. A prayer.

Because the Kaplan Fritz I remember was warm. Kind. Open. And liked me.

He was not anything like the Kaplan Fritz I've been fighting with via text all week because the man refuses to call me back. That's why I'm still here. To prove to myself that it was real. That a connection so vital to me wasn't a lie.

Part of me knows I likely shouldn't have stayed in Boston. I was only here because of Tod, and truth be told, I wasn't all that jazzed when he told me this was where we were getting married and moving to.

I didn't plan my wedding. Tod's mother and my mother did. I was busy finishing up grad school and frankly, I didn't care all that much. The wedding wasn't important to me. What I wanted was the adventure. The new beginning and I had hoped, foolishly, that in marrying Tod I'd be seen as something more than I've always been seen as.

Bunny. That sweet, innocent girl. The one who can't take care of herself. The naive one. The partially broken one—I wasn't lying about that to Kaplan. Bitterness and self-decay battle inside me and I shove it away.

"Stupid," I mutter to myself, standing now and forcing myself to put on my coat. Maybe that's why I stayed. To prove to myself that I'm none of those things I've been pegged as. That I can do this job and do it well and do it for myself and no one else. That I can make it in a new city and a new life all on my own.

Or maybe Kaplan Fritz was a larger draw than I care to admit to myself. "Stupid," I repeat and wholeheartedly mean it.

I was a child the last time Kaplan was in my life.

Do I even want him to recognize me? What would I say? I'd be flustered and embarrassed and no. I am not a child anymore. I was Bunny Parker to him. I'm Bianca Barlow now. I should cut all my losses and go. Nothing good comes of this if he finds out.

But somehow, I know I won't be leaving Boston or quitting this job tonight either.

The glass doors of the building glide shut soundlessly, only to lock directly behind me. My gaze casts left and then right as I bundle myself into my coat. The cold is definitely not something I'm used to yet. I'm half tempted to call an Uber here and head straight to the studio. Dinner be damned. But I need to change my clothes. I also need food.

More importantly, I need to stop thinking about my new boss and what Monday will be like.

Pressing myself against the wind, I head in the direction of the T. Tomorrow I'm going to buy a car. Sunday I move into my new apartment. Tonight is the only time I'll have to work on my art and I'm jittery with that pulsing need. My fingers twitching beside me.

The streets are dark and wet but crowded with Friday night dinner traffic. Women in expensive shoes clinging to the sidewalk, away from the dark slushy mess of leftover snow that hovers along the edges of the curb. The smell of garlic and cooked meats fill the air, the restaurant fronts of the North End warm and welcoming.

"That's totally him," a girl practically glued against the steamy glass of one of the restaurants says. "Kaplan Fritz. I'd know his hot AF face anywhere. The owner of the restaurant practically threw me out when I tried to go in."

"No way. What would he be doing sitting alone in a restaurant?" her friend remarks. "He's dating that woman now, right? Millie Van Der Heusen? I saw it online."

"No. They're just friends, I think. But I'm telling you it's him."

"Friends my ass. Maybe he's waiting on her. It's a totally romantic restaurant, right?"

I don't even realize I've stopped moving until I'm standing in the middle of the sidewalk, eavesdropping.

"Romantic? It's weird. Who rents out an entire restaurant?"

"He must have rented it out for their date. So they'd have privacy."

My gaze hits the window and I scan through the glass along the empty restaurant until I find Kaplan all the way in the back, talking to the waiter. He's not waiting on a date. I don't know how I know that, but somehow, I do. I shouldn't go in there. I shouldn't even be tempted to see him. It's Friday night and he's dining alone likely so he won't be bothered, and I need to get back to the hotel so I can eat, change, and go.

I shouldn't be opening the door of the small, quiet, and yes romantic restaurant with its light-wood tables, flickering candlelight, and roses in small bud vases. Maybe he is here to meet a woman? That woman.

"I'm sorry, ma'am, we're closed tonight to diners. I meant to lock the door." A woman in all black with a black apron covering her front comes barreling out of the back, rushing nervously over to me.

My gaze cuts straight across the room and lands on him.

Kaplan is holding a glass of wine, the rim poised right by his lips as if I caught him about to take a sip. I don't say anything and for a beat, he doesn't either. He just stares at me, his expression unreadable, even as it drags lazily down my body, sticking on my heeled boots and then back up to my face.

I get a *what are you doing here* raised eyebrow.

I return it with an *I have no freaking clue* shrug.

"It's okay," he finally says to the woman without removing his eyes from mine. "She can join me."

"I never said I wanted to join you," I smart, even as I'm crossing the room to his small two-person table in the back.

"I'm not even going to dignify that with a real response. More importantly, how did you know I was here?"

I shake my head as I sit down while the staff rushes to put a place setting, wine and water glass, and a napkin in front of me. I don't touch anything, still undecided.

"I didn't. There were two girls with their faces pressed to the glass swearing it was you in the back and that you were waiting on a date. I simply overheard them as I was heading for the T."

He curses low under his breath, taking a hearty gulp of his wine. "This week has been a nightmare. Worse than normal, and truly, that is saying something. I didn't even want to subject my siblings to dinner with me. That's how bad it's been. Women. Press. Even patients' families and hospital staff and administration. There were several reasons I never wanted the foundation, and these are at the top of the hit list."

"You didn't have a choice?"

"No, Echidna, I didn't have a choice. So again, what are you doing here?"

I lean forward, planting my forearms on the table and erasing some of the space between us. "If you genuinely bought out every seat in a restaurant on a Friday night because you want to be alone, tell me. Have you changed your mind and want me to go or are you just being your cantankerous self, needing to hate me on principle? I don't care who you are, Kaplan, or what your family's last name is. What foundation you run or how many lives you save. And I certainly don't care how fat or thin your wallet is. But you're sitting here alone and I'm not sure that's truly what you want. If you want me to go, I will. I do, believe it or not, have other things I can be doing. But if you'd like me to stay and have dinner with you so we can talk shop or whatever else is on your mind, I'm happy to do that as well."

"I went home first," he says instead of responding to any of that. "The space in front of my condo was completely blocked. My parking space. The private gate that leads into my complex. There were people hiding in bushes and attempting to scale up the exterior of my building and onto my patio and my condo is three stories high and over the water on two of those sides. I haven't brought a woman home with me in well over a year. I haven't dated a woman in the same amount of time. And if there are faces glued to the glass, they will see you dining with me."

"So you want me to go?"

"No. I want you to stay and have dinner with me without all the bullshit that could potentially come with it."

"Between us or if the world sees us?" I tease.

His hand drags a frustrated path through his hair. "Nothing is happening between us. This isn't a fucking date." He's so on edge he looks like he's about to explode all over this restaurant.

"Relax, there, Doctor. Believe it or not, I don't *want* anything to happen between us and you're the last man I'd want to date. And you don't have to worry about the world seeing us have dinner together either. I'm your new assistant. We have plausible deniability."

"Are you a lawyer now?"

I smirk at his growly tone and fierce expression. "No. I'm the step-daughter of a lawyer."

Now I hold. I wait. I watch. Nothing.

Our waiter shows up at our side, handing me a menu. I cock an eyebrow and after a grunt, Kaplan nods.

I glance quickly at the menu, ordering the first thing my eyes touch that sounds like something I'd like—a lot of this is in Italian—along with a glass of whatever Kaplan is drinking because he said he wants me to stay. And he looks like he's on his last shred of patience and sanity. I'm not his friend anymore. I'm not that teenage girl who missed her brother and clung to his best friend.

I'm an assistant he hasn't been coy about saying he wants to get rid of.

But I know what that lonely, lost look in his eyes feels like too and I don't want that for him. Even if I'm still insanely hurt and dejected and furious and well, lying by omission over our past. The Bunny that still lives in my heart wants to believe he had his reasons for ghosting me and that they were valid.

The new Bianca wants his nuts on a platter for the pain it caused so I don't plan to be nice over dinner. Just here so he's not alone. A girl's gotta eat anyway.

"You make art?"

"I make art. And you fix babies' hearts." I grin at how that sounds, not quite a rhyme, but not bad either. I shouldn't be grin-ning but I am. I don't remember him as this surly or good-looking for that matter, but then again, I was fifteen and my heart and mind were shattered. I didn't care how he looked; it wasn't like that between us.

He was like another brother to me. A friend I didn't have anywhere else.

But now it's impossible not to notice. Especially as his sleeves are rolled up to his elbows and there is ink on his forearms I'm seeing for the first time. Sexy fucking ink at that. All black and fierce and telling a story I haven't heard and don't know but wouldn't mind learning.

You know, if he were a different man.

"If you make art, why did my mother hire you?"

I snicker just as my wine is delivered and a bottle is placed on the empty table beside us. Clearly this waiter can tell we'll need refills. "You don't have to say I make art like I'm a six-year-old presenting a stick figure I just drew in crayon. I'm an artist with a bachelor's in fine arts from UCLA. I'm a sculptor who uses metal as her medium."

He ripples in agitation, his hands on the edge of the wood table like he's waiting on a verdict that will determine his fate. I decide to cut him some slack.

"I honestly have no clue why your mother hired me. I ran into the hotel bathroom a mess. You saw me." I point at him. "She arrived almost immediately after and offered me a makeup remover wipe. I cried my life story to her, much as I did with you, and somehow, she told me there was a job and I would be perfect for it. I have the right degrees, I think. It's also come to my attention that I don't look like Jenny, so there would be no temptation on your part." I throw my hands up when his eyes narrow at me. "You can glare all you want, but you know that's part of it. I don't look anything like the women you've been seen dating. Nothing like that Millie Van Der Heusen. Regardless, I had no clue you were part of that package or even that she was your mother until I saw the card she handed me."

"But once you did, you still accepted the position."

I take a sip of my wine, and wow fucking wow, that's *good*. I don't care about money most days and I'm certainly not going to bring it up now, but damn. That's got to be expensive. I normally enjoy living a regular life. My place in LA before this was small and I had a room-mate—my fucking cheating, lying cousin until my cheating, lying fiancé moved in with us. I had a car that was my first stepfather's old Mercedes G-Wagon.

My one vice has always been shoes and clothes and I don't care or make apologies for it.

But I don't typically spend a lot on food or wine.

Kaplan Fritz clearly does if the prices on the menu in the sold-out restaurant I just ordered from and the taste of this wine are anything to go by.

"Listen, Kaplan. Straight deal? I'm an artist. It's my passion. But I also need to keep busy. It's the ADHD in me. So if you're going to be a total asshole and eventually fire me when you're able to, then I should just cut my losses now. I thought I was going to be working for your mother, not you. I don't need the aggravation or headache of you. I like the foundation. I like the work it does because it's important work. I like the majority of the people I work with. I'd like to stay, but if that's truly not what you want, I'll go and find something else to fill my hours."

There. Cards on the table.

His eyes are all over me, more of that untouchable, impassive mask he's so good at wearing. It makes me jittery, itchy in my skin in both a good and a bad way. Any woman on the receiving end of his scrutiny would feel the same because the man is beautiful and intense. A touch mysterious with a sexy hint of bad boy. So my reaction to him is just a byproduct of his natural, raw sex appeal and nothing more.

Sitting here with him is a mistake. I know this. I'm not naive. He has a power he doesn't even realize he wields over me and that's dangerous. I'm not running or hiding either and I'm not using excuses. I don't know what I'm hoping for with this, but I will see it through.

After an eternity of silence, he says, "Bianca. Do you have any clue what you're doing in this role?"

"Not exactly," I answer honestly. "But I'm learning and I'm smart and I wouldn't have agreed or stayed if I didn't think I could do this. Why are you so anxious to replace me?"

He studies me for another moment as our salads are placed in front of us. "Have you heard from your ex-fiancé?" he asks without answering my question. That seems to be his jam.

"Yes." I lift my salad fork and pierce a tomato, shoveling it into my mouth along with a few pieces of arugula, chewing thoughtfully.

"And does he miss you?"

"Wouldn't you? I'm a total catch." I wink cheekily but he's unamused, waiting for a real answer I have no desire to give him. He hasn't earned anything extra from me. Why I came into this restaurant, why I sat down across from him is beyond me.

I don't like the emotions he's intentionally trying to provoke.

I thought I would have a different life. I thought I would be a different woman. I'd marry the guy and... I would have been miserable. I would have been my mother. I know that now. But that doesn't take away the hurt of everything.

"Kaplan," I start, loading more salad onto my fork now that he's started to do the same. "Tomorrow I'm buying a car. Sunday I'm moving into an apartment not far from here. I'm taking this one day at a time, but I plan on staying and seeing this through. I don't care about your money, and I don't want to fuck you. Honestly, I'd rather not have much to do with you personally if I can help it. Do you think that's something you can handle or not?"

10

I don't know why I said she could stay when every instinct I had told me to have her tossed out on her ass the way I had every other woman who walked in here, trying to catch my attention or dine with me. I'm curious about her. I'm distrustful of her.

I told myself I was after answers.

Then she sat down, so honest and unabashedly herself, so perfectly disinterested in me and my bullshit, and I find myself having to work to maintain my assholeishness with her. It's not my default setting though, when push comes to shove, I can be a real motherfucker. Just ask my residents.

This week has been a nightmare. I've been stalked all over Boston, media after a sound bite, women trying to intentionally unintentionally bump into me or get me to notice them. My father tossing out not so casually that this is what happens to unmarried billionaires.

All I wanted was to go home and shake everything off in a bottle of expensive wine, good Italian food from my favorite restaurant in the North End, and Netflix. But the cameras on my building's security were going crazy with motion. My assistant was texting me, asking me why I was hiding from the world, and instead of taking everything to go, I tossed Valencia my black Amex, bought out every table here, and sat down. A migraine I'd never had before in my life brewing like the storm that was my life.

Peace. One fucking hour of peace and quiet. One hour where no one bothered me other than to place food and alcohol in front of me. I'm going to have to hire full-time security again.

Now Bianca, whose eyes glimmer more caramel than chocolate against the flicker of low lighting and candlelight, is asking if I can handle her staying on as my executive assistant. And truth be told, I don't know if I can because while she thinks Jenny is my type, she's dead-ass wrong. But on my life, I'll go to my grave with that secret. Bianca may say she doesn't care about my bank account or my dick, but I've been fed that lie so many times if I kept attempting to swallow it, I'd be eight hundred pounds.

Still, I also unfortunately acknowledge that Luca and Carter are right.

I can't fire her now.

Our waiter takes this brilliant moment to clear our salads and deliver our entrées. Steak and asparagus for me and some kind of hollow spaghetti for her. It looks delicious and she doesn't wait to dive in. She did the same with her salad and before I can stop it, a smile hits the corner of my lips. She eats like she doesn't care I'm watching her. Like she's out with her girlfriends or alone.

I've never been on a date with a woman who eats in front of me.

Not that this is a date. It's definitely not that.

"Oh, yum. Wow. I can see why you bought this place out. Here, you have to try this."

She loads up her fork and offers it to me. I stare nonplussed, wondering what the right move is. Sharing food from the same fork is... intimate.

She rolls her eyes, reading my expression before shoving her fork into her own mouth. "Right, boss. Sorry. If you'd like to try my pasta, I won't object, and I seriously think you should because it might be one of the best things I've ever had in my mouth."

That's because you haven't had my dick in there yet, hits my tongue but thankfully goes no further. Because the fuck? *Yet?* This is why the woman can't work for me.

Still, I stupidly find myself asking, "What kind of car are you buying?"

Her anime eyes blink owl wide. "Oh, so we're steamrolling past the elephant I dropped? Okay. Got it. Something with all-wheel drive, obviously. I haven't driven in the snow, well, ever I don't think, so I need something sturdy. Duke, one of my stepfathers, suggested I purchase a Jeep Wrangler while my mother told me I should get a Mercedes SUV since I'm used to driving one already. I don't usually touch my trust funds, just the interest they accrue, so I'm thinking the Jeep is the more prudent option. Do you have any thoughts or suggestions?"

"Why do you need a car if you're moving close to the office?"

Now she's smiling and I'm an idiot. I essentially just told her she will continue on as my executive assistant without coming out and directly saying it. I don't retract it, nor do I show any outward indication that I'm annoyed I just did that. She has three more weeks to change my mind, which I already know she won't be able to. In addition to liking her tits in that top, I oddly don't find her inability to stop talking while only giving long-winded answers instead of short, polite conversation as annoying as I should.

"The studio space I rent is in an industrial part of Chelsea. I have to drive there. And since I work on my art mostly at night, I don't want to take the bus or constantly rely on Ubers. Plus, I've never lived or even traveled around New England before. I'd like to explore it when the weather turns less frigid and snowy, that is."

"What do you mean you mostly work on your art at night?"

She forks another bite of her food into her mouth, and I glance down, realizing I haven't even touched my dinner yet. I've been too busy watching her. I scowl as I cut into my perfectly cooked steak, spearing a piece into my mouth.

"I don't sleep much. Not sure if it's my ADHD or just chronic insomnia, but I typically get no more than four to five hours a night and that's on a good night. I also work better on my art at night and the place I rent studio space from doesn't care when I come or go."

My fork and knife pause midslice and I stare at her incredulously. "You're telling me you *take an Uber alone to an industrial part of Chelsea in the middle of the night?*"

"Oh please." She waves me away, taking another sip of her wine. The waiter comes over and refills her glass for her and I have no illusions he's likely listening to everything we're saying. "You sound like my second stepdad. He gave me such crap for it last night. I have a Taser on me at all times and I lived in *LA* since I was eighteen. Boston hardly scares me."

Jesus Christ, is she serious? She has prey written all over her innocent, far too trusting, pretty face. Still, I can't exactly tell her not to do it. But I can make sure she has security tailing her whenever she goes. She works for me now, albeit temporarily, but she's a target as my assistant whether she's aware of it or not. It's simply smart business to make sure she's protected.

"You're not going there tonight," I tell her, and I get treated to an eye roll this time.

"Uh-huh."

"I'm serious."

"Noted."

"I'm not fucking around."

"Goody on you."

"Bianca."

"Kaplan," she mocks, using the same tone I used.

"You have two choices. Either you come over to my place after this and we watch Netflix, so I know you're not doing anything stupid and reckless, or I come with you out to this industrial area of Chelsea."

She blinks at me so many times I think her face is about to take flight. "You're serious."

"As a heart attack, and I'm a doctor who deals in hearts."

"No."

"Bianca—"

"I mean it." She jabs the prongs of her fork in my direction.

"That's insane. I'm not going to Netflix and chill at your pad like we're college buddies or fuck friends. I barely know you. No. And you're not coming with me because I art in solitude."

"Fine. Then you're fired."

"You can't fire me."

"I just did. My mother may say whatever she likes but today was her last day and I'm the official CEO."

"You're blackmailing me?" Her eyebrows hit her hairline and she practically chucks her fork down, it clanging loudly as it hits the edge of her plate.

"Blackmail is a strong word. I prefer incentivizing."

"Fine, then I'm fired."

Infuriating woman. "Are you that naive or just have absolutely no sense or care for your own safety? Do you not comprehend who you work for or the world you live in? You are a young, doe-eyed thing asking for trouble and now you're my assistant."

"I think you're blowing this way out of proportion. And I no longer work for you. You just fired me."

I lean back in the booth seat, folding my arms, refusing to back down.

"Kaplan. No! Just no!"

I don't budge.

She balls up her black napkin in her fist and launches it at me. It hits me in the neck and falls to my lap on top of my own. Still, I don't so much as move a muscle.

"Fuck you."

"Not a chance," I retort.

"I don't need another father." A piece of bread this time, the crumbs scratching at my cashmere sweater.

"Honey, if you think that's what this is, you've got the wrong fucking guy. Throw all the shit in the world at me you want. Those are your two options."

"People will see me enter your place," she threatens, thinking she just got me with that.

I shrug as if I'm unconcerned and even though I have zero agenda to ask her to be my fake anything, it worked for Oliver. It got women off his back for a bit. If people assume I'm fucking my assistant, then that's their problem.

"Wouldn't be the first time the press got it wrong, and it certainly won't be the last."

The main problem will be keeping my dick in check if she's in my condo.

"I should have never come in here tonight."

"I'm not disputing that with you and spending more time with you definitely won't be the highlight of my Friday night. Now which one will it be? Netflix or art?"

She glares. It's kind of cute because her nose is all scrunched up while she's doing it. She's not happy, but she's not leaving. Either she's very used to people telling her what to do and obeying them or she wants to spend time with me. Shockingly, when it comes to her, I think it's the former and not the latter.

Which naturally makes my cock harden and the blood pumping through my veins turn into something primal.

"What do you get out of this?"

Good question, Bianca. Good fucking question.

"The knowledge that my former employee's face is not showing up on a missing person flyer in the post office or that her defiled body isn't in the river half eaten by fish. You can imagine how that would be bad for business."

A shrill growl, she runs her hands over her face and through her hair. She lifts the heavy, dark strands up in a makeshift ponytail before dropping them to curtain around her body. "I seriously don't like you."

"Feeling's mutual, sweetheart. You have ten seconds to decide before I decide for you."

"God, you totally suck. Fine. But I get to pick the show or movie."

"No rom-coms or chick flicks."

She gives me a haughty, I've got you exactly where I want you—right by the balls—smirk. "It's not up for negotiation. I give you this, you give me that. Tit for tat, only you're not getting my tits and I won't stare at your tats. Oh, and I want dessert from one of the pastry shops on Hanover. And more wine."

This is the moment that if I were a billionaire who gave a fuck about that or was lazy, I'd call my twenty-four-seven assistant and have them run their scrawny little ass over and do my bidding. But I'm not one of those billionaires. I operate on babies' hearts for a living. I spend my time with my family, out on my sailboat, or our sailing yacht when the weather is agreeable, and on rare occasions go home with a woman without her getting anywhere close to my heart and only after signing an NDA first.

That's it. That's my life.

At least it was.

I'm also refusing to analyze what I'm doing with this move. It ain't smart. That's for sure.

"I pick the pastry place," I counter just to be a dick. Because sure as Jesus in church, I'm not letting her go to do her fucking art in the middle of nowhere in the middle of the night by herself. And again, I don't trust her. She seems like the type who will go off and do it anyway if not properly supervised.

This has nothing to do with spending the evening with her and everything to do with not letting my new temporary assistant end up as a statistic.

"As long as they have good cannoli, I won't argue. So far, your taste in food is proving to be your best feature."

I laugh sardonically, standing and helping her do the same now that we're finished with our meal. "You'll never get to see my best feature. Now let's go."

Thirty minutes later, and after a thorough sweep of the cameras, we enter my condo. I flip on the lights in the foyer, locking the place up tight and setting the alarm.

"Holy shnikes, that view. It makes the one I have at the hotel look like a parking lot by comparison."

I don't have to follow her gaze to know what she sees out the floor-to-ceiling windows through the kitchen and great room. The harbor, because my place is literally sitting right on top of it, and the

Boston skyline beyond it. I live in Boston and for at least five months of the year, I can't be on the water in a boat and since I need the water the way most people need oxygen, I live here. Water views on two sides and water along with the sunrise every day when I wake up. It's my heaven. My oasis.

And I don't bring women here other than my family.

"My crow's nest has the best entertainment set up," I state, still not looking at her as I go about grabbing two wineglasses and two plates.

"Am I really fired?"

Her tone has me rolling my head over my shoulder to catch her eye. Something I've avoided doing since we left the restaurant and I started having palpitations at what I had just gotten myself into. She's holding her cards close to her chest, but this chick is a heart on her sleeve girl, so the attempt is futile.

She wants this job for reasons I don't quite understand and despite my being a total ass, I do know she did a decent job for her first week at it. And much to my chagrin and relief, she hasn't made any sexual advances or tried to marry me.

"I'll give you the agreed-upon month and we'll see how it goes."

She swallows and bobs her head, spinning back around to look out the window. She's very alone here, I realize. Her family seems to suck, though I know nothing of her stepfathers. But she hasn't mentioned a real father and her mother is clearly a judgmental bitch. Yet she stayed in Boston. Took on a position she knows very little about. Ventures to sketchy neighborhoods in the middle of the night. Goes after everything she does with her heart open and on the line.

She's brave.

And whether I care to admit it or not, I respect that about her.

It also makes me feel oddly protective of her since it was my car she slammed into.

I watch her for a moment, my heart hammering in my chest. I could like her. Which is why it's a hell of a lot easier to hate her.

Now I just have to figure out how to stop wanting her.

11

I'm unbelievably warm and comfortable with the softest hint of the sun on my face. It's the type of moment when consciousness is barely a tickle in the back of your brain and you snuggle in deeper, chasing the remnants of your fading dream, anxious to keep this feeling going before you're forced to actually wake up and start your day. That is until I realize I'm not in my hotel room, and the blanket and pillow surrounding my face smell like fresh laundry and *man*.

My eyes spring open only to immediately slam shut at the intrusive sun that's reflecting off the water and just singed my eyeballs. For a moment, I don't move. I hardly breathe. I listen.

No sound.

Other than the very faint hint of water lapping against something —*the building?*—outside.

"Kaplan?"

I bite into my lip, hoping, praying...

No response and I slowly peel myself up, adjusting as I go so I don't fall off the large sectional in his crow's nest as he calls it. It's actually a giant open room on the third floor of his condo, complete with humongous television, the aforementioned couch, a fully stocked bar, a pool table, a card table, pinball machine, and on the expansive deck directly off the room, a Jacuzzi. Can you say bachelor pad?

But thankfully, no Kaplan.

I don't remember falling asleep. We were watching *The Usual Suspects* because even though I might be an innocent, naive little bunny, I do love a good suspense film with tons of action and brilliant acting. We drank wine and ate cannoli and talked about the film and how incredible it is and...

Now I'm covered in a blanket that's softer than a baby's ass with a down pillow beneath my head. Kaplan Fritz tucked me in. Holy wow. That thought shouldn't have me smiling, but it totally does. Mostly because last night was... fun. Unexpectedly so. He was still gruff and closed off and cold as a witch's tit in February in Boston, but yeah. Fun.

And totally weird given our situation.

Which is why I need to go. Like now.

My watch tells me it's just after seven, so after a quick pit stop to the bathroom up here where I pee, wash my makeup-crusted face, and throw my hair up in a bun on top of my head, I sneak down the stairs, quiet as a mouse. I didn't explore much of his place, but I can tell that it was once two side-by-side townhouses that he must have bought and ripped the dividing wall down between and completely renovated.

Why a single man needs this much space is anyone's guess, but there are two wings to the second floor. It's also mercifully dark and quiet with all the doors shut.

Phew! Blowing out a breath, I continue to creep down the floating stairs, anxious to grab my coat, my purse, my phone, and get the hell out of here. My bare feet hit the first floor and I tiptoe back toward the kitchen. Another ridiculously expansive floor with wings and doors, but I know where my stuff is. By the back where I left it.

My phone is plugged in on the table—something I'm positive I also didn't do—and I pick it up, suppressing my groan at what I find waiting for me on it. Shaking my head, I tuck it into my purse, slip on my coat, and just as my hand hits the doorknob a voice calls out, "I wouldn't do that unless you want to set off the alarm and have the police come."

I scream, jolting back in place, my hand recoiling from the doorknob like it's singeing the skin from my bones. "Fuck!" I hiss out, clutching my chest and spinning around. "You scared me..."

Only my voice dies out the second I get a look at him.

He's shirtless, only wearing gym shorts, his entire broad chest, muscular arms and shoulders, rock-hard abs, and holy V-thing on full display. As are his tattoos. And Dear Abby, his left nipple is pierced. He's drenched in sweat. Did I mention that? Beads of it gliding deliciously down his body, over every ridge and valley of perfect muscle. His dark-blond hair is wet, brushed back off his smirking face.

"I... um..." Yep, that's all I've got.

He lifts a bottle of water to his mouth that I hadn't noticed was in his hand—because who cares about his hands in a moment like this —and takes a drink and my mouth is so freaking dry right now I'm tempted to snatch the thing from him and down it all in one gulp.

He wipes his mouth with the back of his arm and why is that so sexy? It shouldn't be, right?

"I was going to make breakfast," he says instead of commenting on the way I'm openly ogling him like a mindless, lust-addled fool who can't help herself. "Do you like omelets?"

Omelets? I don't even know my name right now.

Still, I find myself mumbling, "Sure," in what is very obviously a breathy whisper. He heads for the kitchen and at the loss of his sexy as all sin chest—*that pierced nipple and those tattoos!*—I shake my head, clearing some of the fog. "No. Wait. I should go." *Because if I stay, I might lick you dry.* "You know. Busy day and all." I smack my hand to my forehead and that's when his head pops back around the wall, catching me in the act of visually humiliating myself.

That damn cocky smirk is still there. "Take off your coat. Hang it back up. Set down your purse and come in and eat some eggs with me. I'm going to shower and if you want, you can do the same. After we do all that, I'm going to go with you to purchase your car."

I'm shaking my head before he's even done. "No. No way. Why on earth would I let you do that?"

"Have you ever purchased a car for yourself?"

I shift my stance, my eyes hitting the floor in front of his feet because now he's standing here again half-naked, smelling like a sweaty, sexy god, and I can't think or focus with him like this. "No," I unfortunately admit. "But I can't imagine it's a difficult thing to do."

"You'll get ripped off," he declares and that just pisses me off.

My eyes shoot back up to his.

He holds his hand up. "Listen, it's not a female thing. It's a you look insanely innocent and trusting thing. In case you missed it, my last name goes a long way in this city, and I can help you get a car without being taken for a ride. Pun intended."

I tilt my head, narrowing my eyes. "Why are you doing all this?" I honestly don't get it. Any of it. Last night and now this? It doesn't make sense.

"I just told you why."

I want to argue that. I want to demand answers, but I don't think I'll get any. He's extremely careful with his words. With the things he says and doesn't. I truly should go. It's clear by this point that he's not going to recognize me. And even if he does, our past obviously meant a hell of a lot more to me than it ever did to him.

I'm playing with fire. And not a fire that seals and binds, creating something new and beautiful. A fire that maims, destroys, and hurts, ruins recklessly and without care.

"Kaplan... I..."

I don't want to go though. Even with the knowledge that this isn't anything more than what he's offering and that I could still potentially get hurt, I don't want to go.

"Okay," I say and for a flicker of a second, a genuine smile that makes his green eyes sparkle hits his face only to disappear just as quickly. A mirage in the desert, it was breathtaking for that second, if only an illusion.

"I'm going to run upstairs and take a quick shower because I'm nasty. Then I'll make breakfast."

Nasty is not the word I would have gone with. "You're going to put on a shirt, right?"

"You're blushing again, but thankfully the drooling has stopped."

I flip him off and he chuckles.

"Yes, I'm going to put on a shirt. And pants, for that matter. There's coffee brewing in the kitchen, or you can make yourself a cappuccino with the machine." He jogs off back toward the stairs and I take off my coat, giving myself another few moments to get my head on straight.

He's not even being nice, more commanding and domineeringly alpha than anything else. Maybe this is just how he operates, and the world follows whatever he says because he's Kaplan Fritz. I have no clue. All I know is that this has the makings to be a very strange day.

"YOU LOOK LIKE AN AGING ROCK STAR," I tell Kaplan as we head toward the dealership in some town outside of Boston. He does minus the aging part since he looks a solid ten years younger than he is. He's wearing a black sweater, a black leather jacket, black jeans, black boots, a Red Sox hat, and dark shades even though it's not all that sunny now that the clouds started rolling in. Evidently, we're to get more snow later today.

"And you look like a rich grungy hippie who didn't realize that look went out in the nineties."

"You mean when you were a teenager? Can you tell me what it was like to grow up with dial-up internet and no smartphones or tablets?"

"You're prettier when you're not speaking."

I gasp. "Rude!" I punch him in the arm and all it does is make him smile. "God, why did I agree to this?"

He doesn't get the chance to respond because instantly, there is a salesman in front of us. I decided to go the Jeep route because one, they're sexy-looking, two, I can get one where I can remove the top and it's like a convertible, and three it's four-wheel drive, which you need living in Boston.

"Can I help you, sir?" the man says directly to Kaplan while ignoring me, and for real?

Kaplan smirks at me and again I'm tempted to flip him off. Him and that fucking smirk.

"Actually, he's just my arm candy. I'm the one purchasing and if you're going to be dismissive of the fact that women can purchase Jeeps for themselves, then I think we'll shop elsewhere."

The guy sputters, turning to me as a flush rises up his cheeks. "Oh, yes, ma'am. I meant no disrespect. Typically, we get men here looking for Wranglers, not women."

"Uh-huh. Well, not today." I go about telling the guy precisely what I want, and he runs off to make a copy of my license and get the keys so I can test drive it. I nudge Kaplan, who has been silent this entire time. "Still think I need you, so I don't get taken for a ride? That I'm an innocent, too trusting woman?"

He removes his sunglasses, tucks them on top of the rim of his hat, and pins me with a look that instantly has my heart rate jacking up. "Since we're not at work and I'm not playing the part of your boss in this moment, can I be honest with you without fear of repercussions or you reading too much into it?"

Oh shit. "Yes."

"The way you handled that guy was insanely fucking sexy and if you were any other woman and I were any other man, I'd drag you into the bathroom right now and shove my tongue and fingers inside your pussy until you screamed my name and came on my face."

I squeak, practically swallowing my tongue, my eyes bulging out of their sockets as flames shoot up my face. My thighs inadvertently clench along with my empty core that is growing wetter by the second. No one has *ever* said *anything* even remotely as hot and filthy as that to me before.

"Back with keys, ma'am." The now eager beaver rushes out as he flies back over to us.

"Guess it's a good thing we're us and not anyone else," Kaplan drawls without even a hint of the dirty words he just said to me on his face. He drops his sunglasses back over his eyes and takes the keys from the guy's hand because clearly higher-level brain and muscle function escape me. "Ready to go take a ride with me, Echidna or do you need another moment to collect yourself first?"

Bastard. He knows exactly what he just did to me.

I snatch the keys from him, stomping on his foot in my heeled boots as I walk past him, heading back outside toward the parking lot where there is a waiting Jeep for me to test drive. His warm chuckle rumbles from behind me and I shudder ever so slightly, annoyingly turned on. My nipples are at DEFCON 1, maximum readiness, and I know he saw that through my thin blouse. I zip my coat and snarl out an expletive.

It's not my fault. I've slept with four guys and only two of them have given me an orgasm and that was only one at a time.

Tod isn't included in that two and I was set to marry the shitty lay.

I woefully just assumed this was the way it was and my cousin, who was my freaking BFF never discouraged my theory. Either Tod wasn't giving it to her any better or she was enjoying the fact that he never got me off.

But Kaplan just talked like he doles out orgasms to women the way the Easter Bunny—no pun intended—doles out candy: in mass quantities and to everyone. And I mean come on, who couldn't use a good screaming orgasm after the week I've had?

I tear open the front door of the Jeep and climb up, grateful that I'm not a small woman considering how high off the ground this thing is. Shutting the door, I buckle up just as Kaplan gets in the passenger side. The salesman isn't with us. He's standing back inside the doors of the dealership, waving to us.

"He's not coming?!"

"Feel like you need a buffer from me?"

Ignoring his teasing comment and playfully sexy lilt, I put the Jeep in drive and with my hands gripping the wheel at two and ten, we start off. Praying I don't get us into an accident.

I've never test driven a car before so I'm already nervous and with Kaplan sitting alone in here beside me, smelling all masculine and delicious, I'm a flustered mess. Still, the Jeep is very cool, and I feel insanely high up and powerful in it. I like it instantly. And my new place has an off-street parking spot which Greta informed me is Boston rental apartment gold.

He flips on the sound system, checking it out and I blow out a breath as music fills the space between us. My eyes are laser-focused on the street I'm driving like ten miles an hour down and I can't look at him. Because I can't stop thinking about what he said in there. Or the way his eyes darkened as he did.

"Relax, Bianca. Starting Monday, everything between us will be one-hundred-percent professional and after you purchase your new Jeep, I'll be out of your hair." He turns toward the window and murmurs so quietly I almost miss it over the music playing. "Instead of having my hands up in it."

I swerve, practically veering us off the road only to correct the Jeep at the last minute. I sit up straighter. Clear my throat. Ignore the raging crimson staining my cheeks. "Not a word on that," I warn.

A warm chuckle. "Promise. Despite how tempting *teasing* you is."

12

Monday morning, bright and fucking early, I open my front door, not surprised at all to find all my siblings and most of their significant others on the other side. Why? Couple reasons. One, I haven't seen them all weekend and that includes Sunday dinner, which we always go to as a family at my parents' compound. I was called into the hospital for one of my patients and couldn't go. Two, I was photographed with Bianca, the two of us leaving my place Saturday morning.

And I refused to answer their calls or texts about it other than to say nothing happened, she's my assistant, and I was helping her out.

It makes no sense. Not to them and not to me why I allowed her into my house. Why I allowed her to stay. Why I insisted on spending the day with her, making her breakfast like she had spent the night in my bed with me, and then helping her buy a car.

Why I told her exactly what I wanted to do to her.

I don't do those things with women. Any of it.

Worse yet, I had a really good time with her.

Now here they are, seeking answers under the bullshit guise of we want to wish you luck on your first official day as CEO and oh, yeah, we brought you breakfast from that place you like in hopes it will relax you and you'll start spilling the beans on the girl.

I won't.

"Shouldn't you be, I don't know, wearing clothes?" Grace asks, her nose scrunched up when she sees I'm only wearing gym shorts and sweat. Her reaction is not nearly as adorable as Bianca's and that right there is the problem.

"Considering I didn't invite any of you over, no."

"He's moody. Something is definitely up," Rina comments, casting a glance over to Landon who just shrugs because if anyone knows and understands being moody and not wanting to talk about shit, it's him. Landon lost his wife nine years ago now in a tragic car accident. For years he blamed himself for her death and it's only now that he's starting to forgive himself for his mistakes.

"Amelia and Elle send their apologies for not crashing in on you this morning," Oliver informs me, pushing past me and stalking through my house toward my kitchen. "Both of them had to get the girls to school and get to work and didn't have time to make the trek into Boston."

Amelia is Oliver's now real fiancée, though for a while, she was his fake fiancée. They live together in Chestnut Hill with Layla, Amelia's little sister who Amelia is guardian over. Elle is Landon's woman, his daughter Stella's teacher, and neighbor as it would be, but Elle and Landon are getting serious enough that the house Landon is building he's doing for all of them.

"And Raven said she wasn't going to get out of bed this early to badger you about something you clearly don't want to talk about, so she didn't come," Luca finishes.

Ironically, Raven is probably one of the few I'd actually talk to about Bianca.

"Other than being disappointed in not seeing them, you all should have taken a page from Raven and not come. I have to get ready for work and unfortunately today isn't a scrubs day like it is for the rest of you."

"I'm not in scrubs," Brecken, my baby sister Rina's now husband drawls as he munches on a piece of toast while staring down at his phone. By the looks of it, Rina dragged him here. I like that about Brecken. He knows when to insert himself into family drama and when to back off.

"We're obviously not leaving until you give your siblings something and I'm starving," Grace says, opening a take-out box piled with waffles and eggs. "Why don't you just tell them all the details about this woman—er I mean the new job—and get it over with." She winks at me as she pours syrup over the entire thing and then digs in with gusto only to moan. "God, I'm going to miss eating for two when this pregnancy is all done."

"You always eat like this, pregnant or not," Oliver quips.

"True," she concedes, sucking the syrup off her fingers.

Snagging the egg-white-and-cheddar sandwich I know is for me, I creep backward toward my stairs. "How about I just go up and shower while pretending you guys aren't here?"

"We already told them everything you told us the other day," Luca informs me, waving a finger back and forth between him and Carter. "You tell us you didn't fuck her and we believe you. But you also told us you couldn't stand her and that she couldn't stand you and then you're photographed Saturday morning walking out of here together. Incidentally, Mom and Dad were all over us last night about the picture and the press were all up our asses as we walked in. They're waiting on you."

I groan. "If our bank accounts didn't have nine zeros, would anyone give a fuck about us?"

"Likely not. But we're hot and amazing in bed so we have that going for us too."

I smirk at Oliver because he gets it. Of the six of us, Oliver, Luca, and I are stalked the most by the press. Rina, Landon, and Carter have always managed to maintain a lower profile. Especially Rina and much of that is her big brothers being protective and keeping the press off her ass.

"Just tell us about the girl and then you can eat your breakfast and shower in peace."

"Rina, why do you care?"

Something hits her eye, a gleam I don't quite understand. "Did you see the picture?"

"What?" I shake my head. "No. I only know it's out there because you assholes told me it was." I didn't look it up because I didn't want to think about Bianca any more than I already was and I didn't want to see a picture of us together leaving my condo because deep in my bones, I knew it shouldn't have happened in the first place.

I don't know if it was a fuck you to Millie—who has been up my ass, talking about our future that we will never have and who brought up how magical penthouse apartments in Paris are no less than five times during our one-hour ambush lunch—or my parents for setting up that lunch and planting this stupid arrangement seed. Yeah, that lunch was supposed to be just my mother and me and then "oh, look who's here in the restaurant too, you have to join us"—or to the press because Bianca is so far removed from the women I've always been photographed with.

I've already called Morgan Fairchild, Raven's father and also our family's head of security to get a detail set up. Between the foundation and the hospital and my home it's a mess and I can't do it alone. It's simply not safe anymore.

"Here." Rina pulls up what I assume is the picture on her phone and then flips the screen around so I can see it. It's a picture of Bianca and me walking to my car. It's harmless, other than it's obvious we're right in front of my door. But then I look a bit closer, and I see it. The smile on my lips. The way my eyes cling to the side of her face. The way my head and body are angled toward her. The way her hands are moving as if she's saying something that visibly has me enthralled.

Christ. This is not what I wanted to deal with this morning. Especially not before I have to go into the office and not only face her but the entire office who will no doubt be talking about it.

"She was telling me how she makes her art. She works with metal and has to use hammers and pliers and shit to make it. That's all this is. The crazy-ass woman takes an Uber to some industrial part of Chelsea in the middle of the night to work on her art and I wasn't going to let her do that because it's dangerous as hell. She came over and we watched a movie and she fell asleep on the couch in my crow's nest. That's it. That's how un-fucking-scandalous this is."

"Except you're you," Carter cuts in. "Boston's last billionaire bachelor who wants nothing to do with dating or relationships or marriage. You're the ultimate catch, Kap. Especially now that the rest of us are off the market."

"Exactly," Luca agrees. "What does Raven call you? Doctor Untouchable. That's you to the world and yet now you're photographed smiling with your new assistant leaving your home. We believe you that it's nothing, but the world won't."

"Right." Oliver nods, picking at the food on his plate. "All we're saying is, be careful. Watch your back. They've caught a scent and they won't stop until they've got what they're after."

~

I HAVE to hand it to my family. They're very good at pulling the attention away from me. All of us leave my condo together, Grace and her large belly in the front, her hand on it and a grimace on her face as if she's in pain.

"Carter," she cries. "We have to get to the hospital now."

She's not lying. Both of them are OB-GYNs at MGH and they have shifts this morning, so yes, they do have to get to the hospital now.

"Oh!" And there's Carter on one side of her, Oliver on the other, the waiting press already calling out her name instead of mine, giving me the perfect distraction to take a left toward my car that I had parked on the street off to the side instead of in my spot unseen.

Just as I hit the unlock button, two tall, dark figures stifle my shadow. "Sir," they say in unison, and I breathe a sigh of relief. Morgan Fairchild didn't fuck around. He sent me his biggest guys who are so massive they block out the sun.

"Axl. Slash," I greet the twins whose mother obviously had a thing for Guns N' Roses. "Good to see you both this morning. Thank you for coming on such short notice."

"Our pleasure, sir," Axl replies since he's the only one who speaks regularly of the two of them. Slash tends to grunt instead. "Mr. Fairchild has me in the vehicle driving you and Slash tailing us. Other than the ones in front of your residence, the front of the foundation is surrounded by press."

"Fucking fantastic," I grouse. "What about the staff? Have they been confronted at all?" And by staff I mean Bianca, though Rina told me there was no mention of her name anywhere and the picture they have of us, her face is partially obstructed by her arm and her long, distinguishable hair was up in a bun. Still, if you know her, you know it's her.

"Not that I'm aware of, sir. A perimeter has been set up since they're officially blocking the front of a public building and most staff have been asked to enter through the back using their personal key card."

"Good. Okay."

That's a relief.

"Let's go." Hopping into the driver's side of the car, Axl doesn't hesitate as he peels out and like a stupid asshole celebrity, I duck down in the passenger seat as we pass the front of my building. I hate this. I hate everything about this. I love my family and I'm proud of the foundation, but I just want to do my work without all this other bullshit.

I want to trust the people who enter my life. I want to date women and I don't want to have to question their motives. I want to be able to go to the grocery store or a restaurant in peace without being photographed. I want to fix tiny human hearts and sail and be with my family and fuck women. That's it!

Why does that have to be so goddamn impossible?

We pull into the back lot that's fenced in and partially covered— my mother was no fool when she picked this building—and I breathe out a sigh of relief. The press can't come back here. That doesn't mean they can't get photographs with long-range lenses, but at least there is some protection for the staff.

Axl and Slash wait until I'm inside before they head around the front of the building, and I take the stairs up to the third level, entering through the back door onto the executive floor. But I stop in my tracks at what I'm hearing coming from the kitchen, hovering right beside it.

"No, I don't think that's true," someone who I think is one of the finance people says. "I overheard her explaining it to Greta and Charlie this morning and they're all friends. She'd have no reason to lie to them. Bianca and Kaplan met up at his place because he was going to help her buy a car since she didn't know where to go to do that here and he offered to help as her new boss."

Huh. Some of the tension in my shoulders ebbs. She didn't tell anyone she spent the night after watching a movie at my place or that we had dinner together prior to that. She told her friends she came over that morning so we could go car shopping. She made me sound like the good guy. An honorable guy helping out his new assistant.

A warmth I'm unaccustomed to spreads through my veins. And dammit all if it doesn't make me like her more than I was already starting to. I don't know what I was expecting her to say, but the fact that she isn't trying to sell some story and is even hiding and downplaying some of what went down between us is not only unexpected but a relief.

I've come to anticipate the opposite from women when it comes to me.

"I don't know," someone else whose voice I don't recognize retorts. "They looked awfully cozy and wasn't that the same outfit she was wearing on Friday?"

"I thought it was a different top. Anyway, we all know the press blows stuff way out of proportion when it comes to the Fritz family. Bianca laughed and said absolutely not when Greta asked if they were secretly dating. I feel for Kaplan. I do. It can't be easy to have that be your life."

"But it's worth it to see the murder on Jenny's face this morning. I thought she was going to blow a gasket."

"No kidding."

The two of them start laughing and I take that as my moment to walk past the kitchen and head for my new office. I haven't been here since my mother occupied it and from what Bianca said, it looks completely different.

Speaking of... Bianca comes sauntering out of a small office beside mine, a tablet in her face until she glances up and our eyes meet. She offers me a timid smile and I ignore the way she looks in the snug-fitting burgundy dress she's wearing that hugs her tits and hits just above her knees with matching sexy as fuck sky-high patent leather heels.

"Good morning, Dr. Fritz. I'm glad to see you made it in safely despite the mob outside."

"Me too. Is everything ready for the start of the day?" Indifferent, I blow past her, entering my office, aware she's trailing behind me. She leaves the door open, and I know that's an intentional move.

"Do you want to talk about the paper yesterday?" Her voice is barely above a whisper. "About the picture of us in it? Because for anyone who asked I told them—"

I hold up a hand, stopping her. "I know what you told them. I overheard someone else talking about it. Thank you for that. And no, I don't want to talk about it again."

She nods, smiling a smile at me that has me forgetting about the morning I've had and the fact that I'm currently working a job I have no desire to work.

"I hope you like your office," she says, a hint of nerves hitting her face and just like that, spell broken.

Glancing around, I take everything in, impressed that she threw this together so quickly and somehow, without knowing much about me and prior to coming into my home, hit my style perfectly. Everything is a combination of antique and modern, distressed, and clean lines. From the desk to the bookshelf to the table and chairs in the corner to the worn-looking leather sofa.

I catch sight of the metal piece she made for me, the sculpture of Typhon that's sitting prominently on the top shelf of the bookcase and grin. It's better in person than it was in the picture. She has real talent. And she made that for me. Which means she was thinking about me.

I like the thought of that entirely too much.

"It'll do," I mutter blandly as I set my bag down and fall onto the leather chair behind the desk. "I trust your move yesterday went well?"

I wanted to help like the stupid asshole I seem to be with her but restrained myself. I haven't looked up her address in her HR file. Haven't even looked her up, though I've been tempted. My mother said her background check was pristine and I don't question that. My mother is thorough, and Bianca is well, Bianca.

But the temptation to learn more about her is growing like an itch I need to scratch despite my efforts to squash it. I don't want her around but now she's unavoidable. At least until I go back to the hospital next week, and she stays here.

"It went very well, thank you. I don't have a lot of stuff here other than some suitcases but the rental furniture I picked out came on time."

I wonder if she feels it. This tense, swirling energy between us. Or if it's just me.

"Great. Are we done with the bullshit morning chatter now or is actual work not part of your agenda for the day?"

Annoyance and frustration strike a path across her face, causing her eyes to narrow and her lips to purse. I know I'm being an asshole. I know I've been hot and cold and everything in between, but I can no longer be anything but this with her. Here especially. It's the only way I'll survive her working for me.

She affects me and I can't stand it. I love verbally sparring with her, which is also half the reason I'm an asshole. The other is self-preservation. The way she looks today in her dress with her dark hair down and messy—like she just had sex—is driving me wild. Her curves. Those luscious fucking curves are all I picture when I close my eyes at night. All I think about when I take my cock in my hand.

I return her withering stare.

"Actually, I was coming in here to inform you that your first video conference call starts in less than ten minutes, followed by a meeting with the grant review team. After that is a budget and event planning session for the three charity events coming up."

"And I'm required to attend that one?" Why couldn't Rina have been born first? Or even Oliver since he'd be better at this nonsense than I am. I have no interest. Nor do I know what I'm doing with any of this. What the hell do I know about planning events?

"Yes. It would be helpful for me if you did so I know how you operate in those, and I can eventually take over that position for you. Would you like me to get you some coffee?"

"Are you going to spit in it?"

"I was thinking of blowing my nose into it instead since the last thing I'd ever want to do with you is swap spit."

The air crackles with electricity, a storm brewing between us, and I know I'm not the only one who feels this. It's all over her, from the heavy pants of her breaths to the way her eyes glitter and darken. I'd consider this our own brand of foreplay if I wasn't positive our interactions will never go beyond this. Still, that doesn't stop all the available blood in my body from traveling straight to my dick when she licks her lips.

"Coffee. Minus the snot. Black."

"Like your soul."

"Like my soul, Echidna." With that she turns to leave, only I stop her with, "Starting next week, I'm going to need you to work from the hospital at least three mornings a week."

Because apparently, I'm a man who can't help himself and lives for pain.

The door to my office slams shut behind her and it isn't until I turn on the camera for my video conference that I realize I'm smiling.

13

By the time we make it to the event meeting, I'm ready to kill him and it's not even lunchtime on day one. I have no idea what I'm going to do. He sat through his first two meetings looking bored, his mind anywhere other than on the things he's supposed to be focused on and if he wasn't visibly checked out half the time, the other half the time he was rude and dismissive as he worked on his phone.

I'm the one with ADHD and yet he was the poster child for it this morning.

I nudged him half a dozen times under his desk and gave him the motherly don't be an ass look, but he ignored me too. I can't tell if he's just so miserable by the idea of running the foundation that he's not even going to try or if he just truly, deeply doesn't give a shit.

"You need to pay attention in this meeting," I tell him as we walk toward the conference room at the other end of the floor.

"I'm trying," he lies. "This stuff isn't my thing and I have a patient in the hospital who I operated on last week who isn't doing so well and another case that came in this morning that my residents are having trouble with. I'm needed there. Not here."

I pause, snagging his arm and pulling him to a stop, staring up at his eyes clouded with concern. "Do you need to go?" I ask, feeling bad for thinking he was just being an ass.

He sighs, running a hand through his hair and messing it all up. It was so perfectly coiffed when he came in and now it's a tussled, sexy disaster. "No. I took this week off, and another doctor is handling it, but I don't like it. It doesn't sit well with me."

"Because that's what you do."

He nods as if I'm finally starting to get it. "That's what I do. Not this. The whole reason my mother hired you is so that you can learn this stuff and eventually do it for me."

"You're still the CEO. My position is to help you do that. I can sit in on meetings. I can take notes. I can discuss my thoughts and guide you with my suggestions. But ultimately, the final decisions on things are yours."

"Which is why you're going to work those three mornings a week from the hospital."

My heart instantly starts to pound as a cold sweat breaks out across my forehead and the back of my neck. "About that." I shift, staring down at my feet. "I don't like hospitals." More like hate them to the marrow of my bones.

"Nobody likes hospitals. Not the people who work there and least of all the people who are forced to be there and in this case the patients are children."

His fingers latch on to my chin, dragging my gaze up to his. Oh-so-green eyes burrow into mine, making me feel stripped down. Bare. Yet there's something else too and I can only wonder if he feels it every single time he touches me the way I do. That damn current of energy. A step in and now he's so close, my nose taking a happy bath in his cologne.

His thumb does a small drag along my jaw, clipping the corner of my lips, causing my breath to catch. And just like that, his eyes darken, his body temperature noticeably rising. He does it again, his eyes tracking down to follow the motion, locking on my lips for a beat before returning to mine.

But those eyes... I can't tell what this look is. Anger? Frustration? *Hunger?*

A nearby sound has him blinking as if coming back to the room, his hand instantly dropping to his side. A step back and then, "I can't be in two places at once. That's your job. I'll arrange for you to be in a non-patient part of the hospital."

It's a command, not a request. A cold rush of air settles back on my shoulders, all the heat he engulfed me in moments ago ices over. "Like where, the janitor's closet?"

He gruffly exhales. "There's an administrative wing where my office is. I'll arrange for some space for you there."

I want to argue this more than I want to kick him in the nuts and after the morning I've had with him that's seriously saying something about how much I dislike this idea. "How about a negotiation?"

"The negotiation is you do it or you quit since you enjoy reminding me, I *temporarily* can't fire you."

"I'm not quitting. The satisfaction I get from ruining your day with my mere presence is too rewarding."

"Then it seems you're at the hospital with me three mornings a week, Echidna."

He doesn't give me the chance to argue further as he brushes past me for the conference room.

Damn him.

Without a choice, I plaster on a smile and pretend like everything is fine. That I'm not freaking out over having to spend time in a hospital, and that I didn't just have a moment with my boss where he not so professionally touched my lips.

Because in all likelihood, he didn't, right?

He's a mean, intolerant, arrogant, condescending jerk who outwardly would rather put Icy Hot on his dick than touch me. I probably had a crumb from breakfast on my face that he was cleaning off. Anything that I perceived as something else between us, is just that. Perceived. A point proven as Mean Jenny walks by, throwing me a sneer to end all sneers before entering the same conference room I'm supposed to be in and reminding me precisely what type of women Kaplan Fritz is attracted to.

Not me.

Not that I care.

I wasn't lying when I told him ruining his day is the highlight of mine. Because I hate him. Gorgeous, ghosting bastard dropped me like third-period French. He was something to me and I thought I was something to him. For three years he was the only person who I felt knew me without actually knowing me.

A friend unlike any I had.

He wasn't part of my daily life. I didn't tell him about what high school was like or what was going on with my mother and her marriages. Or that I was moving states again and starting a new school in my junior year of high school. Instead, I told him things about myself I'd never told anyone. Things about Forest and what his death did to me. I asked him philosophical and existential questions and he did that with me too. We shared thoughts and secrets.

Kaplan knew my inner soul and treated it with care and respect while extending that same piece of himself to me. It was purely platonic and innocent and maybe that's what made it so perfect. I trusted him. I relied on the knowledge that someone truly cared.

Now as I enter the conference room and dutifully take the seat as far away from him as possible, I'm starting to question if maybe that was all the conjuring of a lost, lonely child's mind.

He is not the man I thought he was.

So it's time I let go of any residual notion of that. I'll do my job here. I'll get myself acclimated to life in Boston. And if in a few months or a year I find it more impossible to work for him than I already do, I'll quit and find something else that nurtures my soul.

While I get my laptop set up, Kaplan calls the meeting to order, asking Roberta, the head events planner, to start with an update.

"Sure," she says, cuing up her PowerPoint to the SMART Board before twisting in her chair to face Kaplan. "Alright, so as you can see on this slide, this spring we have three main charity events that we're going to be sponsoring. The first is an organization that helps under-resourced children, towns, and school programs by providing funding and equipment for sports, and resources for other extracurricular activities. The second is a reading and math program that targets city public schools in low-income communities and provides supplemental materials and educators for both gifted students, as well as children who require extra help but aren't afforded that through their daily curriculum and school budgets. And the third one provides college prep assistance and guidance for lower-income families. This includes everything from standardized test preparation, assistance with college applications, and financial aid help."

She clicks a button on her laptop and then the slide changes. I scan over the fundraising goal from each charity and the cost to run each event and frown. I hadn't seen any of these figures at the last budget meeting because they weren't available. That meeting was to figure out how much we planned to spend on the events themselves.

"I'm sorry," I interrupt, still staring at the board as I swivel back and forth in my chair. "Can I ask a couple of questions about this?"

"Sure," Roberta replies with a warm smile. Her Kelly-green blouse accentuates her gorgeous dark skin and I need to find out where she shops.

"So, I realize I'm brand-new here, but do you invite the same guest list to each event or are they fresh with each new charity?"

"Well, if you'd done your research and your job, you'd already know the answer to that," Jenny snaps. "There is a forty-two percent overlap between all three events."

"Right," I state, completely ignoring her tone. I use my pen to point toward the screen. "And each of these charities is all academically based or at least related to underprivileged children and school systems."

"So?" Another snap by Jenny, this one even harsher than the first.

"So," I mock. "Maybe if you did *your* research and *your* job, Jenny, you'd realize that these numbers aren't impressive at all. Aren't you the one handling the booking and scheduling for these events? You set the dates for these, right?"

"Yes. I don't see the problem."

"How on earth do you think it makes smart financial sense to have them each one week apart if there is that much overlap in guest lists? If I were invited to all three of these events or even two of these events, I'd likely accept one and decline the others because who wants to deal with that nonsense three weeks in a row?" I turn back to Roberta, completely dismissing Jenny. "Have you considered hosting one large gala instead of three smaller events?"

Roberta leans back in her chair. "You mean combining it into one Abbot Foundation Cares For Kids or something with a better title and dividing the proceeds between the three charities?"

I shrug, tapping the heels of my shoes against the carpet while glancing over at Kaplan, who has remained stoic, his eyes on the screen. I quickly turn back to Roberta. "Yes. Your out-of-pocket expenses for each event are nearly two-thirds of what you *hope* to rake in. People get event weary. There are only so many times they want to get dressed up and open their checkbooks. Especially back to back to back. Knowing that they have three events to spread their dollars, I'd bet people will donate smaller sums to each charity than they might be inclined to if they only have to write one check and attend only one event. These events are also only dinner and light dancing. Nothing else to get them excited but rubbery chicken and too-well-done steak."

Roberta snickers. "No one goes for the food."

"Exactly! But what if we gave them something to get excited about? What if you invited everyone, hosted it in a space that would be more accommodating, get a larger band, did some silent and live auctions, and really pump up the potential earnings for these charities while decreasing overall expenses?"

"As you said, you're new here—" Jenny lays into me again when Roberta cuts her off.

"No, I think that idea holds a lot of merit. In the past, people have attended these events strictly out of respect for Octavia and the Fritz family. Some just so they can be photographed with them. But what if we change all that? Build some buzz and energy for the charities and the foundation rather than the family."

I glance at Kaplan as does Roberta, but she quickly continues when he remains silent.

"Instead of spreading ourselves thin with three mediocre events, we could host one large gala in one location. Think of the cost savings alone. One event space. One band. One meal. One open bar. I love this idea. And I *love* the idea of auctions which is not something we've ever done with our spring events."

"Exactly!" Martin, one of the finance people, exclaims, rocking back and forth in his chair. "Since the foundation matches the sums raised at each event for each charity, I think this will also help with our overall bottom line since we won't be spending so much on each separate event. Those dollars can go to the charities."

Jenny squints at me from across the table, her contemptuous childish antics at trying to make me sound stupid or incompetent annoying. She's seated directly beside Kaplan who doesn't even appear to notice her though she's visibly trying to do everything she can to change that.

Sitting up straighter, she angles in toward him, staring into his profile as if seeking support. She presses her breasts into his side, and I suppress a groan. "Well, I think that idea will ultimately end up not providing enough financial support for each of the charities. I mean, now we're talking about subtracting instead of adding."

I'm so damn tempted to roll my eyes at her and give her a lesson in basic finance and well, math when Kaplan does it for me. "It's dividing, not subtracting. Though technically we were doing that already by having things spread over three events instead of one. As someone who has attended these events countless times over the years as Roberta said, I have to say, I agree that the idea of one large event rather than three consecutive ones is appealing. Being asked to shell out money multiple times in a row grows tiresome. One event bleeds into the next and most times people don't attend all of them because we have lives, so you'll have losses. Especially for the last event. When you say auction, what are you talking about?"

My eyebrows shoot up to my forehead as I blink rapidly. I think hell has just frozen over. Kaplan Fritz agreed with me. His begrudging eyes meet mine, noting my expression. I cock him a well-well smirk and he subtly lifts his hand to his mouth, wiping at his bottom lip with his middle finger.

I chuckle only to stifle it with a miserable attempt at a fake cough.

"By auction, I mean donated or severely discounted items that could potentially raise a lot of capital. Vacations and hotel packages and free meals at nice restaurants throughout the city and handbags and whatever we can come up with. I went to one once where there was both a silent and live auction and it was so much fun. Half the thrill people had was outbidding their friends on things. My mother once won a weekend in Malibu at Naomi Kent's home."

Kaplan laughs, the sound bursting from him startling half the room. "You realize I'm friends with the members of Wild Minds as well as their spouses, right?"

I turn fifty different shades of red, my jaw on the floor. Naomi Kent is a world-famous pop star and is married to Gus Diamond who is the lead guitarist and does backup vocals for the band Wild Minds. They also happen to be my favorite band. Ever.

"Um. No. I didn't realize that. But if you can get them to donate stuff, wow. That'll get the dollars flowing. My mom forked over twenty grand for that auction item and that was just one of the big-ticket items that charity had available."

Excited chatter erupts around the room, everyone talking about things they could possibly get donated and how fun having a gala like this would be.

"So we're in agreement on one gala instead of three smaller events?" Roberta presses, drawing everyone's attention back to the task at hand. Her voice is cool and composed despite the hopeful glint to her expression. I have to imagine planning three events is the last thing this woman wants to do.

Jenny makes some kind of shrill sound while petulantly folding her arms. "I think this is a huge mistake. I'm telling you. This will lose money. Kaplan, I know you're smarter than this. She's been here a week." She jabs her finger across the table at me. "She has no clue how we operate."

"This is my first *morning* here, and I don't know how we operate yet either, but the last thing I want to do is attend three events three weeks in a row or cost these charities potential earnings. Which is exactly what three events would do, Kelly."

I choke on my laugh as does everyone else in here. Roberta gives me a sly smirk and a wink.

"It's Jenny," she fumes, turning redder than the attention-seeking, cleavage-amplifying dress she's wearing. Now I know what Charlie was talking about. You'd feel bad for her if she wasn't such an awful person.

"Good for you," Kaplan mutters dryly. "This is what we're doing. Roberta, make it happen. I will work on getting some auction items that I know will likely bring in some big dollars. Now if we're done, I have to make a phone call. Good work, everyone. Thanks. Bianca." A glare that says follow me and that's it. Just my name to end the meeting and I'm supposed to scurry after him. I half expect Jenny to linger, wanting to throw down with me but thankfully she storms out, chasing after Kaplan.

"Good luck with that," Carlos, one of the grant reviewers, quips, laughing lightly to himself as he closes his laptop and stands up. "Between the two of them, you have your work cut out for you."

"Carlos, I've spent the last seven years of my life living in LA. Trust me, there is nothing I can't handle."

Except possibly my new boss.

14

"I feel like I haven't seen you all week," Greta says as she takes a sip of her soda.

"That's because you haven't," I reply as I pull my salad out of the fridge, shutting the door with my hip.

For a man who can't stand the sight of me and threatens to fire me with every other sentence, he has me in his office constantly. I sit in on every conference call, trudge through every meeting. Most of the time I'm silently working on my laptop, taking notes, or reviewing emails or presentations that come in. Occasionally I shoot him texts on things he should mention or ask or suggest.

But we don't talk a lot. Barely at all. You'd think after spending a week together like that he'd soften a bit, but if anything, he seems harder, more detached.

"This week has been nonstop. I feel like I haven't left Kaplan's office other than to go to a meeting here or there. I swear, I haven't even sat in my own chair once."

I take a seat at the table, popping the top on my glass Tupperware.

Most people leave the building for lunch, myself included—it gives me a break from the man in the suit—but today winter seems to be having some fun with snow and sleet. We decided on an early lunch on the main floor of the building, which no one occupies or works on. Octavia evidently didn't like its easy access to the street or how open the view inside is.

"Oh please. No one here feels sorry for you." Charlie smarts, lifting her sandwich to her mouth. "That man is damn fine, and I wouldn't complain about having to stare at his pretty face all day."

"That's because you all see a pretty face while I'm left with the ass." Someone sharply clears their throat from behind me and I groan. "He's right behind me, isn't he?"

I don't need Greta or Charlie to reply. Their startled "oh shit" faces answer for them.

"Do you think he heard me?" I whisper.

They nod in unison, eyes wider than the sun.

"Fabulous," I grumble under my breath.

"Morning, ladies," Kaplan drawls, the tap of his expensive shoes growing louder as he approaches. His hand grips the back of my chair and I sigh. Yeah, he definitely heard me. "Early lunch, Bianca?"

I tilt my head all the way back to meet his stormy eyes. The man needs to learn how to smile more. Or possibly be less intense. "We don't have another meeting scheduled today."

"That's because I moved them all. Here." He tosses my computer bag, my purse, and my coat at me. "Let's go."

"What? Where are we going? And who on earth gave you permission to go into my desk and touch my things?"

Without answering, he turns on his heels and heads for the exit. "If you don't follow me, you're fired."

"You can't fire me," I yell after him, shoving my uneaten salad in Greta's direction because the girl does not eat enough. "Ugh. See what I mean?" I throw my arms into my coat and toss both my purse and computer bag over my shoulder.

"Good luck with Prince Charming," Greta chirps with a flirty grin.

I roll my eyes, throw them a wave, and then chase after him, my heels clicking loudly against the hard surface of the floor. Kaplan is standing by the front doors, peering out. Most of the paparazzi have cleared out, losing interest in stalking Kaplan here after a week of nothing.

"Please tell me we're not walking. I'm in four-inch heels and you didn't remember my hat or gloves."

He turns away from the door and studies me for a moment, takes in my outfit, frowns, and then turns back to the door. "Button your coat."

"Yes, sir," I mock, and his head snaps back in my direction, his eyes darkening.

"Do you always refer to your boss as an ass to everyone you speak to?"

"Nope." I pop the *P* sound, grinning at his perturbed expression. "Just a select few, but it's not like I have to say anything. You do a thorough enough job all on your own of showing everyone that side of you."

A grunt and he turns back to the glass doors, peering out. "I'm waiting on Axl to pick us up."

"Fantastic. No walking. Are you going to tell me where we're going yet?"

"Nope."

"You know this relationship we have needs a lot of work."

His head whips back around. "Our *what*?"

"Relationship, Kaplan. In case you missed it, we're in one. Deeply. Connected. Together."

He looks pained.

"Yeesh. Lighten up a little, would you? You're a doctor. I'm sure you can safely remove the stick from your ass without causing too much damage. We have a business relationship, Kaplan. I am your employee, and you are my boss and yet you haven't said more than five words to me since Monday. I'm trying to be friendly here, but you're making that oh so difficult. Especially by stealing me away from my lunch."

"By calling me an ass and then telling me I have a stick up it?"

Touché.

"Fine. My apologies for the ass and the ass stick comment. But I'd truly like us to try and get along. Even a little."

Just then a large black SUV pulls up and Kaplan opens the door, fighting the icy, wet wind. Clutching my arm, he guides me straight for the back door that Axl opens, the burly security guard who reads poetry on his Kindle and listens to classical music. His brother Slash is just as adorable, though he's the strong, quiet type.

"Good morning, Axl," I greet him with a cheery smile even as a fleet of icy pins hitting my face blindsides me.

"Bianca. Lovely to see you. You look radiant this morning. Hurry in, the car is nice and warm."

"Thank you!"

Kaplan grumbles something I can't make out under his breath as he practically shoves me into the back seat. The door shuts behind him, bathing us in a warmth that has me sighing and shuddering at the same time.

"When is spring again? Burr." I shake out my hair that within two seconds of being outside is already coated in white ice. With my seat belt buckled, we set off and I immediately turn toward the window, ignoring the man seated beside me because this seems to be our game. Evasion. He didn't answer me about trying to be friendly and I'm done chasing.

He's obviously made up his mind about me.

"We're going to—"

Chime.

"What is that?"

Reaching down, I grab my purse from the floor, slipping out my phone and glancing at the screen. "It's just a notification."

"Of what?"

I throw him a side-eye. "It's from the dating app Charlie installed on my phone. It's nothing. I meant to turn off the notifications, but I guess I forgot."

"You're on a dating app?"

I shrug up a shoulder at his incredulous, and maybe slightly caustic, tone. "I'm single. I'm living in a new city and why not try to meet people?"

"Let me see it." He grabs the phone from my hand that I had already unlocked with my face and pulls up the app.

"Hey!" I bark, reaching for my phone. He swats me away, holding it out of my reach as he angles his body while looking at the message I just received.

"Jesus, Bianca. This is a dick pic."

I scrunch up my nose, giving up the fight. I don't care all that much if he looks through that. I haven't done much with it anyway. Charlie set up the profile for me and I've occasionally scrolled through it, chatted a bit with two guys, but my head and heart aren't into it. I was planning on deleting the app anyway.

"You can delete that. But honestly, not all the men on there are like that. Some of them aren't so bad."

His brow creases as he scrolls through my potential matches, looking more agitated by the second. "Yes. They're all this bad." A hand through his hair and a curse under his breath as he reads some of the messages I've received. "Please tell me you're not going on a date with any of these assholes."

"What does it matter to you?" I fold my arms over my chest, my gaze cutting back to the window, watching the passing frozen Boston landscape as we slowly meander through the streets.

"Because you're too good for a dating app like this. For one, you have money and that makes you a target. All anyone has to do is Google your name to learn that."

That catches my attention. I turn back to him, my heart in my throat. "You sound as though you're speaking from experience. What else did you learn about me?"

"Bianca Barlow, age twenty-five, recent graduate from UCLA with a bachelor's in fine arts and a master's in business and finance. Mother Mariana Barlow and father Duke Barlow."

"Stepfather."

He squints at me. "Stepfather then."

"Blah. You knew all this about me already."

130 J. SAMAN

"There wasn't much beyond that except your stepfather's presumed wealth was there for all to see. It's as if you were born nine years ago."

That's because that's when my mother divorced Elijah Parker and I moved to Texas, becoming Bianca Bunny Barlow.

"What happened to your real father?"

Now I gulp. "Died when I was one. Car accident."

Ask me more, Kaplan. Ask me about my other stepfathers. About my childhood. About where I grew up before I lived in Texas.

His features soften. "I'm sorry. I didn't realize."

I shrug because it is what it is. I don't remember my father, which sucks when you think about it, so I try not to.

"Still, you can't go out with these men."

He tosses my phone at me. It lands softly on my lap, and I frown. So very tempted to tell him everything. To watch his expression as I do. "You realize you have absolutely no right to tell me who I can and cannot go out with, right? If I want to date Dick Pic Guy or any other guy on there or anywhere else, I'm free to do so without judgment or questions from you."

He doesn't have to say anything else. His displeasure radiates from his countenance. But tough shit. He lost the right to comment or act like he cares a long time ago.

"What if I went out with one of them tonight? It's Friday."

"You're not."

"How do you know I'm not?"

"Because you don't seem interested in them."

"Maybe I am," I challenge. "Maybe I'm just putting up a front."

"Bianca, don't test me on this."

I laugh at how ridiculous that sounds. "Or what? You'll throw me over your knee and spank me for misbehaving? I'm not a child."

His entire demeanor instantly alters, the air in the car along with it. His eyes drag down my body in what can only be described as a heated gaze for the way it leaves fire in its wake. "If that's what you need, then that's what you'll get."

Oh hell.

His dark eyes lock with mine and he stares, unabashed and intense. "Are you going to go out with one of them?"

I want to say yes just to see what he'll do. Will he actually put me over his knee, lift up my dress and spank my ass? And why on earth does the mere suggestion of that in my head make me impossibly wet and turned on? I squirm before I can stop it and he notices, his pupils blowing out.

I want to keep arguing with him, but there is no way I can tell him anything other than the truth when he looks at me like that. "I wasn't going to. No."

"Good girl."

Shit. My eyes close and I force myself back to the window, needing to relearn how to breathe at a normal rate. Pressing a palm to my cheek, it's on fire. I feel him lift my phone from my lap, but I can't speak, argue, or look at him.

"I deleted the app. That's not how you should be meeting men."

I listen as he puts my phone back in my purse.

I'm furious with him for being so high handed and doing that without my permission. But I can't speak without betraying myself, so I just stay quiet. If I decide to re-download it, that's my call, not his.

After a few tense minutes, he clears his throat. "We're making a stop at the hospital so I can show you your new workspace and grab you a badge so you can go up to the floor without needing to be let in and then we'll grab some lunch since I stole you from yours."

I flip back around at light speed.

"What? Why are you shaking your head at me like that?"

Fear grips my throat, making it difficult to drag in air. "Kaplan, please. I wasn't kidding about not liking hospitals. Don't make me work from there."

Unbuckling his seat belt, he shifts until he's directly beside me, taking up the entire middle seat with his large frame. He buckles once more, pressing in against me with his size, his thigh against mine. "Tell me."

I open my mouth to tell him that the last time I was in a hospital, I was in the emergency room, and they were declaring my stepbrother dead before my eyes, his lips blue and his neck flaming red, but the words don't come. He knows this about me. I've cried and sobbed and broken down about that day to him more than once. And frankly, I don't trust him with my pain anymore. He hasn't earned any truths from me.

So I pick something else.

"I had scoliosis as a child." Another truth, this one easier to say. "A lot of time in braces. A lot of painful procedures and physical therapy. A lot of time in the hospital."

Ever the doctor, he asks, "What degree was the curvature?"

"Forty-five degrees. Right on the line. They tried and tried to have me avoid spinal fusion surgery."

My face drops to my lap, dizzy, but he's there, cupping my jaw and dragging it back up. "Were they successful?"

"No. I had surgery when I was thirteen, tired of fighting a winless battle."

"And now you wear heels that no doubt tax your spine." He glances down at my silver Versace safety-pin-embellished heels and then back up at me.

It's not a question, but his grimace has me giggling, some of the tension in my muscles easing. "I live for shoes and am no stranger to back pain. But honestly, do you truly need me working there?"

"Having an irrational fear of hospitals isn't healthy."

Neither is the way my body is reacting to you sitting this close to me, but that's life and some things are beyond our control. I wait him out.

"Yes, I need you there, Bianca. I work sixty-hour weeks at the hospital, and I simply don't have the time to be at the foundation."

"But I just redid your office," I protest.

A chuckle. "Feel free to move in there if you like. Don't frown. It's not a good look on you." His thumb hits the crevice of my frown, forcefully pushing it up, and I shove him off me, smiling stupidly, which was obviously his point.

"A frown isn't a good look on anyone."

He shakes his head. "Especially on you. I'll take the statue you made with me. How's that?"

"You're negotiating with me now?"

"So it seems. Is that a yes?"

"I'm terrified," I admit, capturing my lip in my teeth.

His eyes hold mine. "You're stronger than letting something like a building hold you back. You can do it. I'll be there with you and Monday we can ride in together."

"Are you taking our relationship to the next level?" I jest. "Are we becoming friends?"

He grunts, running his hand through his hair, and I shake my head, reaching up and fixing the strands he just mussed. Strong fingers encircle my wrist, gripping it tightly and pulling it from his hair. With his eyes locked on mine, he brings my wrist to his nose, inhaling the scent of my skin, my perfume. Pressing my wrist to his lips without kissing it, he then rests it on his thigh.

A choppy breath comes out as a feverish exhale while warm prickles race up my arm. My gaze drops to my wrist, trapped against his thigh in the manacle of his fingers and then back up to him. His eyes are dark, slightly hooded, and he watches my face as his thumb drags back and forth over the sensitive skin of my inner wrist.

A tremble takes hold of me, and I stifle my whimper. "What are you doing?" It's a gasp and I feel my cheeks heating once more. With lust. With confusion.

He releases me, but he doesn't push my hand away from his leg and he doesn't retreat an inch from how his body is pressed to mine. "I'm not the sort of man you want to make friends with."

"How's that?"

"Do you know why I've wanted you gone so badly?"

A headshake.

"Because I'm attracted to you. And that's not a game I can play."

15

I don't know what made me say that. Tell her, this beautiful, intelligent, sunshine of a woman that I'm attracted to her. Maybe it was her pleading, terrified brown eyes. Her story about her spine or her father dying. The way she's somehow managed to dig into my soul and see its softer, finer parts. Or perhaps it's the way I somehow feel as though I *know* her when I don't.

She reminds me of Bunny.

There. I said it.

She does.

I've tried for more than a week to deny it, but maybe it was Ellis's text on the same day I met her or something else, but yeah. It's there.

I don't have pictures of Bunny. I don't have her real name. I have vague memories of a devastated fifteen-year-old girl with short purple hair and wide, tear-soaked eyes that I would have sworn were blue and not brown. Or maybe I'm remembering them that way because Forest had blue eyes, which doesn't necessarily make sense since they were stepsiblings and not actual siblings. Then I have the later image of her but that never came with a face. So yeah, I don't remember Bunny as well as I'd like. But the way she talks and the way she feels...

They're not the same person. I know this. Just similar.

Which is why I'm reacting this way. All week, it's why I've reacted this way. As a fucking mess. I can't look at her. I can't speak to her. She is a pariah to me and yet, I cannot tolerate her being more than a few inches from me.

I crave her smiles. Her small laugh. The intelligent light in her eyes. The snark in her sharp words. The sexual fire that simmers barely beneath the surface. It's sick. It's depraved. It's the most fun I've had with a woman in forever.

I have the excuse of my job and needing her to learn it to perfection, so I've abused that.

Those eyes blink rapidly at me just as we pull up to the corner in front of Boston Children's Hospital. "Ready?"

"W-what?" she sputters.

"We're here."

"You said all that to distract me? God, you're such an asshole."

She thinks I told her I'm attracted to her to distract her? If only it were that simple.

I don't argue with her though. We're better off if she assumes that's what I was up to. I didn't tell her that to instigate a conversation. I told her that to end one. To end a lot of things between us.

I need her close and yet I can't stand it and that's just how I roll. I want to fuck her, and I can't fuck her. I want to claim her, and she'll never be mine.

I want to care for and protect her the way I used to with Bunny, but she's not fucking Bunny, and I need to separate the two of them in my head instead of tying them in as one. Anything I think about or *feel* toward Bunny is fucked. Bunny was a teenager—one I never gave a thought to beyond our friendship—and then one day she wasn't, and I haven't been right since.

Bianca's hand grips my thigh, her eyes flinging left, staring out at the large hospital. "I can't do it." It's a breathy plea.

I'd argue this, but she's not the first child who had a condition that required multiple painful hospital visits who never wanted to step back within the walls again.

"Bianca Barlow, you ran out on a cheating piece of shit. Moved to a new city in a new state and took on a job you know nothing about. You're fierce and independent and *doing* it. Now get your fucking ass out of the car before I have to drag you."

The door opens right on cue, Axl, already too smitten with her for my liking. Icy snow flies in, covering her hands that now grip the edge of the seat.

"I hate you."

"Noted."

"I can't do it."

"Then you're fired."

"I am not."

"You are if you can't meet my job requirements."

"My pants are going to stay zipped to you."

"Lucky for me, you tend to lean toward skirts and dresses."

A laugh and thank Christ.

"Move. Out. Now." I give her a small nudge in the back. "We're going in. I already told you, I'm not playing that game with you, so you don't have to worry about that. Attraction is curable. Just like hospital phobias."

"Kaplan..."

"I prefer Typhon or Lord Asshole. You're freezing me and ruining my family's car with all the snow and sleet that's blowing in. Out!"

I don't spank her bottom, despite the temptation, but my hand that hits her upper thigh is damn close. She emits a squeal and then hops out of the car. Her fucking hellaciously sexy heels stagger a step and why couldn't my hot new assistant dress like Mother Teresa?

Climbing out, I adjust my suit that feels like shackles on my flesh and walk without glancing back at her toward the entrance. She scrambles after me, her steps clumsy and slippery as she tries to keep up.

"In your sleep when you're contentedly dreaming of the death of small animals, remember that the greatest trick the devil ever pulled was convincing the world that he wasn't a woman."

I clip out a short laugh, reaching down and taking her hand.

"Your misquote of *The Usual Suspects* isn't helping my attraction." I peer down at her with an annoyed glare, but her eyes are fixed on the large revolving door of the hospital. "You're far from the devil with that sweet, wholesome innocence you radiate."

She scoffs, gripping my hand in a viselike hold. "I am not innocent or wholesome. I am fierce and will take you by the balls."

"Promise?"

That grip tightens. Slides up a notch, clutching my forearm and drawing it closer to her quivering body. "Never. Lucky for both of us, you're not my type."

Like hell I'm not her type. I saw just how much I am her type in the car and in my office all week and in my apartment when she fell asleep after dinner with me.

"Lucky," I deadpan, slipping out of her hold and reaching behind her back so I can draw her into my side as we reach the doors, practically dragging her along while garnering curious stares from people passing by.

"I know you're still trying to distract me with this attraction BS, so I won't focus on where we are or what we're doing and I'll go inside, but I can't do it. Please. I can't!" She grasps my jacket, yanking as hard as she can, attempting to stop me before I reach the doors.

"You're going to ruin your heels."

"Argh! No! Stop! I don't feel well. Everything is spinning."

"Move! What are you doing?"

"AHHHhhhhh..."

Her voice dies in her throat as her eyes roll back in her head and her face drains of color. Her body lists and then falls. Somehow, I catch her before she eats shit on the concrete. Wrapping her boneless arms around my neck, I drag her slack body the rest of the way to my chest, my arms around her lower back.

"Bianca!"

Fuck. She fainted.

I get us through the revolving door, hauling her body that is total deadweight. People are going to think I killed her.

It's noisy as hell in the lobby, but she's out cold. I scoop up her lifeless form into my chest as I search left and right. The lobby is filled with children and parents, and I don't want to take her to the ED. That will freak her out more. To the right is a long corridor and that's where I go, all the way down past the bathrooms and the janitorial space beyond.

"Bianca?" I whisper in her ear, but she doesn't so much as stir, hell. Her head hangs limply off my forearm, her hair along with it. What have I done to her? Holding her body closer, I adjust her in my arms, gripping her tighter. My lips plant in her hair, her fragrance sweet and enticing and I feel like a monster.

I had no idea her panic went this far. Stupid. So goddamn stupid and arrogant.

The room back here is an open space loaded with broken hospital beds and equipment and I set her down on one of the beds that appears to be in the best shape. She's like a wet noodle, all uncoordinated limbs and flying hair. The permanent rose tinge that typically stains her cheeks is gone, her complexion ashen.

My hand cups her cool face in my hand. "Bianca?"

Silence.

I check her pulse. It's slow, but steady, same with her breathing. "This is a lousy way to get out of working with me."

No response. Her pupils seem reactive, but it's hard to be sure without a light and with how they're rolled back.

"Typically, when I tell women I want them they throw themselves at me instead of telling me I'm lying about it while trying to run for their lives and then passing out. Is this your way of swooning for me?"

I rub her sternum with my knuckles and still nothing and fuck, that *always* works. Fear takes hold and I cling to her.

"I told you I'm attracted to you, and you thought I only said that to distract you. Do you have any idea the last time I uttered those words or anything similar to a woman? Never, Bianca. Never. I meant them, you crazy girl. Please wake up. You're scaring the shit out of me."

I grip my hair. Dammit! I pushed her too far.

Slipping out my phone, I dial up Luca, who is in the hospital today. He answers on the second ring and relief floods my veins. "I need you to get to the janitor's entrance off the main lobby and bring a pen light and smelling salts."

"Smelling salts? Are you kidding? What is this, nineteen-fifty? Do a sternal rub."

"I did! It didn't work. She's still out."

"Who?"

"My assistant. Bianca."

"Killed her already? Are you ensuring she's actually dead or are you attempting to revive her?"

"Luca!"

"On my way."

The phone slips from my hand and my head falls to her shoulder. "I'm sorry," I whisper into her, my face turning so it's buried in her neck. "I'm so sorry. I shouldn't have pushed you that hard."

I breathe into her for a few minutes and when I hear someone approaching, I force myself back, away from her, sitting on the side of the gurney and adjusting her dress so it's all the way down around her knees.

"What the hell is this?"

"Luca, meet Bianca Barlow, my new assistant that our mother hired to ruin my life." I wave to Bianca's slacken form. "Bianca, meet my brother Luca. Here's hoping he can revive you and we can move past this awkward moment."

"Shit. Kap."

"Yup. Just help her, okay?" I glance over my shoulder at my brother. "I'm freaking out, Luca. She had a panic attack because she doesn't like hospitals and I forced her here and then she passed out."

Luca does a very quick neuro exam on her, checks her blood pressure with a portable cuff, her pulse ox with a finger probe, and listens to her heart with his stethoscope. "She's fine," he tells me. "Vitals are stable. She's just unconscious."

Then he waves the smelling salts beneath her nose. She jolts back, coming out of it too quickly with a fierce cry, waving away the stick Luca is holding before her face. She settles down by the end of the bed, her wild dark eyes all over us, scared and disoriented as she pants out uneven breaths.

"Hey there, pretty lady. Welcome back. I'm Dr. Luca Fritz. This asshole's brother." He jabs a thumb in my direction. "I'm a neurosurgeon here in the hospital and if it's okay with you, I'd like to examine you quickly. Make sure everything is okay. You passed out on this big galumph and gave him a good scare."

Bianca blinks those huge brown eyes of hers rapid fire, taking in the scene around her. She stares at Luca for a long beat and then her gaze flickers over to me. Holds there and then returns to him. "I passed out?"

"Rather dramatically," I inform her.

She licks her dry lips and sits up a little straighter. "I'm fine."

"I appreciate what you're saying, but I'd like to make sure of that all the same," Luca patiently requests. "He deals in hearts." A nod in my direction. "I deal in brains."

"And yet neither of you have a set between you." She cocks an eyebrow, only to cover her face. "Sorry, that was rude. I didn't mean that."

A laugh hits the air from both of us. "I won't argue it though, even if we did just meet and that was a little rude. What's your name?" Luca questions.

"Bianca 'I Hate Your Brother' Barlow."

Luca's green eyes flash over to mine with a smirk I do not mistake. He likes her. Yeah, don't we all.

"Alrighty then. Do you know where you are?"

"Hell. I'm in hell."

She pushes off the gurney, forcing herself up and onto her fucking fuck-me heels. The color in her face isn't great, but it isn't as terrifying as it was when I carried her in here.

"Whoa. No need to stand up yet. You don't want to pass out again," Luca admonishes as we fly off the gurney, our arms outstretched on either side of her, ready to catch her should she fall.

"Stop. I said I'm fine. Look. Not drunk either." She proceeds to close her eyes and touch each pointer finger to her nose while reciting the alphabet backward. Something I can't even do sober.

"Alright, alright. I get it. You're fine." Luca holds up his hands in surrender. "But if you feel dizzy or even if this guy gives you trouble, come find me. I work here two days a week." Luca slips one of his business cards into her hand and closes her fingers around it. "It was an absolute pleasure to meet you, Bianca. Don't stay a stranger, okay?"

Luca tosses me a wink I'd likely just as quickly ignore, and then he leaves.

"Well, that was fun," I deadpan, my heart still beating off rhythm. "Do you think you can make it upstairs this time without swooning all over me?"

She goes for a pink plastic portable toilet we sit kids on when they're unable to get out of their beds and chucks it at me. I duck to the side, and it flies right past my head.

"I hate you."

"You said that already." I take a seat on the bed, staring contritely at her. "I'm sorry, Bianca. I shouldn't have done that to you. I had no clue your fear of hospitals was that bad. Tell me truthfully where you are with this? If you can't go upstairs, I'll drive you back across town to the foundation building and we'll figure something else out."

Her pretty brown eyes that appear more amber under the fluorescent lights blink at me, perplexed. "I really passed out?"

"Yes."

A headshake as she comes and sits down beside me. "I've never done that before. Had a panic attack that made me pass out."

I tilt my head in her direction. "I'm not judging you. It's my fault and I feel terrible."

"But I'm here? In the hospital? How did I get back to this room?" She glances around at the mass of broken hospital parts.

"You passed out on me, and I carried you back here."

Her head whips in my direction, eyes wide. "You carried me?"

"Yes. What's that look for?"

Heat curls up her face in the form of an alluring blush. "Wasn't I heavy? I'm not a small woman."

Jesus. This shit again. I'm going to find her mother and her dipshit ex-fiancé and kill them both for doing this to her. "You weren't heavy, Bianca. I carried you back here just fine."

A gulp and then her eyes meet mine before falling to my arms. "I guess it's a good thing you have all those... muscles under your shirt."

I smirk at just how adorable she is when she's like this. When her guard is down and she's unabashedly vulnerable and honest. "Guess so. You can squeeze one if you want. I won't judge that either."

I get an eye roll instead of a squeeze.

"No? Too bad."

"You don't have to distract me anymore with that."

"Right." Because that's clearly what I was doing when I told her I'm attracted to her. "Well, here we are in the hospital. What happens next is up to you. I realize I just trapped you in the Land of Oz after a tornado fucked up your world, but you have to tell me where your head is at."

"Are you a good witch or a bad witch?" she quips.

I grin. "Why, I'm not a witch at all."

She bursts into laughter, falling to the side, her forehead landing on my shoulder. "Okay. Okay," she repeats, the second time more resolute as I wrap her up in my arms. "I'll go upstairs because no woman wants to be *this* girl. But now that you're aware of my unease, I hope you'll play nice."

My lips, those traitorous, needy, *hungry* bastards plant themselves in her hair. Then my nose takes over and inhales her sweet, *delicious* fragrance.

"Baby, I am not nice. I have the most to lose and the least to gain by being or even playing nice. Especially with a woman." *A woman I find as attractive as I find you.* My hands hit the back of her head, holding her to me, running the tips of my fingers through the silky strands of her hair. "But after watching you collapse like that..." Fuck, I'll never get that image out of my head. "You have my word. If you tell me it's too much, then it's too much. But I need you here, Bianca.

You're smart and by some miracle you seem to know what you're doing with this foundation and I..." *Don't.* "I need you. I won't fire you despite how much I say I want to." A sigh. "Can you do this with me? I can't be here and there, and I need someone who can be."

I press her tighter against me when what I should do is release her altogether. Her hands find the sinew of my back, the blades of my shoulders, gripping me as if I'm her lifeline.

"If I have another panic attack, I'm done."

"Agreed."

"I won't though."

I smile, pressing my lips in tighter to her head. Breathing her in just a touch more. "I believe you."

"Okay." A steady breath and she pulls herself off me, her eyes peering back and meeting mine. "But no more attraction nonsense. Next time just give it to me straight instead of trying to distract me like that."

"Promise," I tell her, even as my gut sinks.

16

"What are we doing here again?" I shout at Oliver over the pounding house music that's been filling my ears for the last hour.

"Watching our women dance," he replies, his eyes fixed on Amelia as she, Raven, Rina, Grace, and Elle lose their minds to the music on the dance floor. Even Stella and Layla are here tonight, dancing like no one is watching.

"And we're not worried about the strobe lights with Grace?" I ask, just making sure since a very pregnant Grace who has epilepsy and is sensitive to strobe lights is in the thick of it out there.

"Nah," Carter tells me. "She's good. It's why we come here instead of going to a real club."

"That and the drinks are good." Landon holds up his glass of vodka with lime.

"Are we going to order food?" I complain. "I'm starving."

"Yeah," Brecken agrees. "Food. Let's get some of that."

He flags down a waitress and asks her for some menus.

"Did you set a date yet?" Carter asks Oliver.

"June, I think, since Luca and Raven leave for Nicaragua after the Fourth of July. Amelia wants to get married in the vineyard house."

Luca is going to do a medical mission down in Nicaragua. A cause that became very near and dear to his heart after he suffered a trauma and came face-to-face with just how far-reaching medical inequities are. He's taking Raven with him because the two of them can't be separated for more than five minutes without him throwing a hissy fit.

"And what about a best man?" I toss out.

"Grace."

I swivel in his direction, taking a sip of my bourbon as I do. "Grace?"

He laughs. "Yes, asshole. Grace. She's been my best friend since we were infants. Who else would stand up next to me?"

"Um, how about any of us?"

Oliver shakes his head at Luca. "You'll be groomsmen, but Grace is my person. We tell each other everything."

"Yeah, but she won't let you deliver my kid," Carter counters.

"She won't let you either and you're the OB-GYN."

"I'm the father. I can't deliver my own kid."

"I'm confused," I say, changing the subject off Grace's impending delivery of my nephew. "If you're all here to dance with your women, why are you sitting here instead?"

Luca laughs. "Because we're babysitting you."

I flip him off.

"Because watching is half the fun of being forced to come here," Brecken states, licking at his bottom lip. "After watching Rina dance like that all night, I'm going to fuck her brains out later. It's a fun form of foreplay." All of us stare at him as if we're about to throw up all over his expensive pants. He tosses his hand up in the air. "Sorry. My bad. Seriously. Sorry. Sometimes I don't think about you guys as Rina's brothers."

"What he said. Only with Elle," Landon says. "And if you ever talk like that about Rina again, you'll find your head dunked in the toilet."

"Yeah. Again, my bad. But you can't deny the watching part."

"You're serious?" I question.

"I read it in one of the romance books Rina made me read," Luca admits. "Seemed hot in that and now that I'm living it, I absolutely agree."

My head spins in his direction. "You're still reading those?"

He cracks up. "Dude, they're like a bible. Rina was one hundred percent right about that. You have no idea all that I'm learning."

"Same," Oliver chimes in. "All kinds of things. And when there is a romantic scene, I read it to Amelia, and she gets all swoony and then the sex is even hotter. Forget oysters, romance books are the ultimate aphrodisiac."

"Yes!" Carter shoots out. "That last one we read was insanely hot. Grace loved the roommate, surprise pregnancy trope."

I shake my head, slightly at a loss for words until something occurs to me. "Wait. Are you all reading them together?" All my brothers, including Brecken, turn to me at once. "Shit. You are. You're in a romance reading book club with each other. Do you read this with your women or just with each other?"

"Both," they all say in unison, and wow, that's some shit right there.

"Whenever you decide to settle down, you have to try it. It's no joke."

I snort out a laugh. "Well, Oli, I think you know that's not happening anytime soon if I can help it. Millie Van Der Heusen can go off and marry someone else. She can stop texting me relentlessly for that matter too. I'm not putting a ring on it." Ever since that lunch, she's been texting and occasionally calling me. Not so subtly hinting at the prospect of the two of us getting together. She even went so far as to say, "when we're married," in one of the texts. I've been pushing it down and trying to be as polite as possible while blowing her off, but she's not getting the message. Soon, I'll have to be straight up blunt.

"So you say now, but a wedding in your future I see."

"Thanks, Yoda," I smart at Luca.

"Not even with your sexy, curvy assistant or does she hate your guts now that you terrified her so badly she passed out in a public building?"

I narrow my eyes at Landon. "How do you know about what happened yesterday?" But duh, dumb fucking question. "Jesus, Luca. Is there anything you don't gab about to the entire fucking world? It's called patient confidentiality, man."

He smirks smugly, his expression wholly unrepentant as he tosses his ankle up on his opposite knee, his hands going behind his neck. "She wasn't my patient. She wouldn't even let me check her, remember? No way I was keeping that to myself. Definitely not about that. You looked like you were about to piss your pants until Miss Feisty Pants with the fuck-me heels came back. I like her. Question, does she *always* dress like that for work? No wonder you have it so bad for her. I mean, *damn*. Those curves are no joke."

And once again, I flip him off. Because sometimes that's all you can do with Luca. "Talk about her curves again and I'll kill you."

Now they're all giving me Cheshire grins. Great. Just tipped my hand with that one.

"This is the same woman you had sleep over at your place last weekend, right?" Brecken questions, finishing off his drink and setting his empty glass on the table, searching high and low for the waitress who never returned to take our order. Now I remember why I hate this place. Shitty fucking service.

"Yes. Same woman. But nothing is happening there." Because she thinks the fact that I'm attracted to her is a joke. And she's my assistant. And I no longer see women and certainly never get involved with them and Bianca Barlow is a woman you get involved with. She screams attached and relationships.

Oh, and then there's the fact that my parents still believe an arranged marriage is the way to go and they think Millie is the woman to have it with. Still, I'll admit, Bianca's the first woman to come along who I'm tempted to bend the rules for. Who might actually be different.

"But you want something to happen there." It's a statement, not a question and I think about what Oliver is saying.

"I don't know. Maybe. But it won't and it would be insanely stupid to consider it."

"Why? Because you've sworn off love because you're a pussy who's afraid of it or because you might actually like her and are afraid of what that might mean?"

"I'm not afraid of love. It's not that simple for me and you know it. You know what I've been through." Some of it. They know some of it. Not all of it. "All you bastards have been miserable at least once because of love. Not to mention, how on earth can I possibly trust anyone that their affection is real?"

"We were miserable, but look where we are now," Landon says simply, and since he was the most miserable of all of us after losing his wife to a horrible car accident when Stella was only a toddler, he's the one I listen to the most with this. "I wouldn't change how I loved Reese because I hurt for so long after I lost her. Her love was worth the pain. Having Stella was worth the pain."

"Fine. You're an exception. You had a beautiful wife and have a beautiful daughter and deserve all the happiness with Elle now. But I've had women do unspeakable things for my name and semen. It's worse now that I'm running the foundation. It's just easier this way for me. Look around." I pan my hand around the room. "Other than your women, how many women are staring at me for the wrong reasons?"

"All of them," they reply.

"See. No thanks."

"And you think that's all Bianca would want with you? Your name and your money and your semen?"

No. That's the first word that hits my mind. No. Whereas I questioned her motives and the coincidence of it all when she was first hired, in the two weeks she's been at the foundation I've come to realize she's an honest, genuine person. She could have told the world she slept at my place that night, but she didn't. She kept that secret when others wouldn't have.

And I like that so much about her.

"Maybe you should give her a try," Brecken says when I don't respond. "See if she fits. Better than stuffy-ass Millie, who actually is after your name and semen."

I shake my head at him. "I'm done with this conversation. I'm going to dance with your women. If our waitress ever comes back, order me a burger and another bourbon."

Peeling myself off the wood bench seat, I make my way through the room to the cluster of Fritz and soon-to-be Fritz women in the center, all the while ignoring all the women saying hi and asking if I'm Kaplan Fritz and if I want to dance with them or if I want to buy them a drink.

"Ladies," I say as I drop my hands on Rina's hips, giving my baby sister a kiss on the temple. "You all look lovely out here dancing. Your men are having a romance-book-level field day."

They all giggle as they continue to dance, moving in around me and making me the center of their show.

"They told you about what I got them into, huh?" Rina asks with a coy smile on her flushed, tacky face.

Before I can answer, my brothers join us, evidently tired of watching and not being active participants. Only Raven is left standing because Luca had to run outside to take a phone call on one of his patients.

"Come here," I command, dragging her small body into my chest and wrapping my arms around her as the song morphs into a slower ballad. "Dance with me, babe. We'll drive your guy wild when he sees us."

Raven's arms circle around my neck. "He's such a baby when it comes to that. You know he flipped out about Antonio again last night?"

Antonio is her conductor at the Boston Symphony Pops Orchestra where Raven is a first-chair cellist. It's also been no secret that at one point, Antonio tried to get in her panties. "I can't totally blame Luca on Antonio."

I grin down at my tiny friend. Four years ago, when Luca broke Raven's heart for her own good, I stepped in and watched over her. They were both a mess—for real, yet another tally on the board for why I don't love love for myself after what I saw those two go through—and I wanted to make sure she was not only okay and safe, but I always intended to help them reunite when the timing was right.

But also in those four years, Raven and I have become very close friends despite our thirteen-year age gap.

"Whatever. You're all a bunch of cavemen for us." A glimmer I want no part of hits her eyes. "Speaking of..."

I shake my head, stopping her. "Don't start. I know my big-mouthed brother told you everything."

Her oceanic eyes sparkle up at me as her lips curve into a sly smirk. "He said she's very pretty and has a mouth on her that rivals mine."

"He wasn't lying," I admit because sometimes it's easier to talk to Raven than it is my brothers. I sway us around, holding her close. I also know Raven won't repeat to anyone anything we speak about. "She's... different."

"What does different mean?"

"It means lately she's all I fucking think about. That's what different means."

"Wow." Her expression grows startled. "That's not something I ever thought I'd hear you say about someone. I'm going to tamp down my joy for a moment because I can see you're struggling. If you're thinking about her this much, why not see if she is actually different? Better than Millie, that's for damn sure."

So everyone keeps saying tonight.

"I... I don't know. There's just all this pressure on me, Raven. I have to settle down. I have to get married. It has to be with the right sort of woman. Everyone is after me. Everyone wants something from me." I sigh. "I like having a quiet life. I like being alone. I don't like people telling me the things I have to do that in no way speak to the things I want." But worse, what if I do try with Bianca and it all goes to hell the way it always seems to?

Raven cups my jaw in her hand, smiling softly up at me. "You have this preconceived notion in your head, Kaplan. Sometimes it just takes the right person to change all that up for you."

Before I can formulate any sort of response, Luca joins us. "Sorry about that. Can I cut in and steal my girl back from you?"

I make a show of kissing Raven's cheek, just to get a small rise out of Luca and then I hand her over with a wink.

"Bastard," he grumbles, making both Raven and me laugh. I turn around, ready to head back to my table and hopefully eat some damn food, when I'm immediately stopped by a tall, skinny brunette wearing a nothing of a dress and a determined look.

"Hey sexy," she coos, her voice a silky purr as she draws in close to me. Her hand hits my chest. "I've been watching you all night. Want to dance with me?"

I step back, removing her hand from me. "No thanks. I'm just here to be with my family."

"But it looks like they're all taken. How about I let you buy me a drink?" she offers, pushing into me and pressing her small tits to my chest. The cloying scent of her alcohol-tinted breath and heavy floral perfume hits my nose and I jerk away.

"Not interested."

"But I bet I can make you interested." This time she cups my junk over my slacks, rubbing me. My dick has never been less interested in my life.

Jesus. "I said no, and I meant it. That means you don't touch." I remove her hand from my body for a second time, trying to worm my way around her when she steps in front of me, blocking me once more on the full dance floor.

A pout with large eyes and batting lashes. "Don't be like that. There's a back room I bet we can have a lot of fun in together."

"Not. Fucking. Interested."

Now all that sex in her eyes turns to venom in a flash and she shoves against my chest. Hard. I take a step back, her over-the-top reaction rendering me stunned for a moment until she shrieks, cutting through the music. "You're going to fucking regret that!" She storms off and I swivel around, finding my siblings and their women just as perplexed by that as I am. They clearly saw the whole thing and I can only wonder how many other people in here did as well.

I shrug, shaking my head and they all shake their heads in return, confused.

"No still means no, right? It's not an invitation for sexual assault?"

"No still means no," Rina says adamantly, and hell, Rina was kidnapped years ago by a crazy ex who did unspeakable things to her.

"I love you all, but I'm officially done here. No food and crazy women are my limit. Have a good night and I'll see you all at dinner tomorrow at the compound." I throw a wave before they can try and talk me into staying and head straight for the exit, stepping out onto the cold sidewalk, still laced with a sheet of ice and salt from yesterday's storm.

I check my watch. It's only eight thirty on a Saturday. I'm hungry. A bit wired after that weird encounter. And my thoughts continue to circle back in one direction after all the talk tonight.

Bianca.

I tell myself I'm just pulling out my phone and hitting her number so I can check on her. Make sure she's okay after what happened yesterday. We never made it upstairs to the new office space I had made for her. Instead, I took her out for lunch and let her go home early. But as the phone rings, with the thrill that she'll pick up and I'll get to hear her sweet voice racing through me, even I can't convince myself that's why I'm calling her.

17

"Mom, I seriously do not care, nor do I want to talk about him anymore. I don't know why you feel the need to continuously bring him up." Clasping the molten-hot metal with my pliers I pull, stretching it out until it cools and then I spark up the blowtorch again.

"Bunny, can you please stop what you're doing for five minutes and speak to me? All I hear is loud clicking and you grunting and metal grating. It's awful."

Twisting the nozzle, I turn off the torch and set it down beside me, lifting my safety goggles onto my forehead and removing my gloves. "Done. Happy now?"

"Lose the tone and I will be."

"No, I think I've earned this tone. Every time we've spoken in the last two weeks you feel the need to bring up Tod to me and I'm not interested. I told him the same and thankfully he's taken the hint for the most part. What else is there to discuss?"

She huffs as I shift over to my small wooden stool, twisting my back around to release some of the muscle cramping I have in my lower back.

"I called to talk to you about Ava. Not Tod."

"Oh, another winner. No thanks."

"She told her mother that you blocked her."

I snort. "That's because I did. Look." I sigh. "I wasn't going to do that to her. I wasn't. But she kept calling and texting me about her and Tod and I'm just... Mom, I'm done. It's all, 'I hope you can be happy for us, and we love each other so much, and it should have always been me up there marrying him instead of you, and I know you can understand why he loves me and not you,'" I mock. "Do you honestly expect me to sit there and take that? I told her I didn't care what she and Tod did. That I think she's an awful human being for what she did to *me*, but she has zero remorse so fuck her. That's right, Mom. Fuck. Her."

"Bunny. She's blood."

"And sometimes water tastes better than blood when you're forced to drink it. Mom, she was sleeping with my fiancé for our entire relationship and is completely remorseless about it. He at least had the grace to apologize and tell me I didn't understand what I saw and heard and that I had it all wrong. A lie, but hey, he tried. I understand she's your niece, and that sucks for you, but I'm done with her."

"Well, I threatened Vicky that if she didn't get her sniveling little slut daughter back on track, I wouldn't give her another dime."

My eyes bolt open wide, staring into the burning flame of the forge that is keeping me nice and toasty in this warehouse. So much for blood. "Mom? You didn't." And while I don't love the word slut, and I'd certainly never use it on another woman, I'm also not about to defend my cousin.

"I did. But now they've both gone postal, and I just don't have the energy or time for this. Duke is telling me I need to arrange for a large soiree for all his ranch employees and hands and Bunny, they only listen to country music and eat barbeque. What am I to do with that?"

I snicker, shaking my head. "I'm sure that's not all they listen to or eat. But if it is, then you have to respect that about them and cater the party to *their* needs. Minus the country, it sounds fantastic."

"I'm hoping you'll fly home for it. Mitchell and Elijah, as well as Ellis and his girls, are planning to come if you do."

Now I full-out laugh. "And I'm sure you love that."

"I love that they love you. Tell me, are you eating well? Avoiding carbs? Exercising daily? Please tell me you're working on yourself, Bunny, because at your wedding—"

"I looked gorgeous and am beautiful no matter my size or weight?" I sharply interject, so very done with all of this too. "Then yes, Mom. That's exactly how I am right now. I'll think about coming home, but I'm hanging up on you now."

"Bunny, you need to—"

I disconnect the call, wanting to chuck my phone into the forge and watch it burn. For all her love, I'm still not enough. Never perfect or even close to it.

I'm the daughter of an NFL lineman and a beauty queen who clearly favors her father's genetics. I'm tall. I'm thick. I also like to eat. I do work out and I do care for myself and I do watch what I eat, but this is my body. No matter how little I eat or how much I work out, this is *still* my body.

It hasn't been easy.

Hell, it's been downright awful to find the strength to look in the mirror and love the woman staring back at me. It's a daily struggle and some of those days I'm better at it than others. The past couple of weeks have been the worst with that. I continuously get caught up in others' expectations of me. Others' hurtful words. I have large breasts, a soft belly, thick thighs, and an ass.

I'll never be thin by society's standards.

And I'm okay with that. Finally. Sorta.

That has to be enough, even if no one else will see what I force myself to see.

That I am beautiful.

The whole wedding, Tod-Ava thing, seriously didn't help my rocky self-esteem and then Kaplan teasing me about being attracted to me hurt. Especially as part of me couldn't help but hope, couldn't help but wonder—

Nope. Not doing it!

Shoving off the stool, I throw my goggles and gloves back on, ready to wield this very fine, delicate metal into something stunning. It's going to be so pretty when it's finished. I can feel it. And all these new things that I've been trying since I moved here are just reinventing my soul with artistic purpose.

I spent all last night here doing this, only going home to sleep for a few hours before I came back. My ADHD did not enjoy the panic attack I gave it yesterday so it's fueling me with unrefined energy and I'm honing it into organized work. When you have ADHD as a kid, your life feels disjointed. Out of control. You constantly feel like you're failing at everything, never good enough because you're always unable to hold still or remember basic things that everyone else remembers.

But I was lucky.

Elijah worked tirelessly with me, helping me daily to take all my restless energy and re-navigate it into my art, leaving my scrambled mind tired and more focused when it came to important tasks. Like school. I didn't start with metal until my mom married Duke and I worked on his ranch during summers. That changed my existence. But as a teen, I learned to draw and paint and sculpt and even throw clay, and now I'm here, using my purposeful focus and concentration for important charitable work and allowing my nights to be consumed by my wandering mind, running wild, and creating beautiful chaos.

The moment the call with my mother ended, old-school Britney blasts back into my ears. I return to my piece, staring down at the shining metal and the second I get back to it, my motherfluffing phone rings, blaring louder than ever. Again. I chuck my gloves and slam down on the green button without looking at it.

"Mom, I think I made it clear, I don't want to talk about Tod, Ava, or my body!"

"But what if I simply want to know what you're doing?"

Kaplan. And just like that my heart rate shoots into the stratosphere as it does every time I hear his voice. Or see his handsome face.

Or even think about him. Despite my best efforts, I react to him like a girl who should know better but craves the rush anyway.

"Why are you calling?"

"I just told you why I'm calling. And I wanted to make sure you're okay after yesterday."

"I'm fine."

I shift my feet, gnawing on my bottom lip as I stare into the flames of the forge. I don't know what to do with him calling me. With the hint of something I can't quite place in his voice that's making my body race with chills despite the sweltering heat I'm consumed in.

"I'm working."

"Art work or foundation work?"

"Art work."

He's silent for a beat. Then... "What did she say about your body?"

"Nothing I'm not used to."

A growl as the sound of the city filters in from his phone. He's out somewhere and yet he's calling me. "They're all stupidly wrong. I hope you don't believe them."

"I'm not that innocent."

"Huh?"

"Sorry. Britney was the last artist on my girls kick-ass playlist."

"I have no idea what that means. But do you remember what I said to you when I pulled over my car before we reached the hotel the day you fled your wedding?"

Do I remember? It's been permanently imprinted on my brain. On repeat. "No."

He chuckles as if he can hear the lie straight from my brain. "I meant every word I said. Nothing hot or sexy about sharp bones and being too skinny. You're beautiful, Bianca. I hope you know that. Have you had dinner yet?"

"Dinner?" I croak at the sharp change in topic when my mind wants to stay glued to what he just said. Once again, Kaplan Fritz has me feeling totally off-balance. I check my watch. "Um. No. I thought it was somewhere just after lunchtime, which goes to show you how off I am. But my lack of dinner would make my mother proud."

A grunt. Then another growl. "Text me where you are. I'm bringing you dinner."

Then he hangs up.

I glare at my phone. What happens if I don't text him?

Kaplan: I will find you anyway even if you don't tell me where you are.

"Argh! Mind reader. Stop! Crap."

Me: You don't have a geotracker on me, do you?

Kaplan: You wish. Send me the address of where you are, or I'll have my family's chief of security locate you. He's also former MI6, so think James Bond only real and way cooler.

He wouldn't. He couldn't.

Kaplan: Don't test me. I absolutely can.

Oh my freaking what the hell? My head flies about, half expecting Kaplan to step out of the shadows like the sinister devil he is. How is he doing that? It's like some sort of Jedi mind trick.

I text him the address and put him out of my thoughts. I do have to eat. I'm starving, actually. But that means he's coming here. To watch me work. And eat with me. On a Saturday night. And he reminded me that he *likes* my body. That he likes curvy and, no. Just no! Liar!

He dates models. Tall. Skinny. Sharp bones.

I go back to work. Full-on goggles and gloves and tools. I pump my music up to full volume, having it slam through my AirPods and I go at it. Britney is followed by Rhianna, J.Lo, Shakira, Lady Gaga, Adele, and obviously TaySway.

By the time I'm recovered in sweat and unrestrained hip movements, I forget all about my mother. Tod. Ava. But I don't entirely forget that Kaplan Fritz is threatening to drive out to Chelsea to bring me dinner.

But after an hour and no-show, I'm over it.

He likely changed his mind. Realized he'd rather not spend his

Saturday night with a woman he refers to as the queen of all monsters.

I jump, my hand in the air as I spin around, rocking my hips to the beat. My head bops flying left and right, allowing the piece I've been working on for too many hours to cool. Then I strike the blowtorch again, rocking out to "Poker Face" as I flame up the metal, bending it exactly how I want it with my pliers.

"Baby, when it's love, if it's not rough, AH!" A hand on my shoulder wrenches the scream from my lungs, mid-Gaga. "Shit!" I set the piece and my tools down—glad I had already turned off the torch —tear a glove from my hand, the AirPods from my ears, and hit stop on my phone. "The hell you doin' sneaking up on a woman with hot metal and tools in her hands?"

Kaplan Fritz. Six foot—*four, five?*—plus of huge. Cut muscles for days and sexy arm tattoos on display since the sleeves of his slate-gray shirt are cuffed to the elbows. Baby faced in the most absurdly gorgeous, sinful way. And what does he do with all that? He smiles at me.

Thump. Thanks, heart. Like I needed you to do that.

He's trying to hide his amusement and failing miserably. "I told you I was coming with dinner."

Yeah, but I didn't exactly take you all that seriously. You know. So my heart and brain wouldn't grow stupid on me. Like they are right now.

"I forgot," I lie.

"Liar."

"Stop reading my mind and go back to hating me while pretending I'm the bane of your existence and calling me the mother of all monsters."

His eyes jolt open wide and yep, I said all that aloud. Awesome.

"Whatever. What food did you bring me?"

"Nice singing. And dancing. It was cute to watch even if you were horribly off-key."

I roll my eyes at him as he sets a large take-out bag on a neighboring table, but his eyes are all over the piece I'm currently working on.

"Is this gold?"

"Yes."

"Like actual gold?"

I roll my eyes again, this time making sure he catches it. "*Yes*. I'm making a necklace."

"*With gold?*"

I toss my hands up in the air. "Jesus Henrietta. Yes! Obviously with real gold. Twenty-four karat to be exact because it's the purest form without any silver, zinc, palladium, or other metals in it. I want this neckless to really exhibit that with its color. Plus, it won't tarnish this way even if I have to be careful because it's softer and easier to scratch."

He's staring at me as if he's about to wring my neck.

"What's your deal?" I tilt my head, baffled.

"You're in the middle of an abandoned warehouse and you're dealing with precious metals. That's my deal," he yells.

"Shhh!" I hiss, glaring all around me, but the majority of the large studio space is vacant. It is a Saturday night, after all. "It's not abandoned. It's an artists' warehouse, Mister Judgy Pants. I don't advertise what I'm using and I'm mostly alone over here in the corner. But I've been playing with making jewelry more and more and I'm not going to do that with crappy metal. It's not like I buy gold by the bar. It comes in sheets and tubes and stuff."

"Do you have a stash of diamonds here too?"

"No." But I had been contemplating getting some precious and semiprecious stones at some point. A few emeralds and rubies and topazes and other pretty things. I don't mention that to him though.

"Christ." He runs a hand through his hair. "I'm going to start having Slash follow you here. I had been contemplating it after that night in the restaurant when I made you Netflix and chill with me instead, but it felt intrusive. No more. You're just asking to get mugged."

"You're being overly dramatic. I'm not the only one here who makes jewelry with precious metals."

"Rosie the Riveter, come and sit with me so we can eat dinner."

I touch the red bandanna on my forehead and stare down at the leather apron covering my crop top and high-waisted jeans. Okay. So he may have a point.

"What did you bring?"

"Cheeseburgers and fries."

I moan. I haven't eaten since breakfast, the scent of greasy fried food hitting me in a hard, delicious way. "If you're doing this for a blow job, you're actually getting yourself closer to that finish line."

Kaplan chokes on the fry he's in the process of chewing and I have to slam the butt of my palm into the center of his back to dislodge it. "Thanks for that," he garbles, finally swallowing it down with a sip of his soda. "No more blow-job talk, okay?"

"So prude, Kaplan Fritz."

A glare.

"Fine. No blow jobs. Want me to show you how to make art after we eat?"

He sits on the edge of one of the wooden stools that's abutting a long metal table, totally fucking up his designer pants since nothing in here is clean. "I'm here, aren't I?"

And a girl could totally fall for that. Especially wrapped in a package like Kaplan Fritz. *Especially* a girl who hasn't always gotten the best attention from her family and men. But whatever. I'm starting to get the impression that despite his close-knit family, he's a bit of a loner, possibly as lonely as I am.

Otherwise, why else would he be here with me now?

18

Once we're finished with our dinner, Kaplan cleans the entire mess up, tossing the trash in a nearby bin and then turns expectantly to me. We talked all through dinner as if it was all so normal and with him here tonight, a nagging guilt is starting to plague my mind. I need to tell him. I just don't know how. It's not the sort of thing you blurt out and I... I don't know how he'll respond.

I'm terrified to lose him again.

Even when he's a grumpy, cold, surly bastard toward me and I openly hate him. It's just that something about being with him feels... *right*.

"Okay, I'm ready," he states, standing from the table and tossing the last napkin into the large trash bin. "Tell me what to do."

I take him in from head to toe, chewing on my lip as I try to suppress my laugh.

"What?"

"I can't put you near the fire when you're wearing Armani."

He glances down at his body and then back up to me. "It's Ferragamo." Now a smirk. "Are you trying to get me to take my shirt off?"

I start to squirm, unable to stop it as I say, "Yes. I'd rather not set you on fire, if that's okay. The cuffs of your shirt stick out."

"Fair enough." With his eyes locked on mine, he slowly undoes one button at a time, starting at the top, and holy hell, what have I gotten myself into? My heart beats off-rhythm as heated pumps of lust rush through my blood. He gets to the bottom, removing his shirt and tossing it onto the stool, leaving him in a black tank top undershirt showing off his arm muscles and tattoos and...

I take an inadvertent step forward, my eyes glued to his chest. To his left nipple.

"Does it hurt?" I whisper, staring at the outline of the barbell through the thin cotton that clings to every ridge and groove of him.

"Sometimes." His voice a deep, rich timbre that gives me chills.

I look up and meet his eyes. "Does it feel good?"

My chest quakes.

The green of his eyes is nearly fully eclipsed with black pupils as he licks his lips and nods. "Sometimes. Depending on..."

"On what someone does to it?" I finish for him.

"Yes. Go on. You can touch it. I know you're curious. It won't hurt me and if it does, well, that's partially the point."

Oh.

Tentatively I reach up, my fingers ghosting over the softness of his shirt. His strong, masculine scent is everywhere, and I take a deep inhale, so turned on when he hasn't even touched me or hinted at it. My clit throbs and my empty core aches. The moment my fingers reach his nipple they trickle along the hard peak of it to the barbell. I swallow down a moan.

I want to lift up his shirt and explore his piercing with my tongue. Lick my way around discovering each of his tattoos. I want to drop to my knees and take him in my mouth, taste him on my tongue. I'm so keyed up I can hardly think, my breaths coming out choppy despite my attempt to even them.

He shifts into me, his bare arm touching mine as I continue to explore the piercing over his shirt. A low, raspy sound emanates from the back of his throat as I pull slightly on it, and I shudder against him. My hand drops and I take a step back. If I don't stop touching him like that, I'm going to climb him like a tree right here.

I clear my throat, turning around and heading for the forge. "I like it. Do you have any other piercings?" I ask airily, trying for unaffected and likely failing, only to realize my mistake a second later because there is only one other place he could be pierced that I haven't seen on him.

Only it's too late to take it back because at his silence, I turn my head over my shoulder. His heated stare makes my pussy pulse with desire, my inner thighs coated in my leaking wetness.

"Yes."

Automatically my gaze drops to his groin. "There?"

Another "Yes."

And oh my God. Ohmymotherfuckinggod!

"You like pain." It's more of a statement than a question after what he said before.

He watches me with an intensity that sets my skin ablaze as he says, "It's more about pleasure than that."

"Okay." Because I have no clue what else to say. I'm so turned on I'm about to pass out. Again. Turning back to the fire, I point toward a leather apron he can put on and go about getting myself ready, but I'm frazzled, my thoughts frayed and dirty. *So dirty.*

Donning my gloves, I pick up the partially finished necklace, ready to start heating some of the metal when I feel him press in behind me, standing over me, his face over my shoulder as if he's watching what I'm doing, but his breath is fanning against my cheek.

Swallowing thickly, I pick up a pair of pliers. "You don't want to bend the metal unless it's hot or you can dent it or even snap it."

I put the necklace on a metal tray and bring it to the edge of the forge.

"I don't want to melt it either, just warm it, so I have to be careful."

"Uh-huh."

I close my eyes for a moment, only to blow out a silent breath and force myself to concentrate. Never been my strong suit, to say the least. This man and his proximity are making my nerves go haywire.

A finger at the base of my neck startles me, jostling the metal tray and I quickly pull it back from the forge before I accidentally dump it over in there. "What are you doing?"

"You have a bead of sweat rolling down the back of your neck."

"Oh-ahhh!" rushes past my lungs as his finger is replaced with his warm, wet tongue that glides up my sensitive skin.

"Now I'm tasting you." His mouth continues to explore the back of my neck, kisses and licks and breath making me shudder and moan. His hand slips beneath my apron, finding the bare skin of my belly, tickling along it before shifting his wicked fingers up to the hem of my crop top.

"Kaplan—"

"You got to touch me. It's only fair I get to do the same." His mouth continues its sensual assault on my neck, all the while his fingers walk up under my shirt, cupping my breast over my bra. We groan in unison and before I know what's happening, his other hand is there too, both of my heavy breasts being lifted, squeezed, my nipples rolled.

"Oh God," I moan.

"I fucking love these," he rasps in my ear. "I've wanted to fuck them since the first second I saw them bounce in your wedding dress."

Jesus. I'm losing my mind. My head falls back to the top of his chest, my eyes closing as he worships my breasts, tugging down the cups of my bra and finally finding my bare nipples. It's exquisite. I can't even explain what he's doing to me. All I know is no one has ever played with me the way Kaplan Fritz is playing with me now.

His body is lined up with mine, his large, hard cock pressed into the crest right above my ass. I can't feel his piercing, but knowing it's there has me moaning again, rocking back into him. He thrusts forward and my eyes roll back in my head as he simultaneously pinches my nipples.

"I wasn't trying to distract you yesterday when I told you I'm attracted to you. I'm insanely, painfully attracted to you." Another thrust. "You're all I've been thinking about. Fantasizing about. Jerking off to. The way I want you breeds madness in my mind. It's not who I am, Bianca. None of this is."

He tugs painfully on them, causing another "oh God" to hit the air. "Someone could see us."

One hand slides back down my belly, dipping into the hem of my jeans, undoing the button and zipper on its way. "No one else is here. It's just us."

"Kaplan."

"Has anyone ever touched you just to give you pleasure?"

I shake my head, hating that response, but it's true. Any time I've ever fooled around with a guy, it's always been about sex. About what they could get out of it. They were college boys and then Tod. I'm not sure I'm ready to handle a man like Kaplan Fritz, but I sure as hell wouldn't mind trying.

His teeth graze my earlobe. "That changes now. I'm going to make you come, but that's it. Nothing else will happen between us and this goes no further than right here. It's just us scratching an itch."

I nod because I know what he's saying. We work together and whether he knows it or not, he's complicated for me. So complicated. Too complicated. I don't even know how I feel about him. I have a lot of things to sort out in my head, but with his hands all over me, I can't stop or think rationally.

With that nod, his fingers dive between my legs and he lets out a groan when he finds me bare and soaked. "Naughty fucking girl, no panties?"

Honestly, I was too distracted this morning and forgot. I couldn't sit still. I had to move, and I couldn't slow down. Sort of like now as I rock forward into his hand, chasing friction he has yet to give. Two fingers find their way inside me, and I cry out, clenching around him.

It's been so long since a man has touched me this way. Which is as sad as it sounds considering two weeks ago, I was about to be married.

My hand flies back, finding his hard length trapped behind his pants and I start to rub him. He may say that it's all about my pleasure, but I want to feel him come apart beneath my touch. I want to know just what my touch can do to him.

"Bianca," he cautions, but I shake my head as sounds and moans tumble one after the other from my lips. His teeth sink into my neck, a warning.

"Please," I beg. "I want to." I grip him tighter, jacking him off as best I can.

"Your touch does things to me," he grunts, biting harder into me as if to punish me for that. And while that should make me feel good, that I affect him the way I seemingly do, it doesn't. He doesn't want me to touch him because he doesn't want to feel anything. He doesn't want my touch to mean anything to him.

So cold. So detached. So untouchable.

"Don't make me stop. I won't take you out if you don't want me to." I move faster against him, and he starts thrusting into my touch, finally fucking my hand the way he's fucking my pussy with his fingers. It drives me crazy. That thought. Us fucking each other like this.

His fingers curl inside of me, hitting my spot with each vicious, sloppy thrust while his thumb presses in against my clit. Hard. He's not rubbing, but the pressure in combination with the rhythm he's set inside of me is unlike anything I've ever experienced.

Stars dance behind my eyes, my toes curling in my combat boots as I get closer and closer, the feral sounds and harsh breaths coming from Kaplan driving me on, building me higher. Getting me there faster than I would have imagined possible.

My legs shake, my limbs turning to jelly, and he takes the hand abusing my breast and wraps it around my waist, holding me up and back into him. My free hand hits the table off to the side, my head back, voice shredded.

I'm searching for his piercing, angry that I can't feel his skin against mine. I move my hand faster, rougher, feeling a small outline. No wait. Two outlines. One on his tip and another on his shaft and I spasm, clenching and dripping all over him.

"I want this," I tell him. I want to feel what I'm touching inside of me. I want to know what getting fucked, truly getting fucked, by Kaplan is all about. Because I know what he's doing to me right now is a sample. A tiny teaser of what the main event could be.

"You want to feel my cock fill you up? Pound into you?"

"Yes. Please, yes."

"Filthy, sweet girl, you want to play, don't you?"

"God, yes! I want that so bad."

His cock pulses against my hand, growing impossibly hard and thick, his body mindlessly fucking into me. His thumb taps my clit twice as his fingers hold in on that magical spot inside of me and I explode all over him. Writhing and shaking and screaming out words and sounds I can't make sense of.

A heady, loud bellow and a "*Fuuuuck!*" and Kaplan is coming too, squirting hot cum all over the inside of his slacks. I want to see it. I want to see his face and watch as he comes, but he's holding me too tight, not allowing me to move as he continues to rub me through my orgasm.

When the last of the aftershocks finish, he slides his fingers from me. I wince when he pinches my sensitive, swollen clit, tremble and spasm one last time before he releases me. I collapse against the table, panting for my life, the world spinning behind my eyes.

A chuckle from behind me has my eyes blinking open, a soft, lazy, sated smile on my lips as I twist my head, cocking an eyebrow. "Something funny?"

He's staring down at the wet spot on his dark slacks. "I just came in my pants like a teenager. Hell, I don't think I did that even when I was a teenager."

No. He's too controlled for that, never giving more than he's willing to lose. He wasn't lying when he said his attraction to me isn't a game he's going to play. I already know he's going to stick to his word about this being a one and done and while part of me is relieved by that, the rest is severely disappointed.

Sadly, that was the best orgasm of my life.

"It's a good look on you," I tell him, straightening myself and adjusting my clothes. Without meeting his eyes, I remove my apron and bend down, shutting off the gas to the forge from beneath. The fire dies instantly, bathing us in darkness with only the limited warehouse lights overhead to see by.

"Are you mad?"

I shake my head as I go about cleaning up my tools and locking the unused gold and the half-finished necklace in the safe I keep here. "No. I'm not." And I mean it. I'm not. I'm just confused and slightly guilty that I'm keeping a secret as big as I am from him, and I don't know. I don't know what's going through my head right now.

His hand clasps mine, both of us staring at our linked fingers. "It's how it has to be."

"I know that. I'm not mad. It was fun, but I don't want this to get weird and I feel like if we stay here any longer, it will."

He tugs me into him, his other hand that smells like me on my jaw, tilting my head up and it's just now that I realize he never kissed my lips. Only my neck. His eyes study mine, attempting to read me to see if I'm lying to him, I presume, and when he realizes I'm not, he smiles, pressing his lips to my forehead.

Releasing me, he holds my hand as I grab my bag and then he's walking me out to my car in the abandoned parking lot. "I hate you coming out here alone like this. It's not safe."

"I'm a big girl. I can handle myself and it's honestly not your concern."

He snarls, not liking that at all, but tough shit. Suddenly I'm unreasonably angry. Bereft and maybe that's why I'm angry. It's not his fault. It's mine and I release his hand, opening my door. He helps me up into my Jeep and leans in, kissing my cheek.

"I'll pick you up Monday morning so we can ride into the hospital together."

"Oh goody. The hospital. I almost forgot to throw up over it today. Thanks for the reminder."

He doesn't smile. His eyes are all over my face, his fingers too as they glide along my cheeks, down the slope of my nose, across my lips and back up through my hair that is now sloppily falling out of the tight bun I had it up in all this time.

"You really are devastatingly, unnaturally beautiful." A kiss to my temple. "Good night, Bianca."

I start up my Jeep and he shuts the door behind me.

I don't watch to make sure he gets in his car, though he's parked beside me. I just drive off, needing to flee both him and my scattered thoughts. It isn't until I walk in my door and flip on my light and read the text he just sent me telling me to lock up and hear his car pulling away from the curb that I realize he followed me home. Making sure I was safe.

Warmth spreads through me, my chest clenching in the most dangerous of ways. I have no idea what I'm going to do about him now.

19

"When you started fucking Grace did that mess with your work?" I ask Carter when he answers his phone. Grace was Carter's resident and since they still work together, though he's no longer her boss, he's the one to ask. Starting up my car, he switches over to Bluetooth and I set my phone down on the charging pad.

"Please tell me you didn't."

"I didn't." That is, I only fucked her with my fingers while she jerked me off through my damn pants, but we didn't technically fuck. Yet. Because while I told her it was only going to be there in that damn warehouse, that we were simply scratching an itch, that itch seems to be growing like a ferocious, unsated, still hungry as fuck beast. The only thing I can come up with to explain that is the fact that I didn't actually fuck her.

"Jesus, Kap," he hisses as I pull out of my spot, headed to pick up the object of my unnatural fixation. "Yes. It messed with work. We said we weren't going to let it and then Grace got all weird. It got so bad that I had to eventually kick her out of the OR to get her to come and talk to me and then we ended up yelling and fucking again. But somehow that seemed to do the trick."

"But you kept fucking her after that."

He chuckles. "Obviously. But in case you forgot, I was in love with Grace for a year before I got the chance to be with her."

"There's something different about this one," I admit. "I can't put my finger on what it is." It's like those sweet, throaty sounds she made as she was coming against my fingers were a siren's call. They've completely short-circuited my brain. Or was I already like this with her?

I inwardly sigh. I was definitely already like this with her.

Carter emits an exaggerated gasp into the phone. "Can it be? Has Kaplan Fritz finally found the woman to bring him to his knees?"

I roll my eyes. "Don't be a sarcastic twat. I barely know her."

"For real though. I don't get it. I mean, I understand why you're done with the random hookups, and I agree that the majority of women who come after you are looking for something from you that isn't necessarily your heart. I also know you've had crazy women do crazy things to get at you. But if this one is different..." He trails off, leaving that hanging in the air.

It's a question I haven't directly asked myself though I've heard the suggestion of it knocking at the back of my mind. Well, and from my brothers and Raven.

"I have to marry a certain type of woman. I've always known this, and those certain types of women do absolutely nothing for me. I don't want that life, Carter. I never did. And after everything that's happened to me and to you guys with women over the years, it just became easier to swear off love altogether."

"There's more to it than that."

I sigh because there is. There always has been. "How do you know you can trust it? Dad was so convinced that woman he loved in college felt exactly the same way, only she didn't. She was after his money all along. Oliver was ready to propose to Nora only to find out she had been cheating on him for six months. Even Bianca's ex was fucking her cousin the entire time she was with him, and she had no clue. How do you know that any of it is genuine?"

I have so much at stake.

"I don't know, man. You just do. Usually, it's a lot of small things that add up in the right way. Or even the wrong way if it's not. I wasn't worried about Grace being after my money or my name because she's Grace and we've known her her whole life. It's the same with Raven and Luca. But Oliver and Landon just knew about Amelia and Elle. It's a gut feeling, and I guess that feeling can be wrong sometimes, but I have to imagine that there were signs. That things weren't right in those other cases. They were either ignored or missed."

"Maybe. Whatever. I've only known Bianca a couple of weeks and most of the time we're fighting with each other. It's too soon for any of that kind of talk."

"But you're thinking of dating her?"

"I don't know. Mom and Dad are all up my ass about Millie." I bluster out a sigh as I get closer and closer to her building. "As sad as it sounds, I've never done that before. Dated someone. Not seriously anyway. Any woman I attempted something with showed their true colors pretty damn quickly. But Bianca's not the type of woman you casually fuck."

"Then I guess you have to figure out how badly you want to fuck her and if it's worth what comes with it." He laughs. "Besides, she might not even want your ugly, insufferable ass."

"True. But I think she does." I hope she does and that's what's sitting strangely with me. "Anyway, I'm picking her up now. Thanks, man. I'll catch you later." I disconnect the call and pull up in front of her building. Staring up at the brick structure for a moment, I debate if I should text her or be a gentleman and go ring her bell. Her building is nice. Secure, which I like. Bianca Barlow has plenty of money. She didn't even bat an eye when she bought her Jeep and considering her wardrobe and insane shoe collection, she's not hurting.

I know her stepfather has big money, but she wouldn't be the first rich princess to try and win over the king. But even as I think that, I don't get that sense from her. At all. It's not who she is. She's so different from the Millies of the world. Not just physically.

Whatever. It's too soon to think like this.

I go to hop out of my car when the front door of her building opens and out comes Bianca Barlow wearing a black figure-hugging long-sleeve dress that has silver studs going down the length of each arm as well as each side. It stops just above her knee and she's wearing those knee-high boots with the silver studs in them, matching her dress perfectly. Her long, long brown hair is pulled up in a high, tight ponytail and damn her. Her lips are a deep, rich red, matching the soles of her boots.

She's a vixen, a goddess, and I'm a fool for thinking one small taste of her would ever be enough.

The door clicks open, and she slides in, hitting me full blast with her heady fragrance. "Good morning," she chirps with a smile that brightens up this gloomy, miserably gray day.

"Morning. You're all sunshine and rainbows today."

"Well, I finished my necklace last night, slept like a baby after, and took a CBD gummy when I woke up to help with my anxiety. I'm feeling pretty damn good at the moment."

I chuckle at just how adorable she is. "Are you sure there wasn't any THC in the gummy?"

"I am. Only CBD, which is a shame, but THC never did well with me and my ADHD. It always made me more jittery than mellow."

Huh. Okay. "No getting Bianca stoned. Noted. Are you ready to go?"

She crosses her legs at the knee, the hem of her dress riding up her creamy thighs. My eyes linger there for a moment.

"Stop staring at my legs and drive me to the damn hospital."

I smirk. "If you don't want me to stare then maybe you shouldn't dress like you're going to a club."

"This is *not* what I wear when I go clubbing. I have much smaller outfits for that."

"No taking Bianca clubbing then. Noted."

She giggles and I drive us to the hospital while she fidgets in the seat the entire way. I've noticed she does that, always moving even when seated and quiet, but there is no mistaking that despite her blathering on about what is now the spring gala and other work stuff that she's nervous.

I pull into the garage, park in my spot, and shut off the car only to be hit with the labored sound of her breathing. I turn to her. "Are you sure?"

Her wide eyes are on the elevator doors as she gives me one curt nod.

"Do you want me to distract you again?"

"No. Just..." A sigh. "This is a stupid request since you're my boss and I'm not a child, but will you hold my hand as we go in?"

I hesitate because me holding her hand will be seen by colleagues and random people who work here and even people who don't but recognize me all the same. Still, I can't refuse her that. She's here when she very obviously doesn't want to be and she's battling a serious anxiety like a champ.

Without answering, I get out of the car and open her door for her, extending my hand for her to take. She does, grasping it like a laboring woman pushing out a kid and I grimace, adjusting our hands. "Surgeon of tiny human hearts, Bianca. I need you to not break my fingers."

"Oh." She glances down at our hands. "Right. Sorry."

Her ninja grip loosens ever so slightly, which I appreciate, but it does little to discharge the way my skin hums every time I touch her.

The elevator doors open immediately upon pressing the button and as we step on, she whispers, "Say dirty things to me so I don't think about the fact that I'm in a hospital."

And just like that, my cock goes from semi to rock-hard. "What? Are you serious?"

Except she's trembling against me, her hand shaking so badly, I grip it tighter.

"No. Not entirely. But tell me something. Something about you. Something interesting."

"My favorite place to be in the world is on a sailboat. I have one, a smallish catamaran, but when I took over the foundation, my father gave me our family's sailing yacht. If I wasn't forced to be here working this foundation, I would have taken all last week that I wasn't in the hospital and sailed around the Florida Keys."

"Alone?"

"Yes."

Her head tilts and her eyes find mine. "Are you lonely or just enjoy being alone?"

"Enjoy being alone. Especially while sailing. It's thrilling. With nothing but you and the ocean and a boat you have to captain. The yacht is huge and does require a small crew to help man it, but they're staff, and they never bother me. And when it's just you on the deck at night with nothing but the ocean rocking you below and the sea of stars overhead... it's humbling. And heaven."

"You know, I've never been on a boat before."

"No?"

For some reason that surprises me.

"No. My mother gets terribly seasick, so cruising was never something we did. Europe. Asia. Australia. Africa. I've visited them all but have never been on a boat."

"I'll take you some time, but if you throw up on my sloop, I'll be forced to toss you overboard and feed you to the sharks."

She doesn't laugh. Her eyes are fraught with panic as we hit the floor and the elevator doors open. I have to give her a solid yank, dropping my other hand to her lower back and pushing her along.

"You have a tattoo on your shoulder. An old nautical compass. It's partially intertwined with a heart. Not a heart shape but what looks like an actual, beating heart, complete with tubes sticking out of it."

"Vessels," I correct. "And yes. My two passions, the heart and the ocean."

"You're like that blue diamond in Titanic."

"Thanks," I deadpan. "Hopefully with a better outcome, though I guess if I'm going to die, doing so at sea isn't the worst way to go." I haul her into my chest and dip her backward, her hair hitting the floor. She belts out a shriek followed by a laugh. "Open your eyes. This is the door to your office. Completely away from the patient part of the floor. You can shut the door and shut out the hospital."

Flipping her back upright, I spin her around so she's facing the door. My hand still in hers, I drag her until her back is against my chest. Exactly as it was Saturday night when I made her tremble and fall apart in my arms.

"Go open it." I nudge her forward and she takes a hesitant step, her hand landing on the nob and then she's opening it up.

"It looks like a regular office."

I smirk. "What were you expecting? Cadavers?"

A glare over her shoulder and then she's stepping inside. It's small. Not much more than a desk and a couch, but since she's only here three mornings a week, I think it should suffice.

I follow her inside and suddenly her arms are around my neck, hugging me. "Thank you," she breathes into me. "Thank you for helping me with this and for giving me a space that is intended to make me comfortable."

A small peck on her neck, one quick inhale, and then I let her go.

"I have to get going to surgery. You good?"

"I'm good." She's beaming at me like I'm her hero and something inside me shifts. Stirs. Swirls. Feels fucking fantastic.

MY MORNING KICKS into high gear with two surgeries that don't go according to plan. The first was a five-year-old on my table whose vessels were extremely friable. She started bleeding out with barely a touch. The second is a fourteen-year-old who was discovered to have a patent foramen ovale, which is a small opening in the septum between the atria, which are the two upper chambers of the heart. Typically that defect closes before or shortly after birth, but not in his case. If left untreated, it can potentially cause a stroke. A pretty standard procedure, except he decided today was the day to tempt the fates and coded not once but twice on my table. I've never seen anything like it with that condition.

What should have been two relatively straightforward cases ended up taking hours longer in the OR. I haven't eaten anything since breakfast. I haven't checked on Bianca. Hell, I haven't even had a chance to check in on my other patients.

Fucking Mondays.

Armed with a protein bar and a sore back, I amble down the hall, knocking on Bianca's closed door.

"Come in," her sweet voice rings out and I nearly sag at the sound. I open the door, find her sitting at her desk, all sexy vamp, and collapse on her couch. "Long day?"

"Is it over? What time is it?"

"Two."

"Shit." My face digs into the soft leather of her couch and I close my eyes. That is until my back tenses up like someone is poking it with hot daggers and I grunt, twisting this way and that to get it to release.

"You okay?"

"Just a back spasm. It'll pass."

"Here." I hear her chair push back, the soft click of her heels on the carpet and then she's... sitting on my butt.

"What the hell are you doing?"

"Relax. I'm giving you a back massage. I'm amazing at them. Years and years of PT and weekly massages for my scoliosis. Trust me, I know what I'm doing."

"By straddling my ass in a dress?"

"Just don't flip over."

I half groan, half laugh. But then her hands are on my lower back and it's a full-on groan. "Up. Left. Yesss. That's the spot. Don't stop."

"That's what she said."

I laugh. "This might, in fact, feel better." As long as I ignore the heat of her pussy against my thin scrub pants. "Please tell me you're wearing underwear today."

"Oh, I knew I was forgetting something."

"Bianca—"

"Relax. I'm wearing underwear. Seriously, your back is a tight ball of knots. Don't move." She climbs off me and I crack an eye open, watching as she digs through her purse for something only to return seconds later, her ass back on mine, only now she's squirting something into her hands.

"You carry lube in your purse?"

"You wish. No, it's hand lotion. Don't worry, it's unscented. Lift up your shirt."

I don't argue with her because whatever she was doing before with her hands was magic and I need more of it. Shifting ever so slightly, I lift my scrub top and long-sleeve shirt up and over my head, tossing them on the arm of the couch.

Her hands hit my back, but I feel her tense on me. "What's wrong?"

"Nothing. I just... I haven't seen your back yet."

Her hands start to move, but I can feel it in the air. Something has changed. Her voice. Her posture on me. The sound of her breath. She works my muscles for a few minutes and then her fingertips trickle over my lower spine, right at the base where my scrub pants sit.

"What made you get this?"

I don't have to ask to know what she's referring to. It's a tattoo of a forest. Only the trees are all evergreens, thick and wide and clustered together. Almost cartoonish. "My best friend in prep school and college... his name was Forest. He died about ten years or so ago. He had this same tattoo on his back in the same place. Actually, I went with him to get it."

"You did?"

Her voice is barely above a whisper.

"Yes. He um... he had a breakdown our junior year of college. Started talking to himself a lot. Had delusions. Was paranoid. When he started blurring the lines between what was real and what wasn't was when I involved his family. He left school and then, six years later, took his own life. Hanged himself. I spoke to him an hour before he did it and I... I didn't know what he was going to do."

"Kaplan..."

Her voice is thick with emotion as her fingers continue to stroke the tattoo.

"It's okay."

"No. I... Kaplan, I have something I need—"

Her voice gets cut off as my pager goes off. "Shit," I groan, reaching down to check it. My five-year-old. Dammit. "I gotta go." Slipping out from beneath her, I toss on my shirts and head for the door. "Sorry. Thanks for helping my back. You can go if you're done for the day. You've already stayed longer than needed."

I shut the door behind me, but something is sticking in the back of my head. Even if I can't quite place what it is.

20

I sent him a text first thing this morning, telling him that we need to talk in person. I lingered at the hospital yesterday, hoping he'd come back in so I could tell him, but he was swamped all day and never returned. His pager cut me off at the worst possible moment. Today I've been in the office, my mind locked on his tattoo, tears clinging to the backs of my eyes since I saw it.

At first, my not telling him was anger-driven. It was hurt-driven. It was animosity-driven. I felt as though I was protecting myself by not saying anything. That if he didn't recognize me, that was on him, and I owed him no explanations.

But now, things have changed between us.

I don't know what's happening and what's not, but regardless of any of that, he needs to know. He's not my enemy and I do not hate him. In fact, with each passing day I spend with him, I care more and more about him. His guarded, self-protecting armor is loaded with chinks. Finding and infiltrating them, discovering the prize beneath is indescribable.

Kaplan Fritz is textured. He's layer upon layer and outwardly, what you see, what the world sees, is not the heart of the man beneath. He tries. Lord knows he tries to stay untouchable, but he's not.

And I can't do it anymore.

His tattoo.

The guilt of him not knowing, of me keeping this secret for as long as I've kept it is eating me alive.

"Hey, are you staying?" My head flies up from my desk to find Charlie, her arms loaded with binders, her workbag over her shoulder. I glance at my watch and realize the time, but I'm not finished with everything I need to do. ADHD kicked my ass today with all that was going through my head.

"Yes. I'm behind. Go on. I'm good."

She hesitates, shifting her weight. "You sure? I can stay and help. I know the gala is now pushing everyone to full force."

"Yes, but it's coming along great." Which it is. The responses we've received from the charities, as well as potential attendees when we ran this idea past them, have been enormous. Everyone is thrilled with this idea and even Mean Jenny is getting on board—sorta. "For real though, I'm just finishing up on some stuff. Go ahead. I'll see you tomorrow."

"Okay. Good night."

I throw her a wave and then force myself back to my laptop. I finish writing up an email, check through Kaplan's one last time, and with a yawn I stand, shutting the top of my laptop and stretching out my back only to scream out in surprise when I find someone lingering by the door.

"Jesus," I cry, my hand on my chest. "You scared me. What the hell are you doing here? How did you even get in the building?" The doors lock to the outside at 5:00 p.m.

"Your friend let me in. I told her I was surprising you. Aren't you happy to see me?"

I frown. "Honestly, no. Seriously, Ava, I have nothing to say to you. You and Tod can have each other, and I wish you all the best, but after what you did, I never wanted to see you again."

Ava's blue eyes go from lifeless to venomous in a nanosecond. "Did you know he broke up with me?"

I press my hands down on my desk. Clearly, we're doing this and there is no getting rid of her. I didn't even know she was in Boston. I sigh. "No, I didn't know that. I haven't spoken to him since shortly after he left Boston."

She takes a step into the large open room, her back rigid and her posture accusatory. "He told me that now that you know about us and it's over between the two of you, that you won't even talk to him, he doesn't have to pretend with me anymore."

I shake my head. "I have no idea what that means."

"He was only with me because he was afraid I was going to tell you what we did and then he'd lose you."

"Ava, I'm tired. It's been a long day. Do we have to do this?"

"I hate you, Bunny. I've always hated you. You with the stepdads who love you. With the stepbrother who loves you. With a mom who loves you. Tod loves you. Everyone fucking loves you and no one ever gave a shit about me. I've been in love with Tod since college. You know he only went to graduate school at UCLA because that's where you were going? He asked *you* out. Not me. Fat, disgusting Bunny. And he wanted you."

Tod's words from when he showed up at my hotel room cycle through my head. "You trapped him."

Another step and my heart picks up a few extra beats. I'm not afraid of Ava. She's a lot smaller than I am and she didn't grow up with Mitchell, who likes to box for exercise and taught me how too. I don't *think* she'll attack me physically. But she's visibly unhinged, which makes her unpredictable and scary.

"We had sex one night after he'd had a bit too much to drink and I told him I'd tell you if he didn't try dating me too. I figured he'd end it with you. I knew all he wanted was your money. That he truly loved me."

"Ava, does your mom know you're here?"

"My mom?" A weird laugh that's a bit hysterical cracks the air like a whip. "My mom disowned me, Bunny. She cares more about the money your mom gives her than she does about me."

Ah. So that's what this is.

She tilts her head, her red-painted lips spreading into a menacing grin. "But, you see, they don't know your secret like I do."

Now my heart is thrashing in my chest. "What secret?"

"I saw him that day you ran from the church. You ran right to his car. Kaplan Fritz. I know all about your relationship with him. I found the emails and texts you saved on your computer years ago."

Shit.

"So what?" I shrug, feigning indifference.

Her clenched fists hit her hips, that smile frozen on her face. "I know how broken up you were when he stopped talking to you. We were freshmen in college. I was your roommate. I watched and heard it all."

"Again, so what?"

"I saw him, you know. Kaplan. At your special eighteenth birthday party Elijah threw you right before we left for UCLA. You were climbing out of the pool in your bikini with your fat, gross body on display just as he arrived. I've never seen a man look more disgusted in my life. He took one look at you and left."

Is that... is that true?

Kaplan and I hadn't talked much that last year. He was working crazy hours. We texted more than emailed or called because it was easier. Just random messages, checking in, asking how things were going. Sometimes those texts came in the middle of the night from him. Random thoughts he was having. Deep, soulful thoughts that I cherished finding when I'd wake up. But they all stopped right around that party. And he never returned my calls, texts, or emails after that. The timing lines up.

Ice water dumps into my veins, my gut twisting, sick to the pit of my soul with the realization she's telling the truth.

"I can ruin him, Bunny. I can ruin both of you."

That snaps me back. "How on earth do you figure that?" My voice trembles and I hate that I'm so shaken by this. By her being here and what she's saying and the thought that Kaplan got one look at me and decided he never wanted to speak to me again.

"You were a minor. He was an adult. You were carrying on a secret relationship. How do you think that will play in the press? Pedophilia is a serious crime."

Oh Jesus. "Those conversations were completely innocent, and we never saw each other after Forest's funeral."

She leans casually against a desk, picking at her chipped red nail polish. The same color she was wearing at my wedding. "That doesn't matter though. Does it? There was already a picture of you in the papers together. All I have to do is make an allegation and there is proof of contact. The press will love it. Boston's favorite billionaire prince falls from his throne into a well of shame and disgrace for entering into a relationship with a fifteen-year-old girl. How old was he back then, Bunny?"

Fuck. Just fuckety fuck fuck.

I round my desk before I know what the hell I'm doing, only to stop short. I don't want to engage her. And now that I look at her a little closer, she doesn't look well. Ava never ate. She was always "dieting" in the form of starvation, but she looks practically emaciated now. Her brown hair, the same color as mine, is stringy, hanging limply down her back. Her eyes are too big on her face and sunken in, the skin around them stained purple despite the heavy makeup she's wearing. Same with her cheeks.

These last few weeks have not been kind to her.

"Ava, let me call your mom. My mom. Let's get you some help, okay? You don't look well."

"I look better than you!" she screams, picking up a glass paperweight off the desk and hurling it across the room—thankfully not at me. It bounces off another desk and crashes to the floor without breaking. I jump, banging my hip into my desk. Hard.

"What the hell is going on here?" Kaplan comes storming in. Jaw locked, eyes blazing as he heads straight for me, and I wish he wasn't here. He needs to leave. Now. Something I try to convey when his eyes meet mine. He's on the other side of the room, moving fast in my direction as if he's coming to save me, and I hold up my hand. The three of us positioned in a triangle of sorts and I shake my head, nodding my chin in the direction he just came, begging for him to go.

He shakes his head in return, acrimony etched on his face. His wild green eyes narrow in on me, checking me over as he now slowly edges for me.

Another headshake, my expression beseeching, and finally he stops. His gaze cuts sharply over to Ava, who is standing stock-still now, barely breathing as she squints at him, her rage appearing to have cut off like the flip of a switch.

Something isn't right. She's too eerily quiet and calm after all that.

"You," he says accusingly, marching in her direction. He points at her. "You. You're the girl from the club. The one who wouldn't take no for an answer."

"What?" flies out of my mouth.

His head flips in my direction, his finger still aimed at her. "She came on to me. Saturday night. She grabbed me and I said no, but she wasn't liking that answer."

Oh crap. Fear grips my heart, making my muscles twitch. That's why she's standing like that. She came on to him and he rejected her. Just like Tod and her mother. I don't know what to do. No doubt she'll blame me for this too. I breathe carefully through my nose, trying to calm the riotous panic swimming through me so I can think.

"Kaplan, you need to go," I say, my voice low and deliberate. "Please go."

He's wrought with fury. "Like hell I am. Who is she and what is she doing here?"

"Yes, Bunny. Won't you introduce me to your new boss? His timing could not be any more perfect," she purrs.

"Bunny?"

A deep, sharp pang slices through my gut. I swallow thickly and stare at him, my face draining of color. I sit on the edge of my desk before I collapse, my legs about to give out on me.

"I was going to tell you. That's why I texted you. I tried to yesterday, but..." My already weak voice cuts out on me.

"Bunny," he repeats, only this time it's not a question. His eyes are all over me, a million different emotions flickering across him. "All this time you knew who I was, and you never told me who you were?"

"Kaplan... I—"

"Wait?" Ava cuts in. "He didn't know who you were?" Now she starts laughing. "Man, that's rich. Speaking of, I want two million dollars. From each of you now that he's here. Or I'll go to the press about your relationship with an underaged child. The proof is all over her computer. I'll ruin both your lives," she promises, grinning evilly at him while twirling a lock of her stringy hair around one of her red talons.

"The fuck you will, little girl," Kaplan snarls at her. "You have no idea who you're trying to mess with."

I hold up my hand, stopping him. This ends now. I won't let her do this.

"Ava, you can do that," I start, standing up again, taking space-swallowing strides until I'm on the other side of the desk from her, my hands pressing onto the wood, my body angled in. "You can go to the press because neither Kaplan nor I will ever pay you a dime. But do you really want to go up against Mitchell? He'll make it his life's mission to destroy yours and I know you know that. He's ruthless and tenacious when provoked. Not to mention, you don't have proof in your possession. You're the woman who betrayed me with my fiancé. You're the one who will look bad. Not us." I pause here, letting that sink in for a moment. "You need help, and this is not the way to get it."

Ava staggers back, teetering on her heels, tears now dripping from her eyes like a faucet. "Why does everyone always pick you over me?" she wails. "I just wanted Tod to love me back. He said he did, but the second you walked away, he told me it was all a lie to keep me quiet. I love him so much and he can't stand me. Now my mom won't speak to me. She's left me with nothing. I have nothing. I have no home. No money. No Tod."

Kaplan pivots, one leg crossing over the other as he side-steps in my direction, attempting to put himself as a barrier between us, but I move around the other side of the desk, closer to her. He reaches out for me, trying to grab me, but I skirt around him and go to her, wrapping my arms around her frail form. Her face hits my shoulder, and she absolutely loses it.

"Tod didn't love me either, Ava. He wanted my money. That was all. He's not a good man, and you deserve someone better." I run my hand down the back of her head and twist to find Kaplan over my shoulder. "Go," I mouth, but he just stares at me. His features locked down. I have no idea what's going through his mind.

"I hate you." Ava pushes against me, the movement so unexpected that I stagger back a step, falling into Kaplan who catches me, only to release me immediately as if my skin is made of acid. She bolts for the door, racing down the stairs, nearly tripping as she goes. I run after her, but by the time I reach the second-floor landing, she's already at the bottom, sprinting toward the front door and out onto the street.

Dammit. I make it outside seconds later, my arms wrapping around myself to stave off the cold, but she's nowhere to be seen. I don't even know which way she went, and she could have gone anywhere.

Pulse racing, I run back inside and up the three flights, panting as I fly through the office, past Kaplan who hasn't moved since I fell into him, and over to my desk. Picking up my phone, I dial my aunt first, who doesn't pick up and then my mother, who does. I explain to her everything that happened with Ava—with the exception of Kaplan and the blackmail—and tell her that she and my aunt need to figure this out. I could chase after Ava, but I don't know how helpful for her that will be.

I'm worried about her though.

My mother tells me she'll call the Boston police and my aunt and get it all taken care of. She says she thinks my aunt knows where she's staying, which is a relief. I had no clue she was even in town again or if she never left after the failed wedding.

After I'm done and all that is settled, I set my phone down. Take a deep breath and then look up at Kaplan. Time to face the music.

21

Kaplan's staring at me, anger and pain etched in his every feature as resentment drips from his lips. "All this time?" he questions, his voice eerily low and rough. "It's been you all this time?"

"Yes."

A hard swallow, his hands meeting his hips, his face cast down toward the floor as he breathes heavily. "You fucking lied to me."

"Not exactly."

"What the fuck does that mean?" he snaps, his eyes pinning mine once more, his voice shredding the air.

"I didn't lie about not recognizing you in the car and I didn't lie about not realizing who you were until after your mother gave me her last name and showed me her business card. I didn't lie about not knowing you were going to be my new boss."

His hands meet the back of his head and he's breathing hard, a war of emotions battling through him. "Do you have any idea what this..." His eyes close for a beat as his voice trails off.

"I was going to tell you. It's why I texted you saying that we needed to talk in person. I tried yesterday, but you got paged right when I started."

"Yesterday?! You should have told me sooner!"

"Maybe."

"Maybe!" he roars, his hands falling to his sides.

"Yes," I shoot back. "Maybe. Because you treated me like shit from day one here. You had no idea who I was and not only did that hurt like hell, but I was already furious with you."

"Me?" he snaps, jabbing a thumb into his chest. "What on earth could you possibly—"

"Because you left me!" I scream, flying around the desk until we're inches apart. "You completely ghosted me. You were my friend. You were important to me. Maybe that makes me childish and stupid, but that's what I believed. But then one day you were gone. You stopped returning my texts, phone calls, and emails. I lost Forest and then I lost you without any explanation."

Silence like a heavy weight falls between us. Tears, hot and painful, burn my eyes, but I don't give them freedom to fall. He steps forward, his eyes a stormy green, an impending tornado ready to destroy what's left of me.

"Losing Forest the way I did was practically the end of me," I cry. "Nightmares and guilt lived in my every breath. All anyone ever told me was how it wasn't my fault. That there was nothing I could have done differently. But you listened as I cried without trying to fill my head with useless words that offered no comfort. You helped me make sense of what happened. Get through it. I told you things I've never told anyone. Thoughts and feelings I had. I thought you did the same with me. I thought our friendship was special."

Kaplan was my salve and then... just gone. I shake my head, clearing my thoughts and shifting gears.

"Ava told me that you showed up at my eighteenth birthday party in Colorado. That you were there, took one look at me in my bathing suit, and left. Is that true?"

"Yes. That's true."

Agony rips a hole straight through me, robbing me of my breath. I swallow, falling back a step and landing on a nearby desk. God, I can't believe it. I can't believe that's why he stopped being my friend.

"Please leave," I beg, on the last shred of my composure, about to lose my mind and not wanting him as an audience when I do.

He makes no move to go, and I can't do this. I thought I could, but after that...

Forcing myself off the desk, I return to mine and gather my things. I'm done here.

I didn't drive today, I walked, so instead of heading toward the back door where the parking lot is, I'm forced to go out the main entrance, past him. A hand reaches out, grabbing my right forearm, stopping me, but I don't look at him. I can't.

"Have you had dinner yet?"

"Dinner?" I bark out an incredulous laugh.

"Yes. Dinner. You texted me this morning saying we needed to talk, and I came here tonight with the intent to buy you dinner."

I shift my weight onto my left foot, my head bowing.

"Have dinner with me, Bunny. Please. You're not the only one who has things to explain."

Reluctantly I twist and stare up at him. I'm terrified to hear what he's going to say, but I think my heart needs to hear it anyway. We'll call it closure if I have to. He called me Bunny. The pain of that is so exquisitely ruining.

"Okay. Dinner."

His hand slides down my arm until his fingers are intertwined with mine, then he's leading me to the back exit, down the stairs, and out to his car. He helps me in, shutting the door behind me and I fall back on the seat, my mind racing. Wrecked.

We're silent as he drives us through the dark Boston streets. Wordlessly he pulls into an alley, parks the car, and hops out, leaving it running and me inside. A few minutes later, he returns with a white bag filled with who knows what and then we're off again. It isn't until we're parking in his spot that I realize he's taking me to his place.

I would have preferred a restaurant. Someplace public. But I guess this isn't exactly the type of conversation I can have out in the open with someone like Kaplan Fritz. Hell, my cousin tried to black-mail him tonight. Me too. I do still have all those conversations saved on my computer. And truthfully, even though they were one-hundred-percent innocent in nature, they could be construed wrongly.

She could do some serious damage if she wanted to. I just hope she doesn't take it that far.

The passenger door opens, bathing me in light and I numbly get out of the car, ducking my head and covering myself with my coat as we walk the short distance to his condo. I don't know if he's still being followed by the press. If there's anyone out here lurking, but I don't want to be seen or recognized.

Kaplan flips the lights on, locking the back door behind us and setting his alarm. "We weren't followed, and no one is here," he says as if reading my thoughts. "I checked my cameras when I was inside grabbing our food."

"Good."

Walking through the first floor, he switches on lights as he goes, setting the white bag down in his kitchen and taking what appears to be subs out, setting them on the counter. I'm not hungry, so I weave through his massive family room, staring out at the inky water and Boston skyline beyond, but something catches my eye first. On the large built-in bookcase that separates what was likely the original division between what was once two townhouses there are shelves of pictures I hadn't explored when I was here the first time.

Pictures of him with his siblings ranging from childhood to present time. His parents. Him at his medical school graduation. Sailing on a stunning white boat. His niece Stella. And Forest. The two of them in college from the looks of it, arm over arm, both shirtless with cigars hanging from their dopey grins.

My fingers touch the glass of the frame, gliding over Forest's face. He looks so happy there. This must have been before his mind started to turn on him. He came home before the end of his junior year and at first, I didn't recognize him. He'd spent weeks in a hospital while they sorted out his medications and my mom and Elijah hadn't let me go see him.

Every day I'd come home from school, and we'd play video games together. Some days were good days. Some days he'd mumble to himself or get in arguments with people I couldn't hear or see.

On the day he died, he had a smile on his lips when I came home. He told me to give him fifteen minutes before coming up. That he wanted to shower first. I made myself a snack but then I heard the crash, and I ran upstairs and found him hanging from a beam in his bedroom, his body thrashing. He kicked me away when I tried to go to him, and I ran and called 911. By the time I returned, he was blue and limp, and I was able to climb up using the chair he'd used to tie himself up and release him. He fell with a heavy thud. A sound I'll never forget as long as I live and then we were in the ambulance.

He knew I'd find him. He counted on it because he didn't want it to be his dad and Ellis wasn't living at home by that point since both boys were so much older than me. I was nearly catatonic until his funeral. Then everything inside me broke open and the one holding me up, crying with me, feeling the same guilt I was, was the man now standing behind me.

"I miss him every day."

"Me too," I croak, wiping at the tears I hadn't realized were falling.

"You knew what my tattoo was."

"I drew it. The image Forest tattooed on his back; I drew for him. My mom and Elijah were starting to fight, and I knew how that always ended for her. I loved Colorado, my life, and my friends there, Forest. I didn't want to leave, so I drew a picture that reminded me of the forest that surrounded our home there. His name."

"He never told me that."

I shrug, still staring at the picture because I'm not sure what else to say to that.

Strong fingers glide through my hair, twisting one of the long strands around them. "I didn't recognize you, but somehow, the more time I spent with you, the more you reminded me of Bunny. I didn't remember your face much and I had your eye color wrong in my head. But there was something about you, Bianca, that had my mind straying to Bunny. I never knew your real name. Did you know that?" He chuckles as if it's the most ridiculous thing ever, which maybe it is.

"Instinctively I knew it wasn't Bunny, but that's what everyone called you, never anything else. My mother has a friend who goes by Bunny, but her real name is Barbara. It's a blueblood thing, I think, so I didn't give it much thought."

"I was never called anything other than Bunny until I went to college, and I introduced myself as Bianca because Bunny sounded childish and a little silly. Not even in high school. Teachers, friends, I was always Bunny. Still am with my family."

"Do you know why I ghosted you?"

I spin around, staring up into his turbulent green eyes, boring into me with an intensity that shakes me to the marrow of my bones. "I'd like you to tell me," I say, unable to voice what Ava said about him being disgusted by the sight of me. "The truth."

Taking my hand, he leads me back through the downstairs to the kitchen, sitting me on a stool at the island. He's plated the subs and there's wine in glasses, but I ignore it all. He takes the seat beside me, pivoting us so our knees are touching and we're facing one another.

With his eyes on the hand he's holding once again, his fingers toying with mine, he says, "I flew out to Colorado to surprise you. I had kept in touch with Ellis, and he mentioned that you were staying there for a week to celebrate with them before you left for college. I was a resident with no time, and even though we emailed and texted, I wanted to see you. I hadn't seen you since I left shortly after the funeral, and I needed to make sure you were okay with my own eyes since you weren't when I had seen you last."

He glances up, his expression soft, head tilted, so close and familiar it should be strange feeling that, but it's not.

"No one answered the front door, so I went around the back and found everyone out by the pool. Just before I entered the gate a woman pulled herself up and out of the water. I only saw her from behind, her brown hair dripping water to the middle of her back, but the sight of her stole my breath. All I could think about was that I had to talk to her. That I needed to meet her. She shifted, her face pointed up to the sky, and I caught a glimpse of more luscious curves and smooth, pale skin, and then someone called your name. Someone called Bunny and the woman I was enraptured with turned her head and replied."

My breath holds tight in my chest, my eyes wide. He sits up, releasing my hand and creating distance between us.

"I was sick with it, Bunny. You were Forest's little sister and the last time I had seen you, you were a child. I always thought of you that way. I treated you as I would have Rina. There was never ever a thought of anything beyond that until I saw you there, eighteen years old and I wanted you. It was wrong. I was twenty-nine and you were you, so I left. Deciding then and there I couldn't speak to you anymore."

"W—" I clear the frog from my throat. "Why didn't you tell me? Give me some sort of explanation? All those texts and emails that went unanswered."

A humorless chuckle hits the space between us. "What was I going to say? That I saw you in your bikini and was so turned on by you that I could no longer be your friend and confidant?"

"And now? How do you see me now?"

His thumb drags along my bottom lip, his gaze following the motion, taking in every line and feature of my face before settling on my eyes. "Now I see you as a woman who has somehow managed to get under my skin with her sharp tongue and razor wit. With her endless bravery and unashamed vulnerability. With her sweet smiles and soft heart. With her gorgeous face and stunning curves. A layer I would have sworn was impermeable, you breached. I'm glad it's you, Bunny, but I'm also relieved I knew you as Bianca first."

"Because you would have thought of me only as Forest's little sister otherwise?"

"Maybe." His hand cups my face. "But that's not how I see you now."

My heart thunders in my chest, my breath catching. "You date models and socialites. Not girls like me."

A smile lights up his face, his grin crooked as he inches closer. "Are you asking me out? Because I only date models and socialites."

I slap at his chest, and he catches my hand, pressing it against his pounding heart.

He laughs, lifting my hand to his mouth and kissing my palm, my wrist before holding it in his lap. "I only dated models or women who look like models because I never had much of a favorable opinion on love or relationships. I'd seen some awful things come out of that and had always been told I needed to be with a certain type of woman. I hated the idea of someone telling me who I had to be with. Not to mention the flip side of that coin, which is women dating me who care nothing for me, only their own selfish gain. More than that, I'm a loner. I liked being that way. Never having to answer to anyone or change my lifestyle. Over the last few years, it just became easier to date women I knew I'd never grow any real attachment to. Honestly, I stopped dating for the most part about a year ago after a woman broke in here trying to get a condom we used so she could try and get pregnant from it."

My eyes bug out of my head, my hand over my mouth. "Seriously? Someone did that?"

"Now you know why I have such high security here."

I lick my lips and take a deep breath. "So... that's not... you know, what you're attracted to?"

He leans in, his lips coasting up my jaw to my ear where he whispers, "I believe I've already made my preferences in that clear to you, but no, that's not what I'm attracted to. I'm attracted to you."

"And pain," I quip, but he just pulls back, staring at me, unsmiling now. My blood thrums through my ears as his green eyes grow a bit darker, a touch more lust filled, yet there is a cautious uncertainty lurking beneath his smooth exterior. A question he hasn't voiced.

His hand hits my thigh, his thumb gliding up and down along the inside of it. "You've stopped breathing." As if triggered by his words, my lungs expel every ounce of breath. He grins devilishly. "Sometimes yes. Does the thought of a little pain scare you? Even if I promise to make it feel like the best thing you've ever felt?"

A warm spiral of desire pools low in my belly, my face heating with an unstoppable flush. Does it? I don't know. I've never tried that with someone who knew what they were doing. Who would make it pleasurable. Isn't that what he said Saturday night? That it's more about pleasure than pain? And if it's anything like that was...

"No. It doesn't scare me with you."

His hand on my thigh squeezes and I know where this is going. His unhinged desire all over his face. "I tried to fight it. From the second I saw you walk into the foundation building, I tried to fight it. This unbelievable need I have for you. And not just for your body. I'm tired of fighting it. I don't *want* to fight it. I just want you."

I shake my head. "Saturday night notwithstanding, I won't be that girl for you."

His hand slips up higher, kneading me. "And what girl do you think you are to me?"

"Maybe that's my question to you," I retort, popping a no-bullshit eyebrow. "You tell me you don't want relationships and I understand that. I just got out of one myself and am not ready for all that again, but that doesn't make me casual and that doesn't mean I share."

He chuckles as if what I just said is the most preposterous thing he's ever heard. "Bunny, I have no intention of sharing you. Ever. Knowing who you are and what that means to me? You're the furthest thing from casual in my head." He leans forward, his green eyes all I can see. "I want you, Bianca. Only you. But can I trust you? I mean, really trust you?"

22

For the last twenty years, since I came to realize what the world surrounding me consisted of and what limited capability it held for wanting to chase my own destiny and free will, this has been my reality. Always thinking of the consequences of my actions. Never living in a time that's only in the now.

College. Med school. Resident. Attending. CEO. Marriage to a woman who will look a certain way on my arm and strengthen my position in the world. The world sees us how they want to see us, whether that's who we are or not.

Other than the doctor part, the rest can go suck it.

I am the most secretive with my life and who I am because I have the most to lose.

It's why I like being alone or only with my family. Or why I love sailing so much. It affords me that freedom. Freedom from the expectations surrounding me. Freedom from what the world sees and demands of me.

But Bunny knows me. The things I've told her, the pieces of myself I've shared...

And Bianca doesn't care about all the rest. She never did.

She's only wanted me as myself.

Bianca's almond eyes stare desperately into mine and I nearly want to laugh at her adorable little innocent, owl-eye thing she has going. She believes she's asking for a lot when it's actually so much less than I want to give. Her. No one else because what the fuck just happened tonight?

Bianca is Bunny?

My insides are screaming, YES! We knew it. She's ours.

While my head is still trying to play catch up. When I went into the restaurant, I made a quick call to Morgan Fairchild about the threat Bianca's cousin made. I don't care if Bianca says her mother and aunt are handling it. That's not nearly good enough for me.

So yeah, it's been a night.

Dealing with an unstable woman attempting to blackmail me and then discovering Bianca's true identity. Or more like Bunny's true identity.

Part of me still believes this should be wrong, but she's not a child anymore. She's the woman I saw by that poolside. The one who robbed me of my heart at first sight. That distant notion of Bunny has held me captive since that day. Made it easier to hide away from the world and women because it was like since I'll never have her, I don't have to want anyone else. But Bunny is here.

Only she's better.

She's the woman I haven't been able to rid my mind of for a second over the last few weeks. The one who fights me and doesn't give a fuck.

Bianca is everything I have been missing without knowing I didn't hate all this time.

She wasn't wrong when she said I like pain. I do like it. I like inflicting it and I like receiving it as long as it's on my terms. Only it's a game I never play. When you don't trust your lovers, despite the legal documents you make them sign, you don't open up often. One whisper. One suggestion. My life is so very public. I treat children. My family is royalty. My face is everywhere.

But I *know* her. I *trust* her.

So the idea of being able to play rough with *this* woman?

My cock is already throbbing.

"You can trust me with anything," she pushes out, almost indignantly. I hurt her with that question just as I hurt her by walking away all those years ago. I have a lot to atone for with that.

"Thought so."

Without another word, I stand, scoop her up into my arms, and drop her on the counter. I stare into her eyes, marveling at how sweet and innocently corruptible she looks. Those pretty doe eyes filled with a burning she can't help but show, while still being the slightest bit nervous. The uneven cant of her breaths giving her away as I find her hips and scoot her to the edge, forcing her legs to wrap around me.

Inching in, I move left, grinning at how her lips follow only to deke her out and fly right, landing on the soft, fragrant skin just beneath her neck. She giggles and I smile into her, nipping and licking at her.

"I wanted to taste your mouth so badly the other night," I tell her, blowing cool air on her hot, wet flesh.

"You didn't," she moans, her head falling back, her hands in my hair as I suck on her. So sensitive, and god, I love everything about this with her. I want to take my time exploring every nuance, nerve, and sweet breath she has to give me. That thought gives me a moment of pause.

Has it ever been like this for me before?

"I don't normally like kissing a lot." I pull back and find her half-mast eyes.

"You just haven't kissed the right girl then."

She has no idea.

Thirty-six years until it all came together at the right time and the right moment.

Diving in, I capture her lips, those soft fucking pillows of sugar, feeling her hot breath against me, sucking me in. My reaction is instant. A stick of dynamite whose fuse has run out. I explode, unable to stop my response to her. Her taste, her smell, the feel of her surrounding me. *Her.*

My hands fly into her hair, and I drag her as tightly as I can against me, her large, soft tits squishing against my chest. A rumbling groan vibrates from deep in my throat and I thrust forward into the apex of her thighs, the heavenly spot I'm desperate to be buried.

Far from the innocent bunny, Bianca tilts her head, her tongue voraciously seeking mine as she grasps at my back, her nails digging into my flesh, holding me against her. Our tongues thrash, passion and frenzy taking over as I rip her blouse up and over her head, my shirt following.

My hands find her breasts and I pry myself away from her delectable mouth, anxious to see what I was denied viewing the other night. I suck in a shaky breath. They're even more beautiful than I imagined. Reaching behind her, I undo the clasp of her bra, my lips kissing along her shoulder. Once it's undone, my teeth drag one shoulder strap down and then the other until the satiny fabric falls away, joining the pile of our shirts on the floor.

Bianca likes sexy lingerie, which is no surprise given her penchant for pretty clothes and shoes. I love that about her. It drives me wild, and I tell her that as I cup her breasts that more than fill up my hands, tipped with perfectly proportioned pink nipples.

I roll my thumbs around them, brushing back and forth over her hard peaks before diving down and sucking one deep into my mouth. She tastes like honey and sugar and sunshine and the sounds she makes drive me absolutely insane. Especially when she does this...

"Kaplan. Oh god, Kaplan."

That. That is everything.

I've had women fake sounds. Give me what they think I want to hear. Put on Oscar-worthy performances. But not Bianca. There is no artifice with this woman. She is real and she is mine. "I'm going to make you see stars tonight."

I want to take her upstairs. Spread her out on my bed and devour her on every surface. But I can't stop kissing her. I can't stop touching her breasts. I can't stop myself from laying her back on the cold stone that makes her back arch and her body shiver while I drag my tongue down her soft belly.

She whimpers and sighs, shaking and trembling as my hands hit her pants, annoyed that she's not wearing a dress or a skirt that my face could already be under. Undoing the button and zipper, I slide them down her legs, catching a peek at her pale-purple panties that match her bra and then those go too.

"Kaplan!"

The urgency in her voice has me glancing up. She's propped up on her elbows, her teeth chewing furiously on her bottom lip as she stares at me with something I can't quite figure out.

"What is it? Am I hurting you?" I haven't even touched her yet.

"No. It's. Um. Maybe this would be better to do upstairs in your room. You know, where it's a little darker. More intimate," she throws out when she notices I'm starting to glare. And once again, I want to kill her fucking ex-fiancé and mother. And likely her cousin too. And a society that places so much pressure on a woman's body.

She tries to cover herself, but I smack her hand away. No fucking way.

I take a step back and gaze at her, completely naked and glorious perched on my counter. The spill of her dark hair all around her. Her large breasts and smooth stomach leading into rounded hips and thighs. Her perfect, bare pussy desperate for my mouth and cock. Then back up to her large, rounded, almond-colored eyes and quivering red lips.

Could she be any more perfect for me?

I force her to sit up while taking her hand and placing it over my aching dick, letting her grip every hard inch of me.

"You feel that?" I growl, clasping her bottom lip in my teeth and dragging it away from hers. "You feel how turned on I am right now? That's you doing this to me. It's never been like that before for anyone else. I'm hard as steel for every *perfect, beautiful* inch of *you*. I've been drooling over you for weeks now. You are so insanely sexy to me." My forehead meets hers. "You take my breath away, Bianca. You are exactly what I would have created if God gave me the choice."

She stares down at my chest, her hand that was gripping me

sliding up, tickling along my abs and swirling around my ink. "I always liked my curves until, well..."

I cup her face, drawing her eyes back up to mine. "I love your body. I love your curves. You love your curves. What else matters? Trust me as I'm trusting you. Love yourself as I'm loving you."

A shaky breath and I lick the seam of her lips, tasting it. Kissing at her mouth and neck, I coax her back into the lull of pleasure as my fingers toy with her breasts and the smooth mound of her pussy. My thumb glides over the seam of her lips, over her swollen clit without giving her any pressure. I've felt her come apart on my fingers, but I'm dying to taste her on my tongue. Her mouth opens on a soundless gasp as I skirt up and down her like this and I smile against her neck.

Bianca is insanely responsive and incredibly sexual when she lets go. The things I plan to do to her body, the limits I intend to test and push are boundless.

"Don't lie back," I tell her as I track back down her body. "Watch me eat you like a man starving."

A sharp, ragged breath flees her lungs as I spread her thighs wide, throw them over my shoulders, and cover her pussy with my mouth.

Running my hands along her silky thighs, a rumble escapes my throat as I taste her, suck on her clit. A loud moan and then her hand is in my hair, gripping me by the roots as if she doesn't know what to do with this sensation. Has anyone ever eaten her pussy like this? I doubt it. That has me growling like a caveman as a flare of possessive satisfaction blazes through me.

This sweet, innocent little bunny is mine now.

Her ass lifts off the stone, seeking my tongue as I slide down to her dripping entrance. I release one of her legs and grab her breast, pinching her nipple until she cries out. Then my tongue thrusts up inside her and her head flies back as that cry turns to a low, long moan. I fuck her like this. With my tongue eating at her. All swirling plunges and deep licks.

Just as her legs start to shake on my shoulders I pull back and she huffs out a disgruntled moan at being denied her orgasm. Blowing cool air on her pussy and with my eyes on hers, I slap her clit. She screams, but I'm already there, sucking it back into my mouth to ease the sting while pressing two fingers inside her. I keep this up, alternating between bites of pain and blissful pleasure, toying with her climax until she's so worked up, she's begging me to let her come.

I'm so hard I'm about to burst in my jeans, my mouth and chin sloppy with her arousal that's leaking from her. My crooked fingers play with the spot inside her, the walls of her pussy quivering, convulsing, just like my girl.

"Please." Another begged cry, and I can't deny her any longer. She's been such a good girl letting me play with her like this and I tell her that making her moan louder than she was before. Even if she has no idea what's coming next for her.

Picking up the pace of my fingers, I blow on her again. She shakes uncontrollably, one hand on the counter, the other toying with her breast. Her legs wrap tighter around me, attempting to press me back into her, and I give her what she wants. My lips capture her clit and I suck it hard into my mouth, flicking it with my tongue while my fingers move faster and faster. She detonates, screaming out a release so powerful for a moment I'm afraid she's going to topple off the counter.

Her body shoots up, practically falling on me, her hand in my hair attempting to pull me closer while yanking me back. It's a lot. A lot of pressure and a lot of pleasure after being denied so long and I'm not being easy or gentle on her. But when I've wrung every last ounce of her orgasm from her body, licking her too-sensitive pussy clean, she sags back on the counter, panting for her life while laughing lightly.

"Stars," she murmurs, her eyes closed. "I definitely saw stars."

Standing, I kiss my way up her sweaty body, over her breasts until I'm at her lips where I give her a gentle kiss. "Was it too much?"

Her eyes pop open, a dopey, sated grin on her swollen lips as her hand comes up, brushing some of my hair back from my face. "You're so gorgeous it's impossible to handle sometimes. Especially when you look like this. No. It wasn't too much. It was... a lot. More than I've ever experienced before. But... I liked it."

"Good."

"We're going to need to clean your counter."

I chuckle into her, kissing her deeper so she knows that can wait. I'm far from done with her tonight. "Wrap your legs around me, pretty girl." She does and I lift her off the counter, holding her against me as I head for the stairs.

"Kaplan, I can walk!"

"I've carried you before and so help me, if you say one word about how you're not small or light or whatever toxic shit is going through your head, I will spank your ass until my handprint shows red."

"I just don't want to fall."

I pull back and meet her eyes halfway up the steps. "You think I'd ever drop you?"

"No. I don't know. Just keep going."

I finish up the stairs and then down the hall into my bedroom where I set her down on the bed. My pants hit the floor and then I'm crawling over her until my eyes meet hers. Lifting one of her legs up, I set it on my shoulder and then, without warning or words, I slide deep inside her. No condom. Nothing separating us.

The pleasure is so euphoric and foreign, every breath in my lungs is instantly expelled.

I've never done this with anyone. Fucked a woman I didn't have a condom and a signed NDA with. What this means for me, for my life and how I've lived it thus far isn't lost on me.

But Bianca isn't just any woman. She's been part of my soul for the last ten years. A permanent resident in my mind. One I never thought I'd get to see again let alone be with like this. Knowing who she is, what she means to me, is sailing me into uncharted waters. Waters I never wanted to navigate before, but now, gazing into her eyes and feeling her around me, I don't know how I'll be able to live anywhere else.

I start to pound into her, setting a good rhythm with her splayed open like this, one knee up on my shoulder, the other wide around my waist.

"Jesus, I can feel it. The metal. Oh my god, Kaplan." Her hands grasp at my arms, gripping the hell out of me as her head twists from left to right.

"Too much?"

"No. So good. So good. Oh my hell, it's so fucking good. But I didn't get to see them."

I chuckle mid-pant as I reach down, grabbing her luscious ass and massaging the globes as I lift her up, shifting our angle. "You will, baby. This is only round one."

"Fuck, I'm going to die or pass out before that."

Leaning down, I bite her nipple. She screams, her hands smacking at the top of my head until I soothe it with my swirling tongue and deep kisses.

"That hurt."

"Too much?"

"I... no. More. Again. Bite me again. I want to see your teeth marks on my skin."

Fuck. This girl. She is made for me.

I do it again, this time on her other breast, her tits bouncing wildly as I fuck her, pistoning like a battering ram into her hot, tight pussy that is the best thing I've ever felt. She's a warm, wet fist gripping me, almost too small to fit all of me.

Sliding out, I flip her over, dragging her hips up until she's on all fours and then I enter her like this, knowing the angle will be deeper and she'll feel more of my piercings on her G-spot. She slams back into me, meeting me thrust for thrust, her head bowed forward, her fists clutching my duvet. Wet slaps fill the air, my balls hitting her clit with each pound.

She's already close. I can tell by the way her pussy is trying to milk me, hold me in, by her loud moans and whimpered cries.

"Bianca, open your eyes, sweet girl, and look up."

She does and finds us in the mirror across the room. Her drunk gaze meets mine and holds there, her lips parted as her cheeks grow rosier, her body flushing all over. Wrapping a fistful of her hair, I hold her like that, forcing her to watch us as I stroke in and out of her like a man possessed. Utterly drugged with her intoxicating feel and heady smell.

Leaning down, I brush my lips along her spine, licking at her sweat, tasting her on my tongue. "You feel so good you make my head spin," I tell her, the words fleeing of their own volition. I'm not typically one who talks a lot during sex. Again with the trust factor, but I want to tell Bianca every dirty, filthy thought and sensation as it enters my mind. I want her to feel this too. This crazy, consuming, life-altering thing that's happening between us.

Pulling on her hair, I force her up, my arm banding around her stomach to hold her to me as my mouth ravishes hers. Our kiss is wet and sloppy, teeth and breath and lashing tongues as I plow into her, getting closer and closer, my balls drawing up in so much pleasure I nearly fear it.

"I'm close," she cries into me, and I reach down, pinching her clit, rolling it between my fingers and that does it. She comes hard, all over me, drenching and squeezing my cock to the exquisite point of pain and I explode inside her on a roar, my cum shooting into her body.

Falling forward, we land in a heap, and I roll us so she's on top of me, my cock somehow still half-mast and partially inside of her.

"I've never come that hard before. That was incredible," I groan, kissing her neck.

"Yeah. That."

I grin, nipping lightly at her, wrapping my arms around her, and holding her close to me. Feeling her heart pound against me as she no doubt feels mine. And for the first time in my life, with a shudder of realization overtaking me, I don't want to be anywhere else but here with her. I don't want her to leave. I want her to sleep in my bed beside me. I want to wake up and fuck her in my shower and make her breakfast and go to work with her. I want to hold her hand and watch her smile when I touch her.

I don't want to be alone if she's not with me.

And I don't want to be with anyone else if I can't have her.

She rolls over in my arms, tucking her head under my chin, my fingers gliding up and down her spine as I stare up at my ceiling. So struck by this I can hardly breathe.

How can the trajectory of my life be so drastically altered in one night?

And am I ready for this new course I now find myself setting? Do I even have a choice but to follow it?

23

He wakes with a groan, my lips spreading into a smile as the sound stirs from his drowsy body. My tongue drags up the underside of his hardening dick, flicking at the piercing just under his head and then the other one in his tip. Kaplan is perfect. I mean, my God. Thick and long and veiny. Velvet over steel as my hand pump him into my mouth. And his piercings? Hol-lee-shit, they're so sexy I can't get enough of them.

His abs clench when his pelvis gives a gentle thrust into my mouth and my core floods with heat. I've never found the idea of doing this sexy before but bringing Kaplan Fritz to the pinnacle of pleasure is doing all kinds of things to me. Filling my head with unexplored desires I never had until now.

He woke something inside me.

Dazed green eyes snap open, and he finds the mane of my dark hair hiding what is an image he seemingly doesn't want to miss. He gathers it, dragging the impossibly long, tangled strands from my face and when our eyes meet, he groans again.

"This might be the best thing I've ever woken up to," he rasps. I flick at the piercing that goes through his hole, making him grunt and tighten his grip on my hair. "I take it back. No might. This is absolutely the best thing I've ever woken up to."

I hum and he moans again, this time longer.

"I told you I wanted to see your piercings," I tell him as my mouth comes off him with a wet pop.

"Baby, I'm not complaining." He glances over at his nightstand. "It's five a.m. and my alarm is set to go off in ten minutes. Come here." Without giving me the option, he drags me up his body until my mouth meets his, his tongue tangling with mine. "If only we could spend all day in bed, I'd do so many wicked things to this body you wouldn't be able to walk for a week and would be sore for a month."

My fingers find his nipple ring as his mouth plunders mine. I give it a small tug and he grins into my mouth.

"You have a thing for my metal."

"And tattoos," I proclaim, the sound turning into a moan as he reaches between my legs to play with me, rubbing a lazy finger over my clit.

He pulls back, his gaze bemused as if he's coming to realize something. "I've never had morning sex before."

"What?" My head pops up, eyes wide in the darkness of his room. He can't be serious.

He fingers a strand of my hair, twirling it around. "Well, at least not that I can remember. I haven't had a sleepover since medical school and even then, we were up so early after so little sleep sex wasn't that appealing."

"We?"

He laughs lightly at my frown. "Well, I wasn't doing it alone."

I shake my head. "I don't like hearing about this."

A thumb runs over the soft pillow of my bottom lip. "That's good because I plan on finding your fuckwad of an ex and murdering him. Don't worry, I'm experienced in these things, and no one will suspect it was me. If you want to give me the names of your lovers before him, I can kill all those birds with one sword."

I roll my eyes at him.

"I'm totally serious. The idea of someone else doing to you what I did last night makes me irrationally jealous and violent."

"No one has ever done what you did to me last night before. That was a first."

"And a last with anyone else."

Grasping my hips, he shifts me until I'm straddling him, rocking me forward and backward over his cock until he's coated in my wetness. I'm so turned on I can't think about anything other than what he's doing to me. His piercings hit my clit with every up glide and it's pure fucking ecstasy.

"God, what do you call that thing?"

"A penis, sweet girl. It's called a penis. I didn't think you were that innocent before last night."

I let out a breathy laugh, taking over and riding him now. "I didn't think I was either, but clearly, I was wrong. I meant that type of piercing. Obviously."

"Obviously." He's grinning like a fool.

He's so damn sexy and fun, I just want to keep playing with him. Make him smile and come all day. Seeing him like this, so relaxed, so happy, it fills my belly with a dangerous warmth I can't think too closely about.

"The one in the tip is called a Prince Albert. The other an apadravya piercing." He pinches my nipple, twisting it until I cry out from the zing. "Though the Prince Albert is more about my pleasure than the apadravya, they're both designed to hit your G-spot whether I'm taking you from the front or the back."

"I can attest to that," I moan raggedly, already getting close. "Can I put you in me?"

"You can do whatever you want to me."

I smirk down at him as he continues to play with my breast, his eyes locked on the spot where are bodies are connected. "Dr. Control is relinquishing it?"

He squeezes both my breasts now, pressing them together and trussing me up. "Not even a little. I want to watch you bounce on me. Doesn't mean I don't have things planned while you do."

"Oh, god," I whimper, closing my eyes as a shiver races up my spine. Rocking faster and faster on him, so the barbell and hoop hit my clit over and over again. "This feels so good."

"It'll feel better in a moment. Go on, put me inside you."

My eyes flash open and my face drops. I tilt my head and bite my lip, batting my eyelashes at him. "But you're so big, how will you ever fit?"

"Cheeky little thing." He grips my ass to the point of bruising and then slaps it.

Why does that feel good too? I whimper, unable to stop it and his cock grows that much harder.

"If you don't do it, I will, and I can't guarantee which hole I'll plunder," he threatens, his voice thick, his eyes growing darker.

I pause my movements, staring down at him in disbelief. "You wouldn't."

"Wanna find out?"

I swallow thickly. "Not this second, no."

Rising up onto my knees, I grip his length tighter in my hand, giving him a squeeze that makes him wheeze and then I'm on him, sliding down slowly only to be met by his up thrust, burying himself in me to the hilt. Both of us hiss out a breath and he gives me a moment to acclimate to his size because even though I was joking, he is huge.

When my body relaxes, I start to move, bouncing up and down and rocking front to back, testing to see what feels good. Each and every time his piercings hits me just right, rubbing that magic spot, my lips part on a silent cry and the hand on his chest presses in deeper. It's so good. So deep like this.

For a few minutes, Kaplan just lies here and watches the show, his hooded eyes all over me.

"You're a goddess, taking pleasure on my dick like the world will end when my alarm goes off. Your tits, those large fucking mounds I haven't even begun to explore and ruin myself in make me so hard when they bounce with you like that."

"Pinch my nipples," I beg, and he's only too happy to comply.

I up my pace, time not on our side, and he grasps my hips, pounding up into me as my body lowers to meet his.

He fucks me wild like this, holding me against him as he pounds me from beneath, fast and furious, hard and unrelenting. Nails claw at his chest and though I haven't checked yet, I'm positive he'll have a new set to add to the ones I put on his back last night. Sounds and words and pleas flee my mouth, the world tilting as a delicious, curling warmth shoots like a tonic through my veins.

Shifting me, his thumb finds my clit, rubbing it just as fast as he's fucking me and with the same amount of pressure. Leaning back, my hands grip his shins, my body wide-open to him, and that's what does it for me. This angle and his fingers and his throbbing cock and I come on a loud cry that turns into a scream when he smacks my clit over and over again.

Electric pulses thrum through my body and just when I've reached the peak and he can no longer hold off, Kaplan clenches my hips, slams me down on him one last time, and comes with a low bellow that goes on and on just like this orgasm.

My body falls against him just as his damn alarm goes off, causing us both to groan and laugh.

"Wow. Morning sex." He plants a kiss on my hair. "Or maybe it's just the girl on top of me."

I smile, everything inside me so light. I should be scared by this. By how this all feels. By how fast it's coming down on me after I nearly married another man a few weeks ago. Only, I've never felt anything like this before. I listened to my mother and believed her words when she described what love and relationships and marriage are all about. And truthfully, I hadn't seen anything else to sway me from that picture.

Until now.

Which is why I need to leave. Kaplan Fritz is Kaplan Fritz and we both agreed that keeping this at a slow, even pace was ideal.

"I need to go home and shower," I lament with a tired sigh, trying to drag my limp, sated, sore body off his.

His hold on me tightens. "Shower here with me and then I'll drive you home to change. We can go into the hospital together again."

"Right. The hospital. Joy."

He pets my hair, kissing my forehead. "Is it because of Forest? Is that why you hate it there so much?"

I stiffen and nod, my heart twists with flashes of that day.

"Fuck. And to think what I did to you. Do you want to stop working there?"

Quiet for a contemplative moment, I then whisper, "No. I'm stronger than that. I'm not a quitter."

He kisses me again. "Don't I know it. Try firing you."

I twist his nipple ring and he smacks my bottom, both of us laughing, holding each other tighter. Savoring this for another moment before we absolutely have to get up. We shower together and Kaplan takes way too much enjoyment in lathering my naked skin in his body wash. Then he drives me home, waiting on my sofa in the living room and working on his phone while I finish getting ready.

No one was there when we left his place, the hour early and the weather awful even for the paparazzi and there are so many things to figure out while I do my best not to overthink. For now, our plan is to just take this day by day and see where it leads us. No pressure. No strain. No expectations. Except the moment I step out of my bedroom, I know I'm already in trouble.

His head turns over his shoulder and his gaze glues itself to me, eyes going just the slightest bit wide. I'm wearing a curve-hugging emerald-green sweater dress that doesn't reveal an inch of skin, but you'd think I was wearing the sexiest, skimpiest lingerie by the look in his eyes.

"I'm not sure I've ever seen a more stunning woman in my life," he whispers, his voice so low I'm not sure the words were meant for me to hear.

But I did hear them, and they make my heart jump in my chest.

"The way the color of your dress makes your skin glow."

Please stop, I want to beg. He was a man who finger fucked me without kissing me, telling me such a thing would never happen again. We've been at each other's throats for weeks. And now it's this. Him finding out who I am seems to have changed everything and I'm... scared. It's all moving so fast.

Rising off the couch, he walks to me as if his body is responding without conscious thought. His hands dive into my hair and his lips fuse with mine in a startlingly passionate and possessive kiss.

"You're a goddess," he breathes into me, his tongue plunging inside, desperate for a taste. I think this is what you call unable to keep your hands off each other as my hands tear at his scrub top, pulling at it so I can touch what's beneath. "All I want to do is strip you down and lick every inch of you. Bury myself inside you over and over."

I whimper, his teeth snagging on my lips, scraping the sensitive tissue until he's forced to release me. Foreheads pressed, he stares into my eyes.

He has surgery in an hour and likely needs to already be at the hospital. But it seems we're breaking all the rules right now. I'm fucking my boss. A man eleven years older than me. A man I knew when I was a teenager who was best friends with my older stepbrother. Someone I know he considered one of his brothers.

"I'm going to be hard all day thinking about how you look."

"So then I shouldn't show you these, right?" I step out of his arms and lift up my dress, revealing the tiny scrap of green barely covering my pussy.

He growls, reaching around and smacking my ass. "Jesus, B. You're going to kill a man with that."

"B?"

His smile makes him look even more boyish than he typically does. "Bunny. Bianca. B."

"Oh no. I get it. I just didn't take you for the nickname sort of man."

"Your entire name is a nickname," he retorts.

"But you didn't know that. Hell, I wonder if Ellis even knows that."

Ellis. Right.

As if this thought dawns on him too, he says, "We should tell your brother."

I laugh, grabbing my purse and computer bag, then opening the door so we can leave. I throw him a look over my shoulder. "Go for it. Ellis actually mentioned he had a friend in Boston who would look out for me. Make sure I'm taken care of."

He winces and I roll my eyes as I lock up.

"Oh please. You all think I'm so weak and helpless. I don't need to be babied. I'm a grown woman and Ellis has never exactly been the overbearing, no one can touch my sister type. If you want to tell him we're seeing each other, then do it. If he has a problem with that, that's on him. He didn't consult me when he started fooling around with Amira and she was my high school lit teacher."

Besides, Ellis is the least of my concerns. I haven't heard back again from my mom or my aunt about Ava. Not that I expect to so soon, but having her out there, angry, broken, blaming me, and knowing about Kaplan has me on edge.

Despite all the exhaustive acrobatics of last night, I couldn't sleep. I tossed and turned and even tried texting her, asking where she was and if she was okay. No response, not that I was surprised. But still... she has power right now and me being around Kaplan could be dangerous for him.

We step out into the rain, and he opens his umbrella, wrapping his free hand around my shoulders and tucking me into his side so I don't get soaked as we run for his car. He opens the door for me, and I quickly scramble in. Shutting the door behind him, he gets in, tossing his umbrella on the floor in the back and shaking out his hair.

This is awful.

"Does it ever stop precipitating here? Ugh." I wipe at the water soaking the hem of my dress.

"This hasn't been the best start to spring. Hopefully this is the last nor'easter of the season."

"Hope so. March shouldn't be this wet or icy."

We drive to the hospital, the heat on full blast, drying us off. I'm quiet as we enter the elevator in the parking garage, my already flayed nerves sparking with an edginess. I can feel his eyes all over me, but I can't quite force myself to meet them. Wordlessly he takes my hand, gliding his thumb over my knuckles.

"I've got you." That's all he says and my heart, that crazy, blood-saturated organ in my chest that has been beating strangely since, well, since I jumped on the hood of a car and locked onto the greenest eyes I've ever seen gives a lurch. The kind that makes it feel like it's attempting to beat its way out of my chest and into his.

Glancing up, I meet his steadfast gaze, his expression intense, introspective, and I wonder if he's struggling as I am.

Stupid to wonder.

He may agree to be exclusive, and he's obviously attracted to me, but I'd be a fool to consider what we're doing anything more than sex. We're too complicated and messy for this. It was easier when I hated him and he didn't know who I was.

The doors part and we step off, his hand still holding mine until we reach the point where I go left and he goes right. His gaze is fixed on our locked hands when he says, "This was almost easier when I was trying to get rid of you."

It's as if he's reading my mind, but his words still hit me wrong.

Stormy green eyes meet mine before he releases me and walks away, leaving me to frown after him. He sounds as tormented as I feel. With a sigh, I realize if we're not careful, this thing between us could turn really ugly.

24

Something has been sticking wrongly in the back of my head since I stepped on the elevator with Bianca. A weird form of guilt. No, maybe not guilt necessarily. I'm not even sure how to categorize it. It's like being rubbed raw with sandpaper and flayed with a knife and I can't shake it. All through my surgeries. All through my morning.

Which is why when I got the phone call right as I finished scrubbing out, it felt like fate. A sign. It's how I end up here.

"Thank you for meeting me," Millie says with the pearly white smile and beauty queen sparkle she's perfected. She's all blonde hair and blue eyes and tiny button nose and minuscule waist and curves. Everything she was trained to be that turns me off completely.

"It was good timing actually," I tell her, staring down at the menu. I hate being here. It feels wrong, but it's necessary. "I've been meaning to talk to you in person anyway." Since you haven't gotten the freaking message via text.

"I feel bad I didn't ask you sooner. Could have given you a chance to change."

I chuckle humorlessly without sparing her a glance. "My scrubs offend you?"

"No. I mean... I don't mind them. But this is a certain kind of restaurant."

It sure is. One of Boston's most expensive and exclusive restaurants.

I'm about to say something when the waiter picks this perfect moment to ask us if we'd like something to drink before lunch.

"Oh. What a lovely idea," Millie exclaims, sitting up straighter. "Yes, Kaplan, let's have a cocktail. Something to relax us a bit. I'll have a glass of champagne, please. Or should we order a bottle? Cristal?"

My menu falls flat on my place setting. "Just water for me and I'm in a bit of a hurry, if you don't mind."

Millie's flawless smile slips a notch. "Surely you have time for a drink first."

Is she kidding me?

The waiter shifts uncomfortably, and I shake my head at him. "The water only please."

"Yes, sir. Very good."

The second he's gone, Millie starts pouting.

"You realize I'm a surgeon, right? That means no alcohol while I'm on shift or call. Not to mention, you sprang this lunch on me and I have to get back. I have patients waiting. I only came here because we need to talk."

She waves me away. "Oh, come on, Kaplan. What's the big deal if you play a little hooky? I'm sure someone else at the hospital can cover for you."

She would think that. A senator's daughter, she's never had an ounce of care or responsibility. Someone was always there to make sure whatever she needed got done for her.

"Millie, may I be blunt with you?"

Shifting in her seat, she crosses her legs and glances around. She doesn't like the way I'm speaking to her in public. But in truth, if she had accepted all the ways I tried to blow her off after our one and only lunch meeting that was far from a date since our mothers set it up, then we wouldn't need to be here in the first place. Typically, I'm not this brash, but I want to get this done and get out of here. I feel like my skin is on fire just sitting here.

Sliding up the sleeves of my long-sleeve shirt, I get ready to get down to business when she gasps. "You have tattoos?"

I stare blankly at her. "Yes. I have lots of them."

"I didn't realize." She scrunches her nose and it is not nearly as cute as when Bianca does it. "Well, I'm sure you could have them removed."

I laugh, leaning back in my seat. "I'm not having them removed."

"They're a bit low rent for someone of your station, Kaplan." I'm about to ask her what station she thinks I'm in when she springs up out of her chair. "Caroline, darling. Oh, so good to see you. You look fabulous. That dress is stunning on you." She air kisses some woman passing by. "You know Kaplan Fritz, of course."

I give the woman a polite nod and half smile. Standing to greet her formally, I shake her hand.

"Yes, I believe we met at the Healthcare for The Homeless charity ball last year. Wonderful to see you again."

"Yes. You too." With a polite grin, I sit back down.

"I have to get going, but let's do drinks soon, Millie. So lovely to see you."

They air kiss again and then Millie sits back down. "Did you see her dress? Disaster. I can't believe she wore something like that in here. It's not vintage, just old and tired."

And that's it. I'm done. Because Miss Sweet Sunshine isn't that at all. She's a two-faced, stuck-up, social climbing, venomous woman. Sitting up, I drop my forearms, tattoos and all, onto the table.

"Millie, while I appreciate that you asked me to lunch, the reason I agreed is because there is something important I want to discuss with you. I know what our parents have been scheming, or maybe hoping for when it comes to us. I know you're very much aware of it too."

She sits up straight, an eager light hitting her eyes. "Yes. I was hoping for a little time with you. You've put off all my requests until now, but I think it's imperative we speak about all that our parents are cooking up." Her hand falls on top of mine, resting there and for a moment, I don't stop the contact. "I realize we've known each other most of our lives with our mothers being such close friends, but we haven't spent a great deal of time alone together before. That said, from the conversations I've had with my mother, who knows your mother quite well as I said, I think this truly will be a perfect match for both of us."

Shaking my head, I slip my hand out from beneath hers and inch closer. "No. You've misunderstood me, and I apologize if you've gotten the wrong impression about what this is between us. But... wait?" I tilt my head, curious. She said perfect match. "What do you think this is between us?"

She laughs as if the question is preposterous. "Oh, come now, Kaplan. You know as well as I do what this is." She leans in, glancing left and then right and then back at me. "The start of our future. Our life together. An arrangement or betrothal if you require such absolute terms. A rather good one, if I do say so. I was not displeased when my parents presented it to me as I'm sure you weren't either."

For a moment, I'm too flabbergasted to speak.

Because until this moment, an arranged marriage had only been mentioned. Suggested. Teased at from my end. And yes, Millie has been my parents' prime candidate. But it had never been planned or pressed and certainly not forced. And it sure as shit hadn't been fucking arranged.

Despite having to "marry a certain type of woman," my parents have *always* valued love above that nonsense. Granted, they know nothing of Bianca and I'm not exactly using that word in terms of her yet—it's too fucking new to even consider that. But...

I came here today to tell Millie that I'm seeing someone and that she needed to officially back off once and for all because I'd feel weird if she were to call or text when I'm with Bianca. I assumed Millie believed this was our parents attempting to push us together. Figured she was going to continue to be relentless in that because she wanted to be a future Mrs. Fritz. That's not something new for me and Millie is that sort of woman given who she is.

But this...

The waiter comes back with her champagne and my water. "Are you ready to order?"

"I think we need another few minutes," I tell him, curter than I ever would be under typical circumstances. But I'm thrown and rattled. I quickly recover. "Thank you. Sorry."

He leaves us and I take in a deep, calming breath. "Millie, I'm so sorry. I had no idea you believed things to be that way between us. An arranged marriage has never been in my plans, despite my family name."

"What difference does that make as long as our common interests are aligned? You didn't think you'd marry for love, right?" She laughs as if that's the most absurd notion in the history of the world.

"Regardless, this isn't going to happen. That's not what this is between us."

Millie's blue eyes are clinging to me, her hand covering her mouth as if this news devastates her. "I don't understand. Why not?"

Pressing my hands into the table, I give it to her straight. "That first meeting we had was an ambush." I have to take another deep breath to get control of myself. "Look, you're lovely, and my rejecting the notion of an arranged marriage is not a reflection on you personally. I just never agreed to any of this and it's not something I want or intend to do."

She shakes her head, her hands now on her lap, her back perfectly straight. "But we're perfect together, Kaplan. Absolutely perfect. With my father's connections and your family's wealth, we can do anything together. The sky is the limit. You could run for senator. President even one day."

"Which is not something I'd ever be interested in doing," I counter. "I get the business side of this, how a match like ours would outwardly appear and how many zeros we'd have that we'd never be able to spend, but is that honestly what you want in a husband?"

She laughs as though I'm being ridiculous. "Of course."

I stare at her, nonplussed.

"Don't give me that look." She waves me away, practically rolling her eyes at me. "I'm not some foolish girl. I'm not expecting love out of this, though if that happened, great. But primarily, I want power and money and the right social connections."

"That's..." I'm at a loss.

"What? There is nothing wrong with wanting those things, Kaplan *Abbot-Fritz.*" She emphasizes my last names with a sarcastic sneer. "Your parents married for those very reasons, as did mine. I'm not afraid to admit it. It's what all women should want from a husband and that doesn't make me old-fashioned. It makes me smart and ambitious. If it's love or even sex you're after, I understand how this all works. Every John needs a Jackie by his side even if they have a Marilyn in secret."

I choke on the sip of water I was taking. Bianca is certainly more of a Marilyn—her stunning curves and lack of bullshit politics pop into my mind—but she'll never be a secret like that. She'll never be a sidepiece.

"Millie, I trust you'll be an excellent Jackie for *someone else* someday, but that won't be me. Ever. I came here today to ask you to stop texting and calling me. To inform you that I'm seeing someone. Someone I care about deeply."

Anger mixed with self-assurance start to curl like the spreading of a disease across her face. "Meaningless," she asserts dismissively. "If you cared at all for this woman you claim to be with, we'd have heard about her before. Regardless, I wouldn't be so sure that this won't happen. In fact, it's already too late. It's currently in discussions with our lawyers. Contracts are being drafted as we speak."

"Contracts I never agreed to, nor will I ever sign."

And truthfully, I'm not sure how true that is. I don't think my parents would do that behind my back. They're a lot of things and they ask a lot of things from me, but they'd never do something underhanded like that. My mother has asked time and time again if I have met someone. She *suggested* an arranged marriage because she was worried for me. Not because she *requires* that of me.

"Again, I'm sorry if you've gotten the wrong impression, but this isn't happening."

She takes a hasty sip of her champagne only to tip the glass back and finish it off when she realizes no one is watching her. Setting the glass down, she dabs at her mouth with her napkin only to toss it hastily on her empty place setting, leveling me with a look that says she means business and isn't accustomed to being brushed off.

"I'm thirty-two years old, Kaplan. I need this to happen now. I can give you children. Heirs. My last name and breeding as part of their pedigree. We can be the power couple everyone looks up to and adores. Is jealous of. Think of that!"

"That's never been something I've sought, and you'd only be disappointed with me as a husband. On paper it all seems great. In reality, it would be anything but. Again, I'm sorry. I wish you only the best and have no doubt you'll find someone who suits your desired lifestyle better."

"You're such a fool if you think that's how this will go," she shoots out harshly. "I'm a senator's daughter. There has already been talk about us."

"So what? Who gives a shit? Certainly not me. I could give a fuck and fucking you or giving you heirs is not something I'll ever do." I'm out of patience. "I came here as a courtesy. To my mother. To you. But I'm fucking done with all of it. And that includes you."

"You don't seem to get it. It's too late to back out now. You can fuck your little sidepieces and groupies all you want. But you *will* marry me, and this deal *will* go through."

Done with this conversation, I stand, slip out two one-hundred-dollar bills for taking up the table and only ordering a glass of champagne, and then hold my hand out to her. It's how I was raised, and she should consider herself lucky I didn't leave her sitting here like a lost doll in a sea of monsters. She eyes it harshly for a moment before plastering back on her manufactured smile and slipping her hand into mine, allowing me to help her up.

I drop her hand immediately and head for the door. "Wait," she cries. "It's pouring rain. Please at least walk me to my car so I don't get soaked. I don't even have an umbrella."

Or I can let your awful, social climbing, monteygrubbing, elitist ass be an adult and walk yourself to your own damn car.

With a grunt of dismay, I open the door to the restaurant, pop up my umbrella, and cover her with it, because I'm a fucking gentleman she does not deserve. The two of us take off, running for her waiting car. Her driver sees us and springs into action, flying out and opening her door for her. That's when the first flash comes. And it's not lightning.

"Kaplan! Millie! Over here." *Flash. Click.*

Millie's head snaps over and she smiles her brilliant billion-dollar smile, throwing the waiting press a wave.

"Kaplan, did you pop the question? When's the big day? How do your parents feel about your romance?"

"You called the press?" I hiss in her ear, ready to snap her bony little body like a twig but only after I throttle her to death. "You set me up."

"Thank you! You're so kind." She gives a Miss America wave.

"What the fuck do you think you're doing?"

Her head whips back over, an evil glint to her eyes despite her unflappable smile. She leans up and presses a kiss to my cheek. "See you soon, darling."

Fucking bitch.

And I never use that term. Ever.

I shake my head, abandoning her to her driver, hoping she gets soaked and looks like a drowned rat in some of those photos. Racing back to my car, I jump in and slam the door behind me. The press are still there. I can feel them like cockroaches hiding in the walls and instead of losing my mind in front of them, I peel out.

The butt of my hand smacks the steering wheel. "Dammit. Goddammit! That fucking bitch."

That's going to be everywhere. Us together. Her kissing my cheek. Shit.

I make it back to the hospital, anxious to go and find Bianca and yet not. I need to talk to my mom. I need to sort through my thoughts on what the hell I'm doing. With Bianca. With my life.

I don't have time for lunch. I don't have time to check on Bianca. An emergency surgery on a newborn comes in and that trumps everything else. I manage to shoot her a text toward the middle of the afternoon telling her that Slash will drive her home and with the nasty weather, she's not to go to her studio.

I get a middle finger emoji I no doubt have earned. But I can't worry about her in the middle of Chelsea in that warehouse right now either. For once in my life, I leave it at that. I don't argue. I don't fight. I don't even reply.

Instead, I round on my patients, fix tiny broken hearts, and try my damndest to figure out what the absolute fuck.

Just as I start losing my mind, my sibling text stream starts blowing up, Oliver telling us he's heading out to the compound to see our parents. Asking if anyone wants to join.

Perfect, I think.

I text back, telling him I'm in and asking if he'll come and to meet me here. I get a thumbs-up emoji and then get back to finish my day. Forcing myself not to think about Millie. About Bianca. About anything other than my job or my life as it was before all this happened. Hoping it will all be okay once I speak to my parents.

Only I know nothing about this will be that simple. It never is.

25

"Hey," a voice slices through the fetal echocardiogram I'm reviewing on my laptop. My head pops up and I force a smile. It isn't all that difficult when the pretty blonde I've known since she was a baby comes waltzing into my office.

"Hey, doll. You're looking glowingly beautiful. What brings you here?"

"Me," Oliver interjects before Grace can answer. He tosses his arm around his best friend's shoulders. "You said you wanted to come, but we're heading out to the compound to talk all things weddings with Mom. I had Grace meet me here. You sure you're in for this?"

"Yes. I need to talk to Mom too." Desperately.

"To talk weddings?" Grace snorts.

I grimace. "Definitely not. Are you sure Mom doesn't already know everything you're going to tell her before you do?"

"You mean how she does with everything?" Oliver laughs. "Remember when I went to tell her that Amelia and I were fake engaged but actually in love and she was all, 'yeah, I already knew that. I'm your mother and I know everything.'"

"Exactly my point." Shutting my laptop, I pull my scrub top and long-sleeve shirt over my head and throw on a clean green long sleeve I have in my tiny closet. "Grace, pants are next."

She squeals, spinning around and digging her face into Oliver's chest as I strip out of my scrub pants and throw on a pair of jeans.

"Grace, Baby Owen is kicking me in the junk," Oliver grunts, angling his body away from Grace's. "Named after me or not, that's not something I'm cool with."

Her head pops up, her hands all wild, whipping through the air. "He's been a madman all day. My back has been aching like a SOB and I swear, it's like my little man thinks my bladder is a trampoline. I've had to pee every five minutes. Do you know how awful that is during surgery? Do you have any clue how gross bladder leakage when you sneeze can be?"

"Um. No," I say. "But since I will never experience the art of growing life and you're growing my nephew, I will not comment."

"Wise," she remarks, tossing me an eyebrow over her shoulder that says if you fuck with me, I'll eat you for dinner and since I'm eating for two, I don't mess around anymore.

"Where is Carter?" I ask, kissing her forehead and giving my brother a punch in the arm. We head toward the exit, and this is what I need. My family. Feeling grounded when I'm anything but. I already know Bianca is gone for the day. Home safe where she belongs. Slash drove her home two hours ago and sent me a picture of her entering her building, but I haven't texted or called since and neither has she. I've been too much of a mess. Needing to get answers and figure things out.

I owe Bunny every real piece of myself and until I can do that fully...

We have more talking to do. More things to figure out. *I* have more things to figure out.

"Working until midnight. He's picking up extra shifts for me because, as of today, I'm on a lighter rotation."

"And you picked tonight to go talk weddings?" I grouse as we pile into my car and head out into the Boston night. The rain this morning is now a heaping pile of sleet and freezing rain, flooding streets, and slowing traffic.

"It's our only free night," they both say together. "And it wasn't this bad earlier. I thought the weather people said the storm was supposed to dissipate by now," Grace finishes.

"They lied," I mutter, rolling my eyes and going with it, merging onto I-90 west toward the compound.

We barely make it to the edge of the city when everything slows dramatically. "What the hell is that?" Oliver leans forward, staring out the windshield. "Fuck. It looks like an accident. A bad one."

"No kidding. We're not moving now." All the cars around us have come to a standstill as what appears to be four or five cars up ahead are piled together.

"Should we get out and go check? Make sure everyone is okay?"

I nod. "Probably, yeah." I unbuckle my seat belt and throw on my hazard lights. "I have a bag in my trunk full of stuff. Let me grab—"

"Oh my god. Oh no."

Oliver and I spin around at light speed, both of us staring at Grace, whose gaze is locked between her spread legs.

"Grace, honey?"

Her head rises, her eyes wide with fear and consuming panic as she stares at Oliver first, then me. "Either I just peed my pants or my water broke."

"What?!" both Oliver and I shout.

"It's too soon," she cries, her face flinching as she takes in the mess between her legs, her eyes watering as they glance back up at ours. "I'm only thirty-four weeks."

Oliver and I stare at each other and then out the ice-coated windshield. We're stuck on the highway in the middle of an ice storm with an accident up ahead. Without another word, Oliver climbs out of the passenger side and immediately into the back with Grace. I fly out of the car too, racing around and trying not to slip and fall and die as I go for my trunk. Pressing the button to open it, I find my duffel bag with whatever medical supplies I have in here, grab the blankets and towels back here, and then close it up, going for the back seat where Grace and Oliver are.

Oliver is behind her now, but he's trying to shift through the narrow back well so he can check her.

She smacks his hand away from her scrub pants. "No, Oliver. Keep your face and hands out of my vagina."

"Grace, are you kidding me? It should be me who checks you. I'm the family physician."

"No. It has to be Kaplan," she demands.

"You want his face and hands between your legs, but not mine?"

"Some boundaries are not meant to be crossed by best friends. My vagina is off-limits to you."

"Jesus, Grace," Oliver shoots out. "I'm not trying to get a fucking peep show."

"Both of you shut up. I'm checking her. Oliver, you help your crazy bestie over there calm down. She's two seconds from losing her shit and we can't have that."

With a grunt and a begrudging growl, he slides in behind her once more, shifting her back to his chest. "I'm sorry," he murmurs, kissing the side of her head. "I know you're scared. But for the record, I'm awesome at checking vaginas."

"That's why you're not allowed near mine. Comments like that."

She smacks at him, only for him to catch her hand and kiss her knuckles.

"Right. Sorry. I won't crack jokes. I love you and I've got you and I'm here for you," he soothes, but you cannot soothe this situation. My back seat is wet with amniotic fluid, the center of Grace's scrubs pants completely soaked through.

Flipping on the interior lights, I take stock of everything. "Fluid is clear, so that's something," I remark. "You sure picked a hell of a time to go into labor."

"Yes," she snaps. "Clearly this was all by design. I thought, 'hey, Kaplan has a big back seat in his car. Why not try it out as a possible spot to *labor my premature child*.' This is why women hate men when it's time to deliver their babies."

"No one is delivering anything in the back of my car. We're going to get you to the hospital right after I check you. Is there any concern about you having a seizure?"

Grace has epilepsy and that's a whole other piece of "oh shit" added onto this.

"I... I shouldn't," she stumbles through, her expression painted in horror. "My last labs were great, and I've been taking extra good care of myself."

Flashing lights and sirens skirt up along the breakdown lane on the left, heading for the accident, and that's a relief. At least one situation is being handled and if there are EMS crews nearby, once we have a better sense of what's going on with Grace, we can have them call for an extra ambulance and—

"Oh! Contraction. Big one." Her back arches, her hand clasping onto Oliver's thigh with a ninja-like grip. "Oliver, I have to push."

"No, honey," he demands, his voice stricken. He brushes her hair back from her face. "You can't. Not yet. Just breathe through it. Try humming."

"Why is this happening so soon?" she shrieks as the contraction tears through her, bringing another gush of fluid, coating her pants and the seat. "Fuck. It hurts and there is a lot of pressure. I need to push."

My heart thunders in my chest as Oliver and I exchange petrified glances. If she's getting the urge to push, then this is happening and it's happening now. Which means I'm delivering my nephew. My premature nephew, in the back of my car.

I throw up a silent prayer and suck in a solidifying breath.

"You've probably either been in labor all day and didn't realize it or you're having precipitous labor." Opening up the bag, I quickly dig through, taking an inventory of what I have and what I need. Christ, I haven't delivered a baby since my intern year and even then it was in a hospital with ten other doctors, residents, med students, and nurses around me. With Owen being premature, I have no idea what his lungs will be like.

Illuminating an emergency lantern, I shift Grace to put a towel under her and toss the blanket over her lap. Oliver speaks to a 911 operator on the phone, telling them our location and that we need a NICU ambulance. My hospital has one and I know Brigham and Women's does too and since we're on that side of town-ish, hopefully it won't take them forever to get here. Then again, we're stuck in an ice storm in unmoving traffic behind an accident.

Unfortunately, other than fluids for Grace, that ambulance won't have shit that can help us and they're dealing with whatever is going on over there.

I snap on my gloves. "Grace, I'm going to remove your scrub pants and underwear. I need to check you."

"I can't believe this is happening." Her head falls back against Oliver's chest, and he kisses her temple.

"Kaplan, do you want me to—"

"No," Grace cuts Oliver off sharply. "I was serious about that. Let Kaplan do it. I need you behind me, Oliver. With me. Please. I can't do this without you. We can both talk Kaplan through this. Where is Carter?"

"I'm calling him now."

Grace lets out a sob, her body trembling, her face burying itself into Oliver's arm as he runs his hand down her hair.

"He should be here," she whimpers. "This shouldn't be happening in the car. What if... what if the baby's lungs aren't developed? What if there's something—"

"Stop," I cut her off. "You have two doctors in the car since you are officially now a patient and an ambulance in route. I have lidocaine, syringes, scissors, a scalpel, various surgical instruments, an Ambu bag with a pediatric attachment, and some basic rescue meds, including epinephrine. Thanks, Dad, for constantly drilling us with the importance of keeping our cars stocked. I don't have anything to start an IV with though, so no umbilical line other than what I can inject with a syringe." I hand Oliver a stethoscope, a pulse oximeter, and a blood pressure cuff. "Check her vitals. You're on point for mom. If you're at all worried about a seizure, tell me. I might have something in here that can help, but I'd rather not spend time digging through looking for that right now."

Oliver sets the phone down on the back end of the center console and gets to work on Grace's vitals when Carter's voice rings out through the car. "Oliver? Everything all right?"

"Carter, we're stuck in traffic behind an accident, brother, but Grace is in labor."

"What?! Grace?"

"I'm here. Carter, it's too soon."

He hisses out a slew of curses. "Can you make it back to the hospital? I'll come get you. Tell me where you are. I'll come get you."

"She's at plus two station," I announce, removing my gloved hands from between her legs and sitting back awkwardly on the small back seat. "The baby's head is fully engaged, which means this is happening now. Carter, you're going to have to talk me through this. Oliver, you're on Grace. Grace, you focus on your breathing and doing everything Oliver and I tell you to do. Got it?"

"Vitals are stable on Mom," Oliver announces.

I glance out the window. No one is moving and we have our hazards on anyway. Nothing to do now but deliver this baby and hope to hell he's breathing, and the NICU ambulance gets here quickly.

"Kaplan. Jesus. Okay."

There's noise in the background as if Carter's moving and I hear him speaking to someone, but then Grace lets out a scream. "I have to push. Now, Kaplan. Now."

"Kap, slide your fingers into her vaginal opening, one hand on the top, the other on the bottom of the baby's head. Do not pull! Just hold it and help guide it. Grace, push. One. Two. Three. Each a slow count. Rest. Then do it again. One. Two. Three. Remember to breathe, sweetheart. You've got this. I love you so much."

Grace screams as she pushes, and I hold on to the baby's head as Carter instructed.

"Add to it, Grace," Oliver encourages. "That's it. Keep it going. Get all the way through the contraction. Perfect, honey. You're doing so well."

"Contraction stopping," I say, still holding the head though she's no longer pushing.

"How's he look, Kap?"

"Your son looks good," I tell him. "Moving along like a champ. Some dark hair, a little bit of his forehead. No face yet and no tearing." Though I can't tell if the baby is in any distress. We're totally blind with this.

"Second set of vitals on Mom are holding. Pupils are equal, round, and reactive. No sign of seizure."

I nod at Oliver, wiping my sweaty forehead with my arm. "I should have stayed in my scrubs."

"You look good wearing my amniotic fluid and blood." Grace emits a shaky, broken laugh. "Sorry."

"You've got nothing to be sorry for," I tell her, staring into her fractured blue eyes. "I needed a new car anyway."

Another shaky laugh. This one more broken than the one before it.

"This could be worse, Grace," I halfheartedly quip. "This could be so much worse." *I hope.* "Oliver could be delivering your baby."

"Asshole," he snaps playfully, trying for levity in his voice too. It makes no difference. We're in the thick of this and all of us know it.

A tear streaks down her face as she stares into my eyes. Desperate. Pleading. Destroyed with fear. She's covered in sweat, panting for her life while Oliver holds her up, his back pressed into the door. He's whispering things I can't hear into her ear—all the things, I have no doubt—but if Carter can't be here, then I'm glad Oliver is.

Like I said. It could be worse.

"Another one is coming," Grace announces, and I get back into position, my knees on the seat as far away from her as I can get, my back hunched over. "I need to get him out. The pressure is unreal. I need him out."

"Let's do this. You got it," Oliver reassures. "Okay. Push, Grace. Push."

"Count it, Grace. Breathe, sweetheart. Let's get our little guy out of you," Carter encourages.

"Head is coming along," I tell them. "Do I just keep holding him, Carter? He feels restricted."

"Keep one hand on the bottom of his head and if you can reach in and grab them, help guide his shoulders. Are they visible? You might have to turn him depending on how he's presenting."

"Yes! He's coming. He's small and he's coming. Keep going, Grace. We're nearly there." With my hand on his slippery little shoulders, I adjust him ever so slightly, so he doesn't get stuck on her pelvic bone, terrified I'll hurt him, but knowing he needs to get out too. My heart is beating like a bitch in my chest, ready to explode. Adrenaline shooting through my veins, keeping me sharp and focused.

"Ahhhh!" Grace screams in pain as I shift him a little more.

"Carter, he's coming. Do I pull him out?"

"Yes. Get him out. That's his best shot now."

"Almost there, almost there. One more push, Grace, and I'll have him out. Just give me one more big one. Oliver, I'm going to need you, brother, the second I've got him."

Another hard push, an even louder scream, and the baby slides out, tiny and blue and not crying. I set him on the second towel I have set up and immediately start rubbing him with it, hoping to get this little guy going.

"Kaplan?!"

"He's out, Carter. I'm working on him. Just shut up. Oliver, I need the stethoscope." He hands it to me, and I listen for a heartbeat.

"Grace?" Carter questions.

"I'm fine." Only she's not. She's sobbing and pale against the glow of the lantern and the inner lights. Off in the distance we catch the sound of fresh sirens, and I can only hope that's for us. "I'll take care of my placenta. You guys take care of him."

"Shut up. Everyone stop talking," I bark, trying to keep my shit together when the desire to lose it is incredible. Never in my life have I been more terrified. "Heartbeat. I'm counting." I tap it out. "Ninety. Let's get it up. Oliver, I need your help."

"Is he breathing?!" Carter yells.

"Not yet. Oliver, now."

He kisses Grace and shifts her so he can climb out from behind her. I clamp off the umbilical cord and Oliver lifts the scissors, cutting it.

"Bag him up now. Let's get him breathing." I hand him the Ambu bag with the pediatric-sized face mask attached.

I keep rubbing his body, but it's not enough. He's limp and still blue and not breathing yet.

"Should we give him some epi?" Oliver asks because even though he's a family physician, he doesn't deal with any sort of trauma the way I do. Certainly not in newborn babies.

"Probably, yes." I give another listen, tapping it out.

"What's his heart rate?"

"Slowing."

"Kaplan!"

"Shut up, Carter, and let him work," Oliver clips out. "He's got this."

Grace is wailing now, sitting up over us and staying back though I know the mother, the doctor in her, is dying watching this and not being able to jump in and help.

"Let's do a round of epi. Give him... 0.1ml/kg as he's about, what, four pounds or so," I murmur to myself, thinking through the math. "That's 0.2ml into the umbilical cord. Into the vein, not the arteries. Do you need help?"

Oliver's eyes shoot up to mine. "I haven't done that before."

"I've got it. You keep bagging him."

Drawing up the epinephrine, I unclamp the remaining umbilical cord, locate the vein, and slowly push it in with the syringe, followed by a small amount of saline to flush it through. Once that's done, I continue rubbing his arms and legs, the top of his head and bottoms of his feet, all the while Oliver continues to give him oxygen through the Ambu bag.

"Come on, little man. Give us something, Owen," I cry. I plead.

Nothing.

Oliver is trembling beside me, panting and sniffling as he attempts to contain his emotions. And just when the abject fear and consuming panic feel like they're about to win and everything we care about is lost to us, baby Owen startles, jerking his tiny arms and legs outward. The smallest of cries pierces the air, but it's there, and I swear, I start to lose it. Huffing and puffing and desperate to hold my shit together.

My hands never shake—it's why I'm such a good surgeon—but everything inside me right now is rattling with relief. Oliver's forehead hits my shoulder as he chokes on his breaths.

"You're doing so well, little man," I tell him, still rubbing his body with the towel, trying to get his skin to pinken up a bit more. He's moving more now. "Give us some more cries, okay? Keep fighting. We love you. Mommy and Daddy want to hear you."

Another cry, this one a little louder and Grace and Carter are inconsolable, both sobbing messes. Oliver too, as he shifts around me and grabs Grace, holding her. I take over with the oxygen, bagging the little man, listening as his heartbeat grows stronger.

"Heart rate is one-forty." I sag against the back of the front seat, managing to crack a smile. "He's good for now, but I'll feel better when the ambulance gets here and we get him to the hospital." Swaddling him up in the towel, I lift him, handing him to Grace. She takes him, tucking her baby into her chest and kissing his head as tears continue to stream down her face.

"Thank you, Kaplan. I don't have words. I don't have a way to express how grateful I am. From the bottom of my heart and the depth of my soul, thank you."

"Kaplan," Carter rasps hoarsely through the phone. "Fuck, man. I owe you everything."

"Go team," I deadpan, drawing a tremulous chuckle from Oliver and Grace. "I think it's officially safe to say I'd do anything for you." I kiss both her and tiny Baby Owen on the head. The sound of the ambulance is growing louder and after ripping off my gloves, I open the back door. "Oliver, you got them? I'm going to pull over and flag them down. Keep tabs on his breathing and heart rate."

"On it." A hand on my back. "Hey." I turn back to him. "Good fucking work tonight, brother."

"You too," I tell him, holding his gaze for a moment and then climbing out of the car.

The door shuts and I lean against my car so I don't get hit, breathing in the icy, freezing air that feels nothing short of incredible on my sweaty, pulsing skin.

Fuck. I just delivered my nephew and for a few minutes there... God. The accident ahead is all but cleared, cars moving around us now, blaring their horns, and it's a wonder my car wasn't hit during all that. I hadn't even noticed what was going on around us.

Climbing back into the driver's seat, I manage to pull us over to the breakdown lane, park, and then get out again, waving my arms so the ambulance that is quickly approaching sees us. Within seconds, they're stopping behind us and I recognize the EMS crew. I tell them everything that happened as well as the status of baby Owen and they're on it. Getting Grace and Owen hooked up with IVs and monitors and oxygen and moving them over to the rig.

"He looks good," Callie, one of the EMS crew, says. "Good work tonight, Doctor."

I give her a nod, making sure my family, my heart, are all settled. Oliver goes with them and as I climb back into my car after watching them speed away, I take a second for myself. Just breathing in and out. Trying to get my shit back together. Trying to slow down the adrenaline and anxiety. Grateful, so damn grateful it turned out as it did.

My car reeks of blood and sweat and heat and hell only knows what else. I need a shower. I need a change of clothes. I need a meal. I need to make sure Grace and Owen are straight.

And when that's all done, the only other place I want to be is inside Bianca. It's been one hell of a day. I can only hope this was the end of the drama for a while. I've had enough for a lifetime.

26

Kaplan

By the time I reach Brigham and Women's, there is a zoo of media camped outside. It's like déjà vu from when my mother was in this same hospital over Thanksgiving and after pulling in and valet parking, I push my way through the bedlam of photographers and barrage of questions.

I'm not alone either. Just as I arrive, so do Luca, Raven, Landon, Elle, and Stella. Their terrified eyes and pale faces very likely match my own. Especially when they get a better look at me. My clothes are stained with blood and vernix and amniotic fluid. My hair is all over the place and likely just as stained as the rest of me. If "wreck of a man" had a place in Urban Dictionary, it would hold my face as a cautionary tale beside it.

"Are you okay?" Raven races over to me, jumping up at me and throwing her arms around me. Not giving two shits that I'm as gross as I am or even if we're photographed.

"I'm fine. Sort of. I need to make sure they're okay and then I will be."

She drops back down to her feet, her hand on my chest over my pounding heart. "You are a hero, Kaplan Fritz. You saved baby Owen's life and possibly Grace's. You saved this family by saving them."

I plant a kiss on her forehead. "Love you."

That's all I got for now.

We head inside the hospital, hugging and talking in quiet murmurs as we take the elevators up to the labor and delivery floor.

Carter had sent out a text to our sibling chat during the delivery and everyone is here, crowding the waiting room with anxious eyes and pacing feet. Amelia races over to me, wrapping me in another hug. "You're a gross-ass mess, but I don't think I've ever loved you more than I do in this moment."

I chuckle, hugging my soon-to-be sister-in-law back. "It was all Grace. Truly. She was magnificent. Where are they? Are they okay?"

Rina smacks my back, pulling me away from Amelia into yet another crushing hug. "She's okay. Oliver is with her because he wouldn't leave her side despite her yelling at him to stay away from her vagina. The doctor is examining her, and the nurses are getting her cleaned up while the NICU team assesses baby Owen. Carter was all over Grace and didn't want to leave her, but neither of them wants Owen to be alone, so he's there with him." She pulls away, her hands on my shoulders as she gazes up at me with tear-soaked happiness. "Have you ever seen Carter cry? Like never, right? The man was weeping like a child. It's the best. But likely Owen will have to stay in the NICU for a bit because he's small and was born in the back of a car and fuck, Kaplan." Another smack, this one on my chest. "He's *alive*. Because of *you*."

I swallow, trying for a smile but not quite getting there. What went down in the car is still rattling me to my bones.

"Wow, look," Stella calls out, drawing all our attention to the television affixed to the wall. "You're all over the news, Uncle Kaplan. You and Uncle Oliver."

Layla, Amelia's little sister snorts, rolling her eyes. "Yeah, they're saying you performed surgery in the back of your car to deliver Owen. Because that makes a whole lot of sense."

Before I can comment, something hard slams into my back, jerking me forward a couple of steps and knocking the wind from me. Strong arms clamp around my chest. "You absolute motherfucker." I grin, spinning around and hugging Carter who is crushing the life out of me. "Thank you," he whispers to me, tears clogging his voice. "Fuck, Kaplan. Thank you so much. I... I just—"

"I know." Because I do. I pat his back. "They doing okay?"

He pulls away, wiping at his eyes that are glowing in a way I've never seen on him before. "They're good. Owen Kaplan Fritz is a champ."

"Owen *Kaplan* Fritz?"

He nods, and yep, now I'm choked up. All the emotion I had been tamping down and shoving away springs like a geyser up my throat and through my face. I grab my brother and haul him back into my chest, gripping his back and clutching him tight. Now he's laughing because I don't do this. Get emotional.

"He's good? He's really good?"

"He's good, man. Already nursing on Grace and only requiring a nasal canula to help him breathe. No mask. No vent. Four pounds, three ounces. Monster dick."

I laugh, a knot I didn't know I had unfurling in my chest. Releasing Carter, I scrub at my face and slap my brother on the shoulder. "As you'd expect from a Fritz man."

"Absolutely. I'm going back to them, but I wanted you to know they're both great and I love you and thank you."

I give him another hug because apparently hugs are my new thing, and when I turn around, I'm met with a pair of green eyes I had been hoping to see since my awful lunch today. The reason I was in the car in the first place. My mother cups my face in her cold hands and stares up at me. No words. They're not needed. Her face showcasing every ounce of wonder and love and gratitude that's flowing through her.

Octavia Abbot-Fritz loves her people with an unrivaled fierceness.

"I was coming to talk to you. About Millie."

She smiles softly up at me. "I heard all about your lunch today. Catherine called me." Catherine is Millie's mother.

Oh, I'm sure she did.

"She's a fucking nightmare, Mom. How on earth could you have wanted me to be with her? Did you know she believed we were headed toward an arranged marriage?"

For once she doesn't comment on my language. "Kaplan, this is neither the time nor the place to discuss this. I understand your position on Millie and we'll talk about it later."

"Are you angry about the lunch? About what I told her?"

"Angry is not something I could ever be with you in this moment."

I need to tell my mom about Bianca. About Bunny. But right now, I can't find the words. She feels like a secret. One I want to keep for myself. Just for a bit longer. Especially after all this.

"I love you, Kaplan," she continues. "And I am so proud of you. Not just for what you did tonight. You are a brilliant doctor and a wonderful man with superior instincts. Keep following them and don't be afraid of where they'll lead you."

I nod, swallowing thickly.

She kisses my cheek, wiping away the stain of her lipstick after. "Now go home and get yourself cleaned up. You're a mess."

She smirks and then saunters off, joining my father who gives me the *I'm proud of you, son,* nod. I return it and then head for the exit. Only home isn't where I want to be.

I need to see my girl.

Just thinking about her calms my racing blood. Bunny, she always had that effect on me. I'd have a rough shift or feel lost or out of sorts and then I'd text or call or her or even email. She was just a kid, but somehow that made talking to her easier. She saw life so differently than I did and I clung to that. I'd tell her the most ridiculous of my thoughts. Trusted her in a way I trusted few others. Loved her like a little sister until I saw her again and everything flipped in an instant.

Now she's the woman who has consumed my every waking hour for weeks. I don't know what's happening. I just know I need her. I need to fuck the raging beast thrashing inside me out. I need her touch and sounds and breath and body. Her. I need her.

There is no going back.

Not to who I was before.

Not to how things used to be.

With purpose in my stride, I press the button for the elevator. I haven't talked to Bianca all day other than our quick text exchange and I'm itchy. Maybe it's the aftereffects of what happened tonight. Maybe it's not knowing where her cousin is—Fairchild is working on it and promised he'd have answers by tomorrow morning. Maybe it's the worry that she didn't listen to me and went off to Chelsea in the middle of a storm in the darkness of night.

Maybe it's that I just need to fucking *see* her.

Whatever it is, it has me ringing her bell with a bit more intensity than I typically would.

"Hello?"

"It's me."

She doesn't ask what I'm doing here. The door just buzzes, allowing me passage inside, where I jog up four flights instead of using the elevator because it was slow as fuck when we used it this morning. This morning. What a world that has happened between then and now.

I raise my fist to pound but she's already there, flinging the door open and staring up at me with such sweet innocence and painful wrath I need to taste all of it on her. My hand glides along her face, my fingertips in her hair and I crash my mouth down on hers.

A startled gasp gives me access to her mouth and I take full advantage, my tongue twirling with hers as I walk her backward into her apartment and kick the door shut behind me. Spinning her around, I press her into it. Flipping the latch on the bolt to lock it, I grind against her, not affording her an inch of space between us.

Her hands are all over me. In my hair. On my face. Down my neck. Squeezing my shoulder. She breaks the kiss, panting as she asks, "What's going on?"

Can she feel it? My urgency. The desperation swimming through me. The wild chaos living, breathing, growing in my chest.

I go to kiss her again, but she pushes me back. "What's all over you?"

I glare down at myself.

"We were driving out to my parents' compound when Grace went into labor in my car. I delivered my premature nephew tonight."

She sucks in a breath, holding me closer, her face wrought with unease. "Oh god. Are they okay?"

I nod. "They are now, but there were some very scary moments with Owen. I'll tell you more about it later." My forehead falls to hers, the tip of my finger tracing the beautiful lines of her face. "He's in the NICU and Grace and Carter are with him."

"Are *you* okay?"

Am I? "I'm better now." I plant a soft kiss on her lips. "It was all over the news. You didn't see it?"

"No. I was painting. Here…" She reaches down for the hem of my ruined shirt, pulling it up and over my head. Then she goes for my jeans next. "Let's get you a shower. Are you hungry? Have you had dinner? I'll throw your clothes in the wash because I'm not sure I have anything that will fit you."

"You fit me."

She laughs. She thinks I'm kidding. The words just slipped out, yet I feel the rightness behind them. The creeping desire to make them real. To say all the things crashing like cymbals through my head.

I deal with life and death every day and some days are rougher than others with that, but what happened tonight, the absolute soul-rattling fear that Owen wouldn't make it or that Grace would have complications is changing something inside me.

Or was that already happening before tonight?

It's as if everything is hitting me all at once, only I don't even know what this is or how to describe it. All I know is that the only place I wanted to be after I knew Owen and Grace were okay was here with her. I had to see her. I had to be near her. It's more than just ripping her clothes off and crawling my way inside her body.

And that terrifies me despite how good it feels now that I'm here. But it doesn't terrify me enough to walk away or pretend it's not real and that it's not happening. Because it is.

"I had to see you," I tell her. "I couldn't think about anything else."

Her eyes flutter up to mine, her hands stilling on my jeans, only to lick her lips, swallow and drop her gaze once more. "Come on. Let's get you cleaned up."

Right. Shower.

Clearly, I'm the only one having a major existential crisis out of the two of us. I don't even know what time it is. I need to get myself in check. My head is all over the place, leading me down paths there might be no returning from. I'm racing ten miles ahead and she's nowhere close. So I keep my mouth shut and let her finish removing my pants while I watch her.

The moment she stands, I rip her sweatshirt over her head. She's not wearing a bra and *yes*. I attack her leggings next and the moment I have her naked, my mouth is all over her as we stumble our way through her apartment in the direction of her bathroom.

We bang into walls. Into furniture. Trip over who the hell knows what, laughing and messy as we go. The bathroom door flies open, banging into the wall, and I smash her against it, sucking on her neck and sliding my fingers between her legs. Wet.

"Always so wet, beautiful Bianca." I glide my fingers through her folds, but it's not enough. I want to see what I'm touching. Dropping to my knees, I spread her legs and resume touching her, my gaze alternating between her lust-drunk face and her slick pussy. "You have the prettiest pussy. And the way you smell." My nose dives in, inhaling her, causing her to jerk, her back arching as she tries to wiggle away.

"You need a shower," she moans as I lick her throbbing clit while my fingers play with her opening.

"I want you." Only it's more than that. "I *need* you." I suck on her, using my teeth to graze her and she cries out at the sharp sting, only to have me soothe it away with the flat of my tongue. I give her pussy a kiss and then rise. "I'm flayed and need to do so many wicked things to your body I can hardly control the urges. Say yes."

One slow blink. "Yes."

"Are you afraid?"

"Will you hurt me?"

"Yes. I'm going to hurt you. But trust me when I tell you, you'll want me to, and you'll beg for more."

Another kiss and then I start the shower while she digests that. Once it's up to temperature, I step in and start washing off the day I had. It doesn't take much for a smile to spring to my lips now that the fear and panic have subsided. Owen Kaplan Fritz. I can't even. As if I didn't already love the little man with everything I am before delivering him and learning of his new middle name.

I make quick work of washing my hair and body, anxious to be with Bianca. Needing to take her like the thundering savage I am. A moment later, I shut off the water and step out, finding Bianca exactly where I left her as I wrap a fluffy green towel around my waist.

Fantastic.

She's still naked and that tells me she's comfortable enough around me with who she is. Finally. I feel like I should be fist-pumping the air with that. But honestly, I'm too keyed up and if my hands and mouth and body aren't all over her in the next second...

Stepping into her, I hold her face in my hands, forcing her dazed eyes up to mine. She's so pretty it makes my chest squeeze. *Mine.* Definitely mine.

"You never answered me."

Another blink. "Okay."

Our foreheads meet, my thumb gliding along her lips that I'm a bit obsessed with. "Okay?"

"Yes. I want that."

"This isn't just sex or kink. I want you. I trust you. I wouldn't be here if I didn't. This is me *only* wanting to do these things with you."

She softens into me, her tongue jutting out and licking my thumb. "Will you teach me how to play? I think..." Hard swallow. "I think I want to learn how to do this, but I also want to know how to please you."

Jesus hell, I'm done. Call the code. Heart stopped. Veins shredded. No hope of resuscitation.

Picking her up, my lips consume hers as I spin us around, only to slam her ass down on her counter. She teeters for a moment, but I steady her with my hands on her hips, while my mouth and tongue and teeth attack her. There is no way I can slow down now. This is going to be hard and rough.

Her hands rake through my hair, kissing me back with equal passion. A fuse lit, we're explosive as I eat at her, suck on her tongue and bite her lips. Two fingers find her pussy, still wet from what little playing we did before, and thrust up into her as deep as they can go.

She bows back, a garbled scream that grows louder when I give her a third finger, plowing into her hard and fast. The sound is wet and sloppy and so good, I tear my lips away from her mouth so I can watch.

"You're not going to come like this," I tell her, bringing my thumb in on the action as it presses on her clit. "You're going to do that on my dick."

I lift one of her feet up onto the counter and push her knee out. And fuck. What a pretty fucking sight this is. She's pink and swollen and dripping all over my hand. But greedy. Her pussy is so greedy, wanting more. Begging me to let it come. Dipping down, I remove my thumb from her pulsing button and blow cool air on her before grazing it with my teeth.

"Kaplan. Fuck. It's too much."

She has no idea what too much is.

"Do you want me to stop?"

"N-no." It's a loud moan that turns into a squeal as I flick her clit with the tip of my tongue, increasing the pace of my fingers. She's getting close. The inner walls of her pussy are starting to convulse. And just before she gets there, I pull my fingers from her body and shove them in her mouth when she starts to protest.

She sucks on them like the sweet, good girl she is. Tapping lightly on her clit, I watch as it pulses.

"Ah! Oh my god."

I do it again and again, not quite smacking it as I did last night. If I do that, she'll come for sure, and I want this to last for her. I want to do this for hours with her. Bring her to the brink and then keep her there. Desperate. Hungry. So needy for me, she'll beg.

Tearing the rope from her bathrobe that's hanging on the back of her door, I tie her hands behind her back, smirking at her wide, startled expression.

"Baby, you tell me if anything I'm doing is too much or too painful or not what you're into. Okay?" I check. "I promise, I only want this to be good for you. Do you want a safe word?"

"Do I need one?"

"Maybe, yeah." A pause. "Tell me what you're thinking."

"I'm good. Excited. A little nervous. I've just never been tied up before. A safe word might be smart."

My face hits her neck and I breathe her in, my fingers still playing with her pussy that I swear I will never get enough of. "Bianca, my sweet, beautiful girl, I'm going to open you up to so many things. But right now, I just need to fuck you."

Her mouth inches to my ear. "Then do it, Dr. Fritz. Fuck me until I'm begging for you to stop. Fuck me until I'm screaming your name. If I don't like something, or I need you to stop, I'll say red, but right now, I want it all."

I'm so crazy about this woman.

In a flash, I drag her off the counter and spin her around, then press her belly against the cold stone. We watched the other night in my room, but this is right here. This is close up. This is me being able to see her eyes in the mirror from inches away. My teeth graze her ear, scraping at her jaw.

"Eyes open. Watch how you look when I fuck you like this."

Without warning, I slam my cock into her and instantly set a punishing rhythm. She screams at the intrusion, my piercings scraping along her inner walls that are already sensitive from my fingers. With her hands locked behind her back, stuck between our bodies, and her body pinned against the sink, she is at my total mercy. One hand clutches her hip, the other squeezing her breast, punishing it as I'm punishing her pussy.

Our eyes hold in the mirror, her brown ones completely blown out, nearly black and I've never done this before. Stared into a woman's eyes like this while I took her. The thought never even occurred to me before, but watching Bianca is like watching living, breathing, moving art. I'm tumbling over the edge, free-falling into her. These past couple days, filled with far too many revelations, are making it impossible to stop or even slow down.

My hand flees her breast, climbing up her chest until it's wrapped around her neck. With my eyes pinned on hers, I squeeze, cutting off some of her air supply. Startled, her gaze slingshots down to where my hand grips her. I give it a tighter squeeze and she trembles, her eyes rolling back in her head as I continue to pound into her over and over again.

It's the sexiest fucking thing I've ever seen, sounds tumbling from my lips, one after the other. Grunts and groans. She's so tight. So wet. So warm. Feels so fucking good, it's all I can do not to come. But I want this to last.

Her lips part, her moans and cries raspy, muted as I play with her air. It's driving me crazy, and I tell her that. Fucking her like this is building me up higher and higher, a fresh coat of sweat covering my body mixing with any residual water still clinging to my skin.

I start thrumming her clit, squeezing her neck just a bit tighter without fully cutting off her ability to breathe and that's when she starts to lose it. Coming so hard and so violently, her body thrashes into the counter as silent screams shred the air. Her inner walls clamp me to the point of pain, dragging a hiss out of me. And just as her body starts to sag, I release her neck, grasp her tits, drag her back against me and unleash myself in her. Kissing and loving her abused neck as I spill everything inside her.

She's so beautiful. Her gorgeous face with her cute little smile and messy long, long hair and eyes that are always hungry and open and honest.

"You're so perfect," I tell her, panting against her tacky skin. "Are you okay?"

"I don't know."

That has me frowning, my eyes popping open. Immediately I untie her and spin her around, gathering her into my arms. "Bianca—"

"No. I mean, yes. I'm good. I'm fine. I'm great. I think you cracked my ovaries in half. Sorry. I can't think. Someone just gave me the most intense orgasm of my life and then asked if I was okay, which obviously I'm not after that."

I chuckle, lifting her face and looking her over. Her neck shows red marks, as do her arms, but I doubt she'll bruise. I rub her arms, trying to soothe the redness away. "You sure?"

"Will you do that to me again sometime?"

"Anytime you want."

My lips meld to hers, kissing her so delicately it almost makes me smile, considering the depravity of what we just did. Lifting her up, I cradle her into my chest and carry her to her bedroom, tucking us both in under the covers and holding her sweet body against me.

I tell her about the delivery and about Owen, and she tells me about what she was painting and how she had to talk Roberta off a ledge today because Jenny is causing drama and how her aunt flew in today to get Ava who she found staying in a hotel in Chinatown. I don't mention Millie because that is the absolute last thing I want to talk about with her.

We talk for hours. The way we used to. Only it's different. So different. So much better because being with her like this is everything. I tell her how I want to take her sailing this summer and she tells me that the best decision she ever made was moving here.

And when I'm positive she's asleep, I tell her something I'm just starting to come to grips with, terrified of all it potentially represents. "I think I might be falling for you."

27

These past couple of weeks have been a clusterfuck. A nonstop circus. Case in point, this conversation. I have many talents, but subtlety isn't one of them. Kaplan says there is no filter between my brain and my face and he's right.

"Jenny, you can't do pastel pink and baby-blue linens and balloons."

She's staring at me—as she always does—as if I'm the Antichrist in her world, which likely I am. Take a number, sweetheart. My cousin has first dibs on that. My cousin who is thankfully now back home in California with her mother and getting some help. My aunt put her in therapy. She still won't return my calls or texts and openly hates me for "ruining" her life. Whatever. At least she's safe and no longer much of a threat.

I think by this point, if she were going to say something, she would have.

"Explain to me why not," Jenny snaps, popping her pink gum just to be annoying.

I glance over her shoulder at Charlie and Greta, who are hovering by the opening of the kitchen, trying not to make their laughter audible and then back over to Jenny. "Because this isn't a gender reveal baby shower. This is a classy gala."

Roberta let her pick the band and I can only pray we don't regret that decision. Jenny has overseen aesthetics for this event and when Roberta initially put her in that role, I'm not sure she considered who we were working with.

For the foundation, Kaplan has been dealing with all the budgetary and proposals as well as some of the operations matters that require his direct oversight, but when it comes to this gala, he's washed his hands of it with the exception of final veto power.

This was his final veto.

He saw the mock-up Jenny hand-delivered—all the way to the hospital, I might add—and he called me immediately after telling me I had to step in on this.

He doesn't have time. I get it. Surgeon of tiny human hearts, he likes to remind me. Not to mention the media storm that has circled around him for the last two weeks. I haven't watched any of it, but he's been followed relentlessly. He's had demands for interviews from everyone from local newspapers to national news networks to freaking late-night talk shows. All of which he's refused because that's Kaplan for you. Doctor Untouchable. Hater of the spotlight despite the world thrusting him back into it time and time again.

He's also spending as much time with his family and new nephew as he can.

That might be one of the most endearing things about him. His unremitting loyalty and love for his family.

Between his job at the hospital, the stuff he has to do for the foundation, my job here, my art, wanting to avoid being seen together by the press, we haven't seen much of each other this week. It's Thursday and Kaplan told me he was going to try to get off early and I told him I wasn't going to go to Chelsea tonight.

The plan is food and sex. A lot of hot, dirty sex. Toe-curling, multi-orgasmic, vagina-ruining sex. It requires discretion and craftiness if we're going to keep this thing—whatever this thing between us is—quiet. I'm trying to find the rosy side of this latest media madness.

Pretending that all the sneaking around is fun. A bit dangerous and slightly taboo. That is if screwing your boss who was your stepbrother's BFF, is eleven years older than you, famous as a Kennedy, and has a wild side you're desperate to explore more of could be considered *taboo*.

More like stupid and reckless and asking for heartbreak and disaster, but a girl can play, right?

Which brings me back to Jenny. Jenny who looks nothing like the woman Kaplan Fritz actually wants. It has me smirking and she notices.

"Why are you smirking at me like that?" It's a frustrated half shriek

Oops. "Because I think you're intentionally trying to sabotage this whole gala because it was my idea and you had us assigned for three separate gigs."

There I said it. It needed to be said.

She flushes ever so lightly, shifting her stance and looking to her left. With a scoff she flings her long, blonde hair over her shoulder. "Why would I do that? I love what I do here. I'd never hurt the Abbot Foundation."

Uh-huh. Tell it to a judge, honey, because you ain't foolin' this jury.

"Because I'm Kaplan's assistant. Because I work at the hospital three mornings a week with him. Because you feel entitled to the job I have since you've been here longer than me and are just as equally if not more qualified. I get it, Jenny. I do. But ruining this gala in the name of vengeance won't make you look good. You're smart. You're beautiful. You've got so many things going for you. Ask yourself honestly why I'm in this role and you're not. You said it on day one. But you're missing the point in all of this."

"What, that you're the ugly, fat girl Kaplan won't fuck or fall for, so it's you in this job and not me?"

Sigh. Then I give her a louder one that is purely for show because, women, when did trashing each other become what we do? Especially in the name of a man. Just no! I don't even need to point out how wrong she is. That Kaplan doesn't seem to want what society dictates he should. Everything that Jenny has been trying to be, which again, is sad.

"You don't need to work a job just so you can try to woo a billionaire into a loveless marriage. Because let me tell you, as someone who was on the flip side of that, my ex was not going to get a penny out of me because prenups are no joke. And honestly, you can be so much better than that. You *are* so much better than that. Do yourself a favor, okay? Work your ass off. Showcase your brain and your talent. Make your own billions and blaze your own trail in this world. And never put yourself in a position where a man is your endgame."

She blinks at me as if I just spoke pig Latin to her.

"You're just saying that because you want him for yourself."

Ugh. "Jenny! Fine." I throw my hands out in the air, ready to strangle her scrawny neck. "Be nutty about this but quit trying to throw off the gala with ugly-ass baby shower decor. Elegant flowers in eye catching but not flamboyant shades. Candles on tall pillars. Votives for ambience. Uplighting along the walls and hard surfaces. Silky fabrics in muted colors. Cool lighting displays with the charities' names floating across the dance floor. No balloons. No hokey-fucking-pokey, and if I hear another damn word about baby goddamn pink or blue, you will quickly learn just what us fat, ugly women are capable of when we're pissed off."

I get a sassy grin that makes her look more constipated than smug. "Is that your way of saying you're going to sit on me with your fat ass?"

Oh no, she motherfucking didn't. My patience at the end—have you seen the month I've been living?—I get ready to go all crazy on her when an arm swoops around my waist, lifts me in the air, and suddenly I'm facing the complete opposite direction. A direction that gives me a lovely view of the audience I've accrued.

Fabulous.

"Things. Out. Now."

Three sharp words, but wow, they cut through the air like a scalpel. I can't even turn around, the arm on my waist practically crushing the life from me. Turning my head to the left, I catch both Greta and Charlie with matching wide eyes and hands over their mouths. Roberta actually jumps in the air, her hands silently clapping with her obvious joy.

"Kaplan—"

"It's Dr. Fritz to you," he seethes at Jenny. "No one, I repeat, no one speaks to anyone like that. Not in my building. Not in my presence. Not in my foundation or hospital. It's disgraceful. It's repulsive. It's just plain old *wrong*. Grow up. The high school mean-girl bullshit was old even then."

I try to slip out of his hold, but his grip tightens, and I quit struggling, knowing I'm not going anywhere until he lets me.

"I'm done with this. I'm done. You've been doing a shitty job since Bianca showed up and if I have to tell you in live action, then here it is. You and I will never happen. I am not attracted to you. I do not want to date you or sleep with you and I will never ever make you my wife. Whether Bianca was here or not, that was always how it was going to be. So get your shit and get the fuck out of my building before I have security come up and do it for you, Kelly."

And that's it. Him calling her Kelly when her name is Jenny. I die. So does everyone else in here. And I fall. In love just a teeny, tiny bit. And I swoon. Because no one has ever come to my rescue or stood up for me like that.

Jenny hisses something I can't even make out over the thundering of blood through my ears, but then she stomps off, making a grand show of it and somehow I'm no longer pinned to Kaplan's back. No, his green eyes that look like the coming of a tornado fill every inch of my vision.

"Get your stuff. We're leaving. Now."

"Um. But. I still have more work to do."

"Charlie," he calls out into the wide-open room of gawkers. "Bianca will not be here tomorrow. Do everything she just said to Kelly about aesthetics for the gala."

Charlie waves her hand in the air, giving us a thumbs-up. "On it. I'll make it fashion fabulous, only better."

"Greta, you're on point for all of Kelly's other work."

Greta looks like she's about to pass out when Kaplan turns his blazingly gorgeous face to her, but she manages a nod and sputters out a, "Sure."

He spins us around, addressing the whole room now. "We are not half-assing this gala. It needs to be everything these charities deserve. Bianca thinks that seasonal galas featuring three different yet similar charities each time will make them a ton of money. That they will be the 'It' event of the season and in case it is not fucking clear, I trust her judgment on this."

"Yes, sir," echoes throughout the room.

"She will not be here tomorrow because I need her at the hospital with me. Have a good night, everyone. Thank you for all your hard work. Go home. I'm sorry I haven't been around much, but it's not because I don't appreciate all you do. It's because I already know you're rock stars and don't need me interfering."

And with that, Kaplan Fritz, doctor, CEO, master of my universe, whispers into my ear with that sexy rasp thing he does, "Get your stuff. You have two minutes." I'd argue just to watch the charge build in his eyes, but I'm thinking that might be more fun to do later.

I grab my purse and laptop bag and am by his side in less than my allotted time. "Do I get a reward?"

"That all depends on how fast you can pack your stuff."

"Pack my stuff? I just did that," I squawk as Axl opens the door of the building for us, shielding my side while Slash takes Kaplan's side. "Evening, guys." I throw them each a wave. I don't see any press, which is a miracle, but one never knows.

The car door shuts behind us and Kaplan drags me onto his lap until I'm straddling him in my dress. His hands clutch my thighs, and his eyes pin mine.

"You just fired Jenny."

"No one needs someone that toxic in their work environment. She came on to me again when she showed up at the hospital this morning and I likely would have just dealt with that, but no way in hell was I going to tolerate the way she was speaking to you. No one says stuff like that to you. Ever."

I do my best to rein in my smile, but it's impossible after he says something like that. "Lucky for her I didn't know she came on to you or she'd have claw marks for a face."

"Territorial and jealous. I like that."

I run my fingers through his hair, toying with the strands. "I like that you did that. Stood up for me. Totally turned me on." I grind against him with a wink, and he smiles. A real smile. A relaxed, almost happy smile.

"I'm taking you home and you'll have exactly ten minutes to pack a bag."

I pause, tilting my head because I'm not sure I heard him correctly. "A bag?"

"You can bring clothes or not. Either way, it doesn't matter for where we're going."

"Kaplan."

"Bianca," he mocks with a smirk that makes me wetter. Damn him for that.

"Can you tell me what's going on? What exactly am I packing for?"

"I'm taking you somewhere tonight because I haven't seen you all week and I need some alone time. It's been entirely too long since I've had any of that without the madness that is my life getting in the way and I want to do that with you even though it won't technically be alone time for me since you'll be there. I'm sick of being followed and work and people and drama and I need to fuck you to the point of both of us requiring fluid resuscitation. I brought IVs and starter kits, by the way. You know, just in case we do actually reach that point."

I blink about ten thousand times. "I'm sorry, I think I just had a stroke. Somewhere in that rant, did you say you're taking me somewhere tonight?"

The car stops way too fast and suddenly the door is flung open.

"Ten minutes," he reminds me, smacks my ass, and then his eyes are on his phone and he's typing away.

Numbly I step out of the car and peer up at Axl, who is trying so desperately not to be amused.

"A little help?" I beg.

"Think warmer weather," he recommends with a sly grin.

"Warmer weather?" Does this mean he's taking me away for the weekend, not just tonight? Am I missing work tomorrow with all that's going on? Did Jenny actually get fired? I bang on the glass of his window. "I have questions, Kaplan Fritz."

"I don't care," he mutters through the door. "You've got nine minutes now."

Damn him!

"What if I don't want to go?"

"You do. You hate this weather. Now move or you'll have to live with only what I've packed for us. Eight minutes."

Packed for us? What the... whatever. Best not to overthink.

I race into my apartment, determined not to be naked for whatever Kaplan Crazy-Ass Fritz has in store for me. Locating a bag, I snatch it down off the shelf and fill it with... I have nothing. Like nothing. No bathing suits. No hot, tiny, skimpy dresses. I was living with a piece-of-shit guy for the last six months who made me want to hide my body at every turn and was dating him for a year and a half before that.

I was headed to Scotland in winter for my honeymoon, not Maui.

"Fuck it." I face myself in the mirror. "Fuck it!" I screech louder.

I find T-shirts and nightie shorts and panties and bras and the sexiest stuff I have in my naughty drawer. A couple pretty sundresses catch my eye and I throw them in too. I only have one ugly one-piece bathing suit and that makes me want to cry. I decide I'll buy something wherever we're going. There must be a shop somewhere. Then I go for my toothbrush and basic toiletries and snag a pair or ten of sandals and other shoes.

I'd rather be naked than shoeless it seems.

Staring down into my ridiculous bag of mismatched stuff, I start thinking only to force myself to stop. If the shoes make the woman then what else is needed? And then, oh my God, Kaplan is taking me away. For tonight or the weekend, who knows, but he's taking me on a surprise trip. And he fired Jenny for being a nasty bitch to me.

"Slow your roll, Bianca. This doesn't have to mean anything."

Only the giddy flutter of my heart and the excited flush on my cheeks aren't selling it.

I do a small freak-out dance and then once that's done, I grab my bag, shut off all my lights, lock everything up, and fly back down the stairs out to the waiting car.

"That was more than ten minutes," Kaplan states as I launch myself onto the back seat beside him, his eyes still on his phone. "I was getting ready to leave without you."

"No, you weren't. Incidentally, I don't have a bathing suit. Will we have a chance to stop somewhere so I can pick one up if swimming is going to be on the menu?"

"No. But as I mentioned, for you, clothing is completely optional."

I shake my head. "Sometimes I think I know you so well and then in moments like these, I can't tell if you're being a joking sarcastic dick or a serious, sarcastic dick."

"Serious."

"Kaplan, will you please tell me what's going on?"

He sets his phone down and meets my eyes with a grin that makes my pulse jump. "You'll see soon enough. For now, enjoy the suspense."

28

Bianca

K aplan just kissed me when I told him I didn't read suspense, only straight-up romance that has a bit of a dirty twist to it. He thought I was kidding. I play innocent and physically, I kind of am, but total overshare time, I enjoy MMF books. But he doesn't have to know that.

I digress.

Because Kaplan stays quiet as we drive through Boston, the signs becoming obvious as we hit the tunnel. The airport. A deranged, almost sickly, excited feeling I've been trying to minimize since he told me to pack explodes and suddenly, I'm bouncing like a six-year-old who was just told she's going to Disney World.

Wait.

I spin to face him, my hands still glued to the window. "Are we going to Disney World?"

He gives me the *don't be absurd* look. And right. Can't be naked at Disney. Steals the whole magic of the place.

"Do you ever sit still?" he comments dryly, his face still on that damn screen of his.

"Honestly, no. We can try to blame it on the ADHD, but right now, I'm a fourteen-year-old with his first hooker."

"What?"

"Legit, I don't even know. Two seconds ago, I was thinking about Disney World and my mind just flew right off the Mine Train."

With a chuckle, he takes my hand, finally tucking his phone into his pocket. That's all he does as the car weaves through Logan airport to the private side where the jets are smaller, sleeker, and increasingly more expensive.

We stop in front of an impressive plane that's all white with gold-rimmed windows. The door opens and I peer up at Axl as he extends his hand to help me out. "Are you coming with us?"

"On the plane and a little beyond that. After that it's just the two of you."

Oh. Oh!

Now, I've been a rich girl all my life. But my wealth has been strange. It's been in the form of trust funds bestowed upon me by my birth father and then my stepdads. It was never a life of dripping diamonds and swimming in champagne, much to my mother's chagrin. I mean, I never wanted for anything. Far from it. I had everything I ever needed, never needed, and more. My stepdads are very wealthy, and they buy me stuff and we lived an incredible life. But *my* wealth is the accumulation of the men who loved and raised me.

And it's not something I spend all that often. I simply live off the dividends from investments when needed. Most of the time, I try to make do with what I've got.

So flying on a private jet... That's all Abbot-Fritz and it's all new for me.

"Is this yours?" I hiss to him as he helps me up the small ladder and we meet Allegra, the flight attendant and Mike, the pilot.

"My family's." Kaplan slips onto a cream-colored leather bench, kicks his ankle up over his opposite knee and pretends to ignore me while I ogle everything in sight, though I can feel him watching me out of the corner of his eye.

The smirk on his lips that he's trying so hard to hide tells me that he finds me amusing and I can't help that.

"Is this to impress me, or is this just how you roll?"

"Do I need to impress you?"

I shake my head. "No," I tell him honestly.

"Good," is all he says and leaves it at that.

It's gorgeous on here. Long and not as narrow as I would have imagined, the main cabin consists of twenty or so seats that vary between benches and deep-cushioned chairs. There are tables, an eating area, a bar and a small kitchen at the far back, as well as an office with monitors, two mounted televisions, what appears to be two bathrooms, and... "Is that a bedroom?"

"Hmmm."

Wow. Just wow. "It's nice." I go to take the seat across from him only to have him snatch my waist and drag me down beside him.

"Nice?"

"I guess. You know. If you're into this sort of thing." I scrunch my nose and he grins at me.

"Not impressed?"

"I thought you weren't trying to impress me. Because if you are, there are easier and cheaper ways."

He shakes his head, leaning over and nipping at my earlobe while sucking on my earring. "I'm not trying to impress you. This was easier than attempting to book a commercial flight and dealing with the timing of all that. I told you what this is."

"You did." I beam at him. I don't think I've stopped. "Thank you. I don't even know where we're going or what we're doing, but I'm already having the best time."

His lips press to mine. "Being with you is the best time. This just makes it easier for us to do that."

His hand slips between my thighs and I smack him away.

"Oh no. No mile-high club, mister."

He chuckles, returning his hand to the same spot. "That's Doctor and why not exactly?"

Why not exactly? "People will hear us," I hiss, glancing around at Axl and Slash and Allegra, who are all grinning knowingly at me.

Another chuckle. "Only if we do it right."

Oh.

The plane starts to pick up speed, racing down the runway until it lifts in the air, my stomach going along with it. I grip his arm, holding on even though I'm belted now.

His lips tickle my neck just below my ear. "Relax, baby. Have a drink. Have some dinner. We've got three and a half hours and even though fucking you in a tiny bathroom or even on the bed with a host of witnesses within hearing range does have its appeal, I'm more anxious for what I have planned for us after."

Oh boy.

I turn to him, chewing on my lip. "Have you done this a lot? Flown women to unknown destinations for the night or weekend?" I'm not even being snarky. Just genuinely curious if this is how a Fritz operates. A Kaplan Fritz at that.

His thumb glides up and down the column of my neck, his gaze earnest and intense. "You're the first." Something in his eyes sparkles when he says that, lighting my soul up with their shine.

I kiss him. Letting him feel just what all of this means to me. How special he makes me feel. How... loved. We haven't said those words, nothing even remotely close and I know that's not what this is. It's far too soon for any of that.

But this month and a half with him has been the best of my life. Even when we were fighting, and I swore to all that is holy, I hated him. I'm trying not to think. I'm trying to focus on the now. But with Kaplan, I'm starting to want all the things. Picture all the things.

And I don't know how to stop it.

His hand grips mine and then I settle in only to wake with a jolt when the plane touches down hours later. My eyes snap open, my head listing on his shoulder with an awesome wet spot of drool staining the dark blue of his shirt just past my lips. I blink up at him, my cheeks flaming, but all he does is kiss my forehead followed by the tip of my nose.

"Sorry." I nibble sheepishly on my lip as I try to wipe away some of the evidence.

"You're fine. Stella drools way worse than that. The first time I let her fall asleep on me, she was four and her mother had recently died.

She spent the whole night sleeping on me, woke screaming any time I tried to move her. My T-shirt was soaked by dawn. It became a thing with her for a while and I went through a lot of shirts."

There are far too many things in that statement to focus on. Him letting his tiny, brokenhearted niece sleep on him—I remember when Landon's wife died, it was only a year after Forest did. The fierce way he cares for and protects his family and those he loves. The sexiness he exudes without trying or even caring if he is. The way he goes to extremes to keep his life private and out of the spotlight when all the world wants is a taste of him.

But knowing him... the real him... he's impossible not to love.

All his jagged ends and sharp pieces fit together to make the most incredible man.

One I'm growing day by day to realize I don't want to lose or let go of. Not again.

The plane taxis and suddenly the door to the cabin opens, the ladder lowering. I stretch, the scent of warm air, flowers, and... possibly the ocean filtering in through the door along with a balmy heat that attaches itself to my skin and hair.

"Where are we?" I ask, squinting out the door into the darkness of night. Standing up, I watch while Axl and Slash go about getting our things. I have no idea what time it is, all I know is that it's well past dinnertime, and I slept through it.

"Key West."

"Key West? For real? Like Margaritaville Key West?"

"Yes, but this isn't where we're staying."

"It's not." I can't help the frown, only to realize how ridiculous it is. I'm in the Florida Keys with Kaplan. What could possibly be bad? He could take me to a hostel and it would still be amazing. We exit the plane, another large, black car waiting for us, and a girl could get used to traveling like this. He doesn't even bat an eye and why would he? He's a billionaire who comes from a family of billionaires. Hell, his parents' families were billionaires even before they married.

Sliding in beside him, I let out an embarrassingly loud yawn and he wraps his arms around me, tucking me back into his shoulder.

"You must not care about your shirt."

I feel his smile as he kisses the top of my head. "Tired still?"

"Honestly, no. I'm too excited now to be tired."

"Do you know one of the things I love most about you?" he whispers into my ear, and my eyes shoot open wide, staring straight ahead, unblinking.

My heart just started a mariachi band. I lick my lips and take a breath and when I'm positive I can control my voice, I say, "No. What?"

"You have such a pure, honest heart. Your cousin betrayed you with your fiancé and threatened both of us and yet you still tried to help her. I heard you tell Jenny that she could be better than chasing a billionaire, and she plowed right past that. Most people wouldn't have even tried to get through to them."

"Yeah, well, a lot of good trying to help Ava did and Jenny is a nasty person, but part of me feels sorry for her. Even if she was scheming for you."

"That's exactly what I'm saying. You're you. You've always been you."

I tilt my head up to him, my eyebrows pinched. "What do you mean? Who else would I be?"

His fingers tickle along my face as he stares into my eyes. "The fact that you're confused by that is what I love about you. There is no artifice to you. No bending or attempting to conform to what someone else wants you to be. If you're afraid of something, you say it. If you're embarrassed or make a mistake, you own it. You laugh and smile and genuinely see the best in everyone with no judgment. I've told you before that you wear your heart and mind on your sleeve, and I love that you don't even attempt to hide or change that." He sighs, his sweet breath coasting over my lips. "I've never had that with a woman before. They've always tried to be something or someone else. They've always been women like Jenny. It's all been an act, but with you, I can be me—something I've never been with anyone outside of my family—and you can be you and it's just... natural."

"I never knew how to do that. Be something I'm not. Ava and Tod mastered that art, and I had no clue. It's why people view me as weak and naive. A pushover. Little helpless Bunny who can't take care of herself."

"I don't see you that way. I think you're one of the strongest, bravest, smartest, most capable women I know. Being yourself takes courage. I convinced myself I was better off being alone. That after all the bullshit, after all the years, it was just easier. I've never been with anyone who is genuine. Who was with me for me."

I scrunch my nose. "I find that very hard to believe."

"I'm not saying they didn't like me to a certain extent. I'm saying that they liked what I could provide for them more. Jewelry, clothes, front-row concerts or sporting events, celebrity meetings, a certain level of fame, social ladder climbing, bragging rights, whatever it was. It was always something."

I nod numbly, at a total loss for words.

"I gave up. Detached. Swore off love and relationships altogether. A point that was only solidified when I saw all that my brothers went through with it. It was easier to use all of that as an excuse than to try and weed through the miasma of women for something legitimate." His hand comes up and his features soften as his eyes dance about my face. "Then I met you, B. You have me rethinking things I swore I'd never rethink."

My breath hitches and he smiles when he hears it.

Our foreheads press together, his nose gliding back and forth along mine. "I'm crazy about you."

I swallow. Clear my throat. It's no use. "I'm crazy about you too," I croak.

"Good. Because we're here."

"What?"

Snapping toward the window, I peer out, climbing over Kaplan in the process. The door opens and I practically go tumbling out, only to have Slash catch me and help me up.

"I hope your sea legs are steadier than that," Kaplan quips, but I'm too busy staring at where we are to care about his teasing me over my less than graceful exit.

"You're taking me on a boat? Which one?" Only the second the words leave my mouth, I know exactly which boat it is. There is a massive sailboat down at the very far end of the dock. It's long. Sleek. Has two colossal white sails raised high in the air and cool blueish-purple lighting in the water.

Kaplan comes in behind me, his chest to my back. His arm slips around my waist and he points to the one I was just marveling at. "That pretty lady."

"You can steer that thing all by yourself? She's huge."

A kiss on my neck. "No. There's staff on board. I'll steer some though during the day. I'll teach you how and then this summer I'll take you on my smaller sloop and then we can really feel the ocean move."

Oh god. "Am I going to get seasick? My mother does."

"This is a luxury yacht, so even though you'll feel her move, she's not that fast and has a more balanced hull. I brought stuff with me for you just in case though. I remember you mentioning that about your mom."

"How many does she sleep?"

"Fourteen plus up to ten crew."

Wowzers.

I spin in his arms, wrap mine around his neck and kiss the hell out of him. "Can we go on?"

"She's ours to do with as we like," he breathes against me.

"What's her name?"

"Amphitrite."

My eyes glitter as I spin back around and face her. "Goddess of the sea. Poseidon's wife. Queen of the ocean."

"That's the one. Come on. The sooner I get you on there, the sooner I can get you naked."

29

With the wind whipping my hair about, sunglasses shading my eyes from the blinding sun, a beer in one hand, the helm in the other, and a stunning woman in a tiny bikini sitting with her legs kicked up and a hat on her head, today might be one of my happiest days. Period. Well, that and the news that baby Owen was finally sent home from the NICU.

So yeah. Happy day right here.

Bianca shifts, adjusting the slightly too small triangle of her top and I can't fight my grin. I might have caught a bit of crap for what I had my head steward pick out for her. I called him from the plane after she mentioned not having any bathing suits, knowing that during the day, with the staff helping me keep Amphitrite in a good wind, she'd need to wear something.

"Where are we?" she asks, her voice getting lost in the wind. "What's that island?"

"I think that's the Marquesas Keys. Yep. Look." I point over to the leeward side.

Bianca sits up, her hands gripping the rail, her body angling over. "Oh my gosh! I've never seen dolphins like this. They're so close. What if you hit one?"

I chuckle, taking a sip of my beer. "I won't. Believe me, they're very used to boats and know exactly how to swim. They'll follow us for a few miles. They like the current we make."

"They're so beautiful."

"We'll stop in a bit and maybe you can try to swim with them."

Her head whips around, her smile uncontainable, and I'm glad I took this risk. Brought someone along on something that had always typically been just for myself. My dad and I would take this ship out a lot together when I was younger, but my mother never liked sailing, always preferring her larger cruising yacht. But in the last few years, it's just been me and it's been something I looked forward to.

The quiet. The peace. The solitude.

But last night I made love to Bianca in my bed and again this morning and then we had breakfast together, both of us reading on our tablets. Since then, we've been up here, sailing around the Keys and being able to watch her reaction and excitement and interest in learning one of my greatest passions has been everything.

She's been everything.

She's become everything.

Something I had all but given up on.

I'm falling so hard for her. And there is no stopping it now.

"Come here, B. Take the helm."

Jumping to her feet, she saunters in my direction, slipping under my arm and tucking herself between me and the wheel, giving me a little booty shake against my dick because she can be a delicious tease like that.

"Do you think you can do this?" I rasp in her ear, kissing a trail up and down her neck.

"Just tell me what to do."

"That's my girl. Alright, we need to change our point of sail as the wind changed directions on us. Can you feel it?"

"It feels like we're heading into the wind."

"Good. Exactly. And we can't sail into the wind. We're going to starboard tack. Do you remember which direction that is?"

"Right."

"Perfect. I'm going to help with the lines and rigging that will move the mainsail and jib how we want them. When I tell you, cut the wheel starboard."

"Aye aye, Captain Kaplan." She gives me a salute and I smack her ass, giving it a firm squeeze. Most everything on the boat is motorized. I simply have to push a few buttons and it does what I want. Not as fun as my catamaran, but what can you do? I just wanted to watch her man the helm. Especially because she starts singing "Yo, Ho! (A Pirate's Life for Me)" as she does.

This summer I'll take her out and really teach her how to sail.

Not even a hint of seasickness, she's made for this as much as I am.

Bianca does as I tell her, sailing us around for a bit, and just as the afternoon sun starts to dip more toward the west, we drop anchor in the middle of nowhere and then it's just the two of us relaxing on the sundeck. The chef made us a cheese board, a crudité along with some dip, and left us a chilled bottle of wine. We also have two fishing lines hanging out in the water, kept steady by the rod holders.

"This is so much better than being in Boston in March," she muses, popping a piece of cheese into her mouth and washing it down with a sip of the wine.

"Now you know why I do this a few times a year if I can."

"I'm shocked you don't live down here."

"I thought about it," I tell her honestly, chewing on a grape. "After med school, I looked into residencies in Miami, but Boston Children's Hospital is the best in the world and Boston has always been home. For better or worse, it's where I belong. Carter did his residency in Virginia Beach and Luca did his in Minnesota. Rina lived in New York for a while, but we all came back to Boston in the end."

"I never really had a home. I mean, no place I ever felt rooted to, so I understand why you all moved back home. I lived in LA the longest, between when I was a little girl and then in college and grad school. But between those two periods of my life, it's been Colorado and Texas. And with my mother, nothing ever felt permanent. I like that you're all so close. That you all value family and your city the way you do."

"Family is everything. You know that. You're the same way with yours." Standing up, I pick up the bottle of sunscreen and start spraying her shoulders and back. "Your pretty white skin is starting to turn pink," I explain when she shoots me a bemused look.

"As much as I love the sun, my skin isn't used to it," she remarks just as the line on her fishing rod starts to jerk and then pull. "Oh! Holy crap, I caught something." Leaping to her feet, she races over to the pole, attempting to lift it from the rod holder only to have the top of it bend and pull against her. She belts out a scream. "I can't turn the reel. What do I do?"

Running in behind her, I grab onto the pole along with her, yanking it back toward us before it drags her over the edge. "You're not hooked onto the boat. Let go before you get hurt or fall in. I'll reel it in." I start to turn the reel as best as I can, but whatever she caught is putting up an amazing fight. Both of us angle our weight back, pressing our heels into the deck of the boat.

"Whatever this is, it does not want to become dinner." She laughs as we continue to struggle. "Should we let it go?"

"I can't until we get it out of the water unless I want to let the pole go with it, which might hurt it even more." I continue to alternate between pulling the rod up and then reeling down, over and over, the muscles in my arms and back killing me.

"Wait," she calls out, leaning over the side and squinting down at the blue-green water. "I can see something. An outline."

"What does it look like?"

"A fish. What do you mean, what does it look like?"

I roll my eyes. "I realize it's a fish, but what *kind* of fish?"

"How the hell should I know what kind? Do I look like a marine biologist? A big one. It looks like a big freaking fish, Kaplan. This is insane. We're like *The Old Man and the Sea.*"

I pull up on the rod with all my might and whatever it is finally breaks through the surface of the water, thrashing around.

"Ahhh! Shark. It's a shark. How the hell did I catch a shark? It's like Jaw's cousin."

Sure enough, a huge blue-gray shark with a pointed nose, round black eyes, massive jaw, and sharp spiky teeth flaps around, struggling like mad, desperate to go back into the water. "Jesus. That's a Mako shark."

"Okay. Goody for it. What do we do now?"

"I think it's a baby."

"A baby?" She gives me an incredulous "are you crazy, that shark is huge" glare. The thing continues to flail and snap. "My, what big teeth you have, baby Mako shark. The better to eat us with."

Yanking with every ounce of my strength, I pull up and reel down, but its tail almost hits Bianca the closer it gets to the deck.

"What are you doing?" she shrieks.

"I don't know," I yell back. "I thought about bringing it on board, but now I'm thinking that's a terrible idea."

"On board? You can't bring it on board. Let it go. It's going to eat us."

"Just you. You're closer."

She flips around, throwing me a scathing look only for us both to start cracking up. "You're bigger than I am. Better eating."

The freaking shark snaps at us, calling our focus back to it, and yeah, it's going to eat us. "I could stab it. We have a spear."

"Are you crazy? You can't *stab* it." She points at the rebellious fish.

"Mako shark is delicious."

"Kaplan, there is no way I'm eating this thing. Let it go."

"What kind of sea woman are you?"

"The kind who has been doing this for less than two days and would rather drink wine and eat cheese than kill a shark. This is another one of those times when I can't tell if you're being sarcastic or not."

"No sense of adventure," I tease. "B, grab the scissors and cut the line."

"Me?"

"Baby, I can't do it and hold the pole. This thing is fighting too much, and it's very strong. I want to get it back in the water safely. We're using circle hooks. It will eventually rust away or fall out without killing it, but we need to release it and to do that, we have to cut the line."

"After this, no more fishing," she threatens, picking up the braid scissors and going for the orange line.

"Promise. Cut it up by me. Don't get anywhere near the shark."

She snips the line, and the shark falls back into the water with a massive splash, swimming away, its fin already entirely back underwater. The pole slips from my hand, falling to the deck of the ship with a loud clatter, and then we're both panting and laughing.

"Wow," she gasps, a hand over her racing heart. "That actually happened. I can't believe that actually happened. We caught a freaking shark." She points to the ocean and the fleeing fish.

I haul her against me, my lips layering with hers. "Next time it's great white or bust, baby."

～

"THIS IS MAGICAL," Bianca whispers on a dreamy sigh as we stare up at the endless ocean of stars, the sea gently rocking us from below. After a quiet beat, she says, "Do you remember when you once asked me where my happy place was?"

"Yeah," I murmur absently as I take in the constellations.

"Mine had been with Forest. Playing video games and hanging out. He never made me feel less than, only more, and it was the same for me with him. I hadn't done much art until I moved in with him and his family, but I started drawing and painting after my spinal surgery and I was laid up for a while. I loved it, but it wasn't what called to me. After Forest died, I was so lost. You know that. But then after Mom married Duke and we moved to his ranch, I started playing with metal. That became my happy place. Doing metal work, making things with my hands. But I can see how this is your happy place now and I'm thinking this might be a very close second for me too."

"I told you back then my happy place was the hospital. The OR. That was true. It's *still* true. It's what stirs my soul, but the only place I feel true peace is here. On the water with the sky and the stars and the quiet of my mind around me. You're real, B and you remind me what it feels like to allow myself to be that way too."

She leans deeper into me, kissing a spot over my sternum and then working to the left side of my chest. Over my heart.

"You once texted me in the middle of the night that you did this when the hospital became too stressful for you. You'd go on the rooftop of your building and stare up at the stars or the sky to give yourself a moment. Gain some perspective. Do you still do that?"

I hold her closer against me, kissing her temple as we lie on the large sunbed on the aft deck. She's wrapped up in a blanket, snuggled in close, and I think this is my favorite moment ever. I might have already said that. In fact, I know I did. But I'm quickly discovering that with Bianca, every moment is my new favorite.

"No. Not anymore. I was a newbie resident back then. Scared out of my mind. If I had a patient go south on me, it wasn't just a patient. It was a child. And that's what gutted me more than anything else. The young life with so much potential lost. It still guts me. There is no getting used to that. But now I've learned to focus on the ones I do save. On the kids who go on to live full, happy lives."

She twists toward me, abandoning the stars in favor of me. Her fingers comb through my hair. "I think what you do is incredible. You fix tiny human hearts. I can't even wrap my head around something like that and you do it. Your whole family. You're a bunch of billionaires. Each of you. So many of your kind—the children of very wealthy families—live like that. Off their trust funds and money and create a social media presence and contribute very little other than eating disorders and unreal expectations of life to others. They do nothing for the greater good. But you all sacrifice and work impossibly hard and give back so much of yourselves through your work. You save lives and that makes you a hero, Kaplan Fritz. That's why you should be famous. Not because you're hot and have money."

I smirk down at her even though my heart is racing at what she just said. "You think I'm hot?"

She smacks at my chest. "Jerk. That's what you got out of everything I just said?"

I chuckle, tearing the blanket off and rolling on top of her. My forearms press into the stiff mattress, and I stare down into her eyes, barely illuminated by the glow of the ship lights. "No. That's not what I got out of that. But right now, all I care about is that I've got you. Out here, it's just us. No money or fame or press or sick patients. We're man and woman versus the ocean and the elements. It's an adventure. A ride. And it's one I only want to take with you."

I let that settle for a moment, watch as it swirls across her beautiful face, through her sparkling eyes and across her curled-up lips.

Her hand cups my jaw and she stares up at me, spellbound. Just as I am with her. "You keep talking like that and you're going to make a girl fall in love."

"That might be a risk I'm willing to take so long as the girl doing the falling is you."

I sink my weight down on top of her, my lips claiming hers in a kiss so deep I can't tell where I end and she begins. I've taken her so many times in so many ways, in every position there is all over this ship, but none of it feels like enough. Some moments, the need to bury myself inside her is too intense to control. There is always this voracious pounding in my chest when it comes to her. A chant that cries for more, more, *more.*

Our mouths feast on each other, ravenous and wild. Primal with an eternal hunger that will never be sated. We make quick work of each other's clothes, my mouth licking and kissing a trail down her neck to her incredible tits. My hand squeezes and lifts one, my teeth scraping along the upslope until I reach her perfect pink peak. Sucking it into my mouth, I take in as much of her as I can.

Her fingers grip my hair by the roots, her body rocking up into me, seeking friction I'm refusing to give her. Bianca gets greedy. Frenzied. And it's so fucking beautiful the way she grows desperate for my cock. But tonight, I have so many plans for her. Tomorrow is Sunday and we have to fly home. Back to reality and I need this with her as much as she needs it with me.

Rising up off the bed, I smile at her displeased whimper. "Where are you going?"

"I'm getting this," I tell her, grabbing a length of white rope that was sitting on the starboard edge by the lower aft deck.

"Kaplan." My name is a nervous, breathy whisper. "Rope?"

"B, I'm a sailor and a doctor. I can truss you up in rope in six hundred different ways without breaking any of your beautiful skin. I can do breath play. I can do anything you can begin to imagine with a rope. All of it, you'll love."

"Okay."

So trusting. My hands claim her wrists, dragging them up and over her head. I fasten the rope around her forearms, angling her hands for her to hold on to the line and then I tie her to the base of the sunbed.

"Wiggle your fingers for me," I command, and she does while I test her circulation.

Coming back around, I climb back onto the bed, straddling her hips but not putting any weight down on her. And god, just how sexy is she like this? Splayed out and tied up on the bed, wanting and waiting for me. With her arms over her head like this, her tits are pulled up and practically smooshed together. My tongue dives into her cleavage, licking a trail from the bottom of her sternum to the top. Bianca shivers beneath me. She loves it when I play with her tits and that reminds me.

"Don't move."

"What?" she shrieks in alarm as I run off yet again.

I race for our room, locate the item I was seeking, and then in less than a minute, I'm back with her.

"If you leave me a third time, especially like this, I'll throw you overboard and let Matty the Mako eat you."

A chuckle hits the air seconds before I kiss her. "I'm sorry. I promise I'll make it up to you. I started getting all kinds of ideas and couldn't stop."

"Maybe you should plan your kink ahead of time, Doctor."

"Definitely." I take one nipple into my mouth, sucking it up into a hard pebble. Then I place the clamp on her wet nipple and slide the tension bar up until it's firm but not too tight. To the point where Bianca's moaning and whimpering at the bite, but not squirming or writhing in pain. "Good?" I check.

A jerky head nod. I'm pushing her past any limit she's ever tested and it's so beautiful to watch. I do the same with the other one and with both her nipples clamped, my mouth comes back down, covering one and then the other before blowing cool air on them.

Her back arcs and she pulls against the restraint on her arms.

Standing up, I shift toward her face, her eyes glued to my every move. My cock bumps her lips, and she opens for me immediately, her tongue coming out to lick at my tip piercing. "Get me nice and wet," I tell her, pushing my cock into her mouth. "Yes, B. Suck me down like a good girl. That's it. So good."

She slurps on me, bobbing her head as best as she can, but with how she's positioned, she can't do much. Once I'm nice and lubed up, I pull myself from her mouth and straddle her again, my cock sliding between her breasts.

"Oh, God," she moans as I press her tits together even tighter, pulling ever so slightly on the nipple clamps. My cock continues to fuck her gorgeous tits, thrusting up into them. Her mouth opens, her chin pressed down as the head of my cock hits her lips. She licks me as I do this, all the while playing with her tits and sensitive nipples.

Her tits feel so good like this. Warm cushions sliding against me, eating my cock up, the visual is nearly enough to have me coming like this. But it's when I flick on the bullet and press it against her clit that she starts to go wild.

"Kaplan!" she screams.

I fuck her tits while playing with her clamped nipples and pressing the vibrator tighter against her throbbing clit. I can see her pussy leaking from here. Her legs shaking. Trembling. Thrashing.

"I'm going to fucking come."

"No, you're not. You're not coming yet," I tell her.

"I have to. It's... it's so good."

And when I start to feel my balls drawing up and a tingling in my spine, I slide out of her tits, climb down her body, and cover her pussy with my mouth, pressing the vibrator into her opening.

"Christ, you're soaked. You liked that, didn't you? Me fucking your tits with this little toy against your dripping cunt?"

"Yes," she cries as I slip my tongue up inside her, alternating between the toy and my mouth. I splay her thighs open wide, playing with her clit. Up. Down. Tickling. Pressing in deep. Anything I can do to keep her guessing. Keep her pleasure on the edge. She's moaning uncontrollably. Writhing, begging me for more. Needing to come so bad, but I won't let her.

"Please," she begs, and her begging... I could come just from that too.

"You're so sexy. I can't stand how fucking sexy you are when you get like this."

My tongue flicks her clit on one side, the toy on the other and she shrieks, yanking on the restraints, jerking, her body thrashing against the bed, unable to move. "Kaplan," she groans. "Oh god, it's so much."

"If you need me to stop, say red and I'll stop everything immediately. Remember?"

"Yes. Yes. Oh hell. *Yes!*"

My mouth continues to eat at her pussy while my fingers work her breasts and nipples in the clamps. I pull the toy from her and press it against one nipple. Then the other.

"Fuck! Fuck! *Yessss!*"

"More, or have you had enough?"

"More. Please, Kaplan. More."

"Where do you want it?"

"Everywhere."

Damn.

I pull and tug and flick and vibrate. I press the vibrator, wet with her arousal, against her other nipple, my mouth eating from the one it was just on. Then I slide it off and back into her pussy. Her body catches fire. Her eyes a missile of heat and lust.

All the while, my tongue and lips devour her tits. Her trembling legs wrap around my back, her feet scraping at my skin. It's a lot. A lot of pleasure and pressure and pain and she's getting so close to exploding.

Diving back down, my tongue circles her clit a few times, the vibrator inside her. I suck her deeply into my mouth and she comes apart, screaming out her orgasm. I release one clamp, then the other, rubbing her breasts and nipples, and her scream intensifies, along with her orgasm until she squirts into my mouth. I lick every drop of her up, continuing to pleasure her until she's absolutely spent and sagging down into the bed.

Turning off the toy, I toss it aside and stare down at her.

A goddess. *My* goddess.

Climbing up her body, I kiss a trail along her sweet skin, massaging and worshipping her breasts. And when my mouth reaches hers again, I hike her leg up over my thigh and slide inside of her. Her teeth sink into my lip, and she whimpers into me, her inner walls still quivering and sensitive from her orgasm.

I give her a moment to adjust to me and when she relaxes, I slide slowly out of her, only to thrust back in all the way to the hilt. I fuck her. Up on my knees, eyes locked, her legs clamped around me, pounding into her. All the while, she lies here helpless. Immobile as I control her body. Her pleasure. Loving every second of it.

"Wanna flip over, or do you like it like this?" I ask on a ragged breath.

"Like this. I want to watch you. I want you closer."

I drag her knees up to my shoulders and then bend forward, my hands on either side of her head, bringing our faces inches apart. "This what you wanted, pretty girl?"

"Yes. I like feeling you deep inside me while watching what that feels like for you."

Christ. This woman. What she does to me. I'm so gone on her.

Our moans fill the air, swirling above us and getting lost in the stars. I bury myself in her over and over. Never wanting it to end. My forehead presses into hers, my tongue jutting out, licking at the seam of her lips.

I pick up my pace, skin slapping against skin, my balls smacking into her ass as I piston in and out of her. "You want to know what you feel like for me? Slippery hot and tighter than tight. Your greedy cunt squeezes my cock every time I slide in you, desperate to keep me there. You feel like heaven. And sin. There is nothing better than being inside you, Bianca. Nothing. And when you come, watching you do that…"

I trail off, pressing my thumb into her mouth so she can suck on me and then I take my wet digit and rub her clit with it. Marveling as her skin flushes pink. As her eyes glaze over even more, her pupils totally blown out. As her breaths tumble one after the other past her pillowy lips.

"You take my breath away," I whisper into her mouth just as she starts to come again, her body convulsing and clenching around me, her legs clamping, holding me tighter against her. I fuck her through it and when she's on the other side of it, I come too, bursting inside her, grunting and groaning as my face slips into her neck.

Afterward, once I can breathe and think, I climb off her and untie her. Holding her against me, I massage her wrists and arms, kiss her face, and come to the brutal realization that everything I ever told myself about how my life would be is a lie. There is no living without this woman now. And no matter what, there will be hell to pay for that.

30

Bianca

W alking hand in hand through the crowded streets of Key West, wearing Kaplan's Red Sox hat to cover my slightly too-sun-kissed face, I can't help the frown on my lips. I don't want to go home today. I want to stay in our bubble of "everything is absolutely blissfully perfect."

"I feel you frowning," he whispers into my ear.

"You do not."

"But you didn't deny that you are."

Busted.

"Just pouting like a spoiled little princess." I peer up at him. "I don't want to go home."

His hand slips out of mine in favor of my shoulder so he can draw me against his side. "Me neither. But now that I know you can handle a sailboat and a shark, we'll do something again when we can."

For a moment, I let that ride, thinking. Because I feel like we should talk. You know, considering we have a lot of things to talk about. He's my boss and sooner or later, the media will spot us together again and there will be talk. So that must be addressed. We said we're exclusive and all that, but we also said we're just fucking, and no. That's a serious nope on the nope scale. Because I wasn't lying last night when I told him I was falling.

I am.

Totally. Completely. Irreversibly.

So even though he doesn't want a relationship or any of that and I told him I wasn't ready for one either, I'm not sure I can do just fuck buddies with him. I like to imagine he's there too, given all he's done and said, but hey, you never know until you ask. I don't need or want him to put a ring on it and I don't even require a fancy title.

I just need to know I'm not alone in this.

And if I am, then, well, what we're doing has to end. My heart is already involved, and it's not as if things get any easier or cleaner the longer this goes on.

But I don't want to ruin the last few hours we have here. Talking can wait. Margaritas and tacos for lunch cannot.

"Hey, how about after lunch, I take you to a couple of art galleries? That seems like something you'd enjoy doing on your last day, right?"

"Kaplan—" My voice cuts off, freezing in my lungs as I stare into one of the open bars, straight at a mounted television.

"B? What is it? Are you alright? You look like you've seen a ghost."

"Look."

That's all I've got as I read the headline. Again. As I watch the images flashing along the screen.

His gaze follows mine and locks in on the television, and immediately, he stiffens beside me. "Fuck."

That's all he says. And it's a resigned fuck at that. An angry fuck. But not a "What the fuck?" It's not incredulous. There is no shock in his voice. It's not "How can there be pictures of Millie Van Der Heusen kissing my cheek. Smiling at the press while clinging to my side?" He's not surprised to see scrawled in bold, "Kaplan Abbot-Fritz and Millie Van Der Heusen Engaged."

"Kaplan?"

Again, that's as far as I go. At least this time, it sounds like a question because I'm full of them. He tries to turn me away from the screen but I'm not budging.

"Bianca, we need to talk."

Oh. He's starting it off like that.

I read the subtext now. "Rumors have been circulating around Kaplan Abbot-Fritz, famous Boston billionaire doctor and Millie Van Der Heusen, daughter to Senator Van Der Heusen for weeks now. The couple has been spotted together on numerous occasions and a spokesperson for the Van Der Heusen family has confirmed the couple is very much in love and headed toward nuptials. The Fritz family has yet to respond to our requests, but we already can't wait to talk all things Fritzheusen and their high-profile relationship."

Slowly, I turn and stare up at him. His eyes are all over me, green and turbulent, but there is no denial in them. "Are you engaged?"

"No." That's it. That's his only response.

"Are you..." I lick my suddenly dry lips. "Are you with her?"

"It's not like that."

"What's it like then?" I demand, my eyes and nose stinging from my unshed tears. It's like déjà vu. Once again, I'm this Bunny. The one who everyone deceives and betrays because I'm too stupid and naive to know better. "They already gave you a fucking love nickname." I look back at the television. "When were those pictures taken? Not the day I saw you with your mom outside the foundation building. No. This is from another day after that. Wasn't it?" I point at the screen. "It's pouring rain there. She's in a different dress. You're in scrubs."

An agitated hand through his hair. "Bianca, can we please go somewhere private to have this conversation?"

"Because you're afraid I'm going to make a public stink? Run into traffic and throw myself on a passing car?"

"You're being dramatic."

"I am not," I seethe. "Don't you dare fucking patronize me."

He grabs my arm, jerking me away from the television and getting right up in my face. "I'm not patronizing you. Not even a little. But I can't have this conversation with you out here. You trusted me as of five minutes ago. Please hold onto that for a little longer and let me take you somewhere so we can talk."

Without waiting for my reply, he drags me along, searching left and right but we're in the middle of Duval Street in Key West. There is no private or quiet. It's all loud bars and drinking and shops. He cuts up another street and then down half of one and finally, he finds an alley and shoves me in it, right up against the side of a house.

"When I agreed to be CEO of the foundation, my mother started pressing upon me the importance of marriage. They always wanted us to find love, but I never had, and frankly, I'm not a kid anymore. More than that, I was always resistant to the prospect. So, her pushing harder for marriage wasn't a shock. Hell, I fucking expected it. But not just any marriage. A certain kind of marriage. A marriage that would grow our family wealth and power and station if it wasn't going to be for love."

I shake my head. "I realize I don't know your mother or your family all that well, but she never struck me as the type who cared about any of those pretenses. And your siblings are not with people who fit that bill."

His hands are in his hair and he's pacing now. "I'm the eldest. I'm the heir. My parents' marriage was arranged, as was their parents'. It's how things are done."

"So, you're in an arranged situation with Millie Van Der Heusen." It's not a question. After what I just saw and what he's describing and seeing his mother and her mother and them together that day, it all fits. I lean back against the building, sweating in the blistering heat and humidity and heartbreak.

My insides feel like they're being ripped out of my chest, and I can't help but want to flip off the small touch of irony that comes with that. I was set to marry Tod and when I found out about his betrayal, I felt nothing even remotely similar to this. I didn't love Tod, but I sure as hell love Kaplan Fritz, and wow, how bad does that suck right now.

"I never agreed to it," he barks as he paces a small path in front of me. "To any of it. My parents mentioned it, but nothing had ever been arranged or even discussed beyond suggestion."

"And yet it's all over the fucking news, Kaplan." My hands fly through the air. "You knew there was a possibility of venturing into an arranged marriage, and you started fucking me. Not just fucking me but knowingly stealing my heart. How could you do that to me?"

A growl slices the air, and then he's all over me, pressing against me. "I met with Millie the day after I found out who you were. After you and I got together. She asked me to lunch, and the timing was perfect. I went there to tell her to back off. Since that first lunch, she had been calling and texting a lot. I went there that day to tell her I had met someone, thinking that would be enough, and she'd just move on. But she started talking about how we were a perfect match and how our mothers were putting things together for us. She was adamant that we'd be the perfect power married couple. I told her I wasn't going to do that. That it wasn't going to happen. She went a little crazy and basically said too fucking bad. We walked out of there and the press was everywhere because she had her people call them as a setup. That's what you just saw. A setup. But none of that mattered. Not really. I wasn't going to do it and I told my mother that."

"And what did your mother say when you told her that?"

A grunt this time. "She said she understood my position on it, but that we'd talk about it later."

"And did you?"

"No. Not yet."

"And you didn't think to mention to me the fact that you were in negotiations with another woman to potentially be married?"

His fist slams into the wood beside my head, but I don't so much as move or jump or flinch. I just continue to glare up into his stormy eyes. "I was never going to do it!" he yells. "That was never going to be my life. I had sworn it years ago. That's why I'm a loner. That's why they call me untouchable. Women like Millie Fucking Van Der Heusen and the motherfucking expectations of being an Abbot-Fritz."

A tear somehow manages to escape—the bastard—and tracks down my cheek. He attempts to wipe it away and I shake him off. "You should have told me about her. About that lunch. I shouldn't have been blindsided by this." Again. Blindsided again.

"Between Owen and the subsequent press with that and how little I saw you last week, I honestly didn't think about it. As far as I was concerned, I was done. Out. Finished with all of it."

I suck in a ragged breath, my face falling toward the dirty gravel lining the alley. "Regardless, you can't be with me. Right? I mean, you have to be with a certain type of woman, and I am not that type of woman. You just said it. A loner. Untouchable. Never one to get involved, no matter what. So." Deep breath. "It was simply going to be us fucking around until I caught feelings—which I obviously already have—and then it was going to end."

"No, B. Look at me." He cups my jaw, forcing my face up. His thumbs brush at my tears and his eyes bleed into mine. "That's not how it was going to be. You don't understand. We forged a friendship years ago out of the worst of situations. Then I saw you again years later, and you caught my eye in a way no one else has ever done. Not before or after you. You are the object of all of my fantasies, including the ones I have yet to imagine."

"You liked how I looked in a bikini."

"Bianca, I fell in love with you the second I saw you that day in your bikini, staring up at the sky. There was something about you that struck me and wouldn't let go. Especially after I learned who you were. It's always been you. But I never felt... I couldn't have you. You were young and I felt wrong about all of it. So I put it out of my head and after all the craziness with women, I gave up on all of it. And then there I was, in the right spot at the right moment. It's as if fate ran you right to me. Since then, no wait, with *all* of it..." His forehead meets mine, eyes holding tight. "It's as if you were created just for me. It was never going to be anyone else because it could only be you."

"What about Millie? What about what it said on the television?"

His body fuses with mine, holding me up, forcing me to feel the thunder of his heart against my own. "I told her there was no way I was ever going to do that with her. And I will tell the world that there is no relationship and no engagement and that there will never be a wedding."

"But... what about your mom? Your parents?"

"B, I'm a thirty-six-year-old man. I love my family, and I love my parents and I'd do anything for any of them, but I was never going to do that. My mother has always made it clear for us that she wants us to find love first above everything else. She..." he trails off, taking a sudden step back and staring at me as if he's seeing me with new eyes. "Son of a bitch."

"What?"

He blinks. "Oliver said something to me, and I didn't..."

"What?" I repeat more emphatically.

"I need to get home. Now. We need to leave now."

"Kaplan, can you please tell me what's going on?"

Stepping back into me, he takes my hand. "Not yet, okay? I need to figure some things out, but I swear, we're not over, and I'm not marrying Millie, and I love you. Okay? I don't say that. I never have, but I do. I fucking love you so much, so stay with me and trust me. Please," he tacks on when I don't immediately respond.

"You love me?"

A breathy laugh escapes as he cups my jaw and presses our foreheads together. "Yes. I love you. How could I not love you? Look at you? You're absolutely perfect. Everything about you from the way you can't sit still for two seconds to the way your face shows every thought and emotion you have as if I'm watching a movie to the way you talk back to me and don't care about anything that has to do with my name, fame, or money, to how sweet and loyal and loving you are. How could I not love you, Bianca Bunny Barlow? I never stood a chance at anything else from the second you walked back into my life."

I fall against him, my cheek to his chest. Over his heart that is beating for me. "I love you too."

"I know."

Now it's my turn to laugh. "You do?"

"Yes, baby." A kiss to my hair as he holds me against him. "I just said it, didn't I? You wear your heart and your mind all over you. You can't hide anything."

"Oh. I'd feel embarrassed about that, but you said it first, so I don't."

"You said you were falling for me last night."

"Falling. Not quite there yet, so not the same thing."

He chuckles, the sound vibrating into me. Pulling back, his hands dive into my hair and then he's kissing me. So fully, so deeply, so passionately that my toes curl and my mind unwinds. It fills me. Plasters over those cracks where doubt and insecurity were attempting to leak through.

"I said it first," he whispers into me. "And I'll be the one to say it last. You changed my whole world and while that's not something I ever wanted to have happen, I can't imagine going back to how it was before. Let me take care of this. Let me clear it up. And after that, no more hiding us."

"I like the sound of that. Good luck though. You're going to need it. You've got one hell of a mess to clean up."

31

Millie Van Der Heusen is an idiot. She thought she'd peer pressure me into getting engaged to her like I'm some grade school weakling. She thought she'd media bully me into it like I give a shit what the media says or does with me.

Whatever she was thinking, she was not only wrong, but she also grossly underestimated who I am. The power I can wield if I want to turn the tides in my favor. Her father is a senator, but the Abbot-Fritzes are the gods of Boston, and after delivering Owen in the back of my car, I rock a cape along with my lightning bolt in the eyes of the world.

But there's more to this than that.

Bianca passed out on me again the second we got on the airplane. Honestly, it's a relief because my mind was too wild for any sort of chitchat and there was no way I was going to take her on the plane the way I need to take her with all this madness swirling about.

We landed at Logan and even though I hated to do it, I put B in a car with Slash, and I got into one with Axl. My sibling text stream has been blowing up since before we got on the plane and other than telling them that I'm not marrying Millie, I haven't said anything else.

But it's not like I have to.

Because here it is, Sunday night and my entire family is at my parents' compound for dinner because that's what we do on Sunday nights. So as the car pulls to a stop and I step out, I'm swarmed before the door can even shut behind me.

"Where have you been, and why are you so tan?" That's Rina.

"The press has been all over us. Hounding us for comments and information." Oliver.

"The Van Der Heusens faxed over a crazy-ass contract. Is this shit actually happening?" Carter's turn.

"Just tell them all to fuck off. That's what I did, and eventually they left me alone." Landon.

"I could tell them Raven is pregnant." Luca and—

"Wait," I snap. "What?"

"I'm not pregnant," Raven comes in with an eye roll. "Jesus, Luca. Slow your biological clock because mine hasn't even started to tick yet." She grabs my hand. "And the rest of you, back off. Let the man breathe." A jerk of my hand and I'm following after my pretty black-haired friend. "I mean it, Luca," she threatens with a menacing finger pointed back at them. "Back off or no naughty play later. And as for the rest of you, I'll tell the same to your better halves."

They're groaning and arguing, but no one messes with Raven. Or Amelia, for that matter, now that I think about it.

Raven brings me up the front porch steps and into the house. "Thank you," I tell her, dropping a kiss on the top of her head.

"Daughter of Morgan Fairchild, former MI6 and chief of Fritz security at your service."

I let out a small laugh, pulling her closer and dropping an arm over her shoulder. "I hope you're taking me to see my mom."

"I am, but she's in the back with Grace and Owen. She has a whole room set up on the first floor for them."

Of course she does. Octavia Abbot-Fritz loves her people. I'm counting on that.

We reach a parlor room off to the garden room and Raven knocks. "I have Kaplan with me. Everyone decent?"

"Yes. I'm done nursing. He can come in," Grace calls out and when we open the door, it's like walking into a full nursery.

"You know you have a whole nursery set of rooms upstairs, right?" I comment dryly as I look around the gender-neutral room of grays and greens with smatterings of yellow. Grace is sitting in a large, cushioned rocking chair with a sleeping Owen tucked against her. My mother is on the daybed, sitting as she always does, though I can see the unease all over her.

"I didn't want Grace to have to go up and down stairs and Owen is so small, I wanted to have him closer to us."

Without hesitation, I cross the room and kiss Grace on the forehead and then do the same to my little man, running my fingers gently along his soft hair and tiny nose. "How are you doing being home? You being good for Mommy and Daddy?"

"He's being as you'd expect for a newborn," Grace tells me. "You can hold him later." I get the meaningful look and I roll my head over my shoulder to meet my mother's eyes.

"I guess that's my cue."

I stand to my full height and extend my hand to help my mother up. "It is indeed."

She takes it and then the two of us find our way through the expansive downstairs all the way to my father's office. The door is open as if he was expecting us, and when I enter, he's sitting on his couch with a stack of official-looking papers in front of him along with a glass of his expensive bourbon. My mother takes the seat beside him, leaving me one of the chairs, and wordlessly I go about fixing my mother a glass of wine and myself a glass of what my father is having.

I take a sip, but I don't sit down.

When I was in Key West, talking to Bianca in that alley, something hit me. It hit me hard. And before anything else can be discussed, I have to ask this first of my mother.

"Did you know who she was?"

My mother's green eyes, the same shade as mine, drag slowly away from what I assume is a contract for marriage up to me. Her hand falls from her face, revealing the barest hint of a smile. When Oliver was fake engaged to Amelia and the shit hit the fan with them, he came here to tell my mother that the engagement was fake, but their love was real.

My mother already knew all about it.

I've said it before, my mother is cunning.

She also doesn't play by the rules. Especially when it comes to her children. Or their love lives.

"Did you know who she was?" I repeat, unblinking. "That Bianca is Bunny."

She rises from the couch and stands before me, so perfect and lovely, even when she says, "You don't smile a lot."

A bemused, humorless chuckle flees my chest. "What?"

"You don't, Kaplan. Unless you're with your siblings. But otherwise, no. And it isn't because you're like Landon and had your light stolen from you. You've just always been cautious with yours. Wary of people and their intentions with you. Slow to trust or show people outside of your family who you truly are. That's my fault. Your father's too, as we ingrained that in you from birth. And though I wish I could say I regret that side of you, I don't. You're the heir of both the Abbot and Fritz names and we understand all too well what that comes with. The lengths people go to for a piece of it. Your father and I had an arranged marriage because of it."

"Mom, I—"

She holds up her hand, cutting me off. "Yes, I knew who she was. Not at first though. I saw your car pull up in front of the hotel that morning, and I decided to wait for you, only I noticed someone in the passenger side. I watched as she leaned over and gave you a kiss on the cheek, only to fly out of the car and into the hotel. You smiled, Kaplan. She kissed your cheek, and you smiled, watching her run inside. You had this look about you. One I had never seen before. I had no idea what was going on. I mean, the woman was wearing a wedding dress with makeup all down her face, but there was something about her, so I followed her into the ladies' room and started talking to her."

"Did you know it was her then? Bunny? Forest's little sister?"

"I met her when I came for Forest's funeral. I doubt she remembers. The girl was broken, understandably so. She looks very different now than she did then and at first, I didn't recognize her. When she told me her name and a bit of her backstory, something started clicking into place, and then when she mentioned your name, saying her brother had known you, I knew then it was her."

"And you didn't think to tell me? Mention that the girl you saw flee my car was Bunny Parker?"

"You didn't mention her to me either, so I assumed, for whatever reason, you wanted to keep her a secret from me. Honestly, I don't know why I held my tongue about it that morning. Maybe I wanted her to be a surprise if she took that position. Maybe it was instinct."

"Instinct? For what?"

That smirk again. The one I've perfected over the years, I'm staring at now on my mother. Taking my hand, she guides me to sit. I do and she sits back beside my father, who takes her hand, giving her an encouraging nod.

"Once I discovered who she was, at first, I assumed you must have as well. But then Monday morning, when you saw her in the office, I realized you didn't know. You were adamant on firing the girl once you saw her, whereas when we spoke about it in the restaurant, you were willing to let me hire someone for the position without asking a whole lot of questions. That right there told me everything I needed to know. The girl lit a spark in you in a way no one else ever has. I assumed either she'd tell you who she was, or you'd figure it out eventually. I also knew once you learned who she was, there would be no going back for you if it wasn't already too late for that."

My hands dive into my hair, my elbows pressing into my knees as I stare down at the floor, shaking my head. "I don't understand."

She laughs. "Yes, you do, my darling boy. You're already very much in love with her and my guess is you have been for some time."

"But, if you were planning on pushing Millie down my throat—" I cut myself off, leaning back in my chair and grabbing my drink off the coffee table as realization (once again) kicks my ass. "You never intended for me to marry Millie or get into an arranged marriage. Did you?"

My mother and father exchange looks. "Well. Not fully."

"Elaborate on that," I grunt to my father.

"We were worried about what your life would be like after you accepted the position as CEO. And the thought of an arranged marriage when you were so against falling in love didn't seem like a bad way to go. The Van Der Heusen family has been in contact with ours over a possible arrangement for years," he explains. "We had consistently claimed that you were a man of your own course who did not want a wife and it was not something we would attempt to force."

My mother laughs. "That sounds so old-fashioned when you say it that way."

"My love, so is this archaic notion of wealth must breed wealth and power must only stay among the few. True power, in my opinion, lives in the people who overcome adversity and grow to challenge. Who stare evil and easy outs in the eye and flip them off. They are the ones I want to see ruling our world. Not some pompous old bloat who was handed a Harvard degree because their daddy is an alumnus and gave millions in endowments. Certainly not people who have the world at their fingertips and still whine and complain about how unjust and unfair it all is for them."

"Now you know why the foundation is the passion of my life," my mother retorts.

"But not the love of your life. I still hold that title."

"Forever."

"We don't do that," I argue, bringing them back to the discussion at hand. B reminded me of that on the boat. We work our asses off. We spend hours of our days, weeks, months, and years toiling in the hospital with the sole purpose of helping others. Saving lives. We sacrifice and we *care*. All of us do. No exception. Our wealth and name and power have no affiliation with that decision other than medicine is our passion. Yes, we have money, but our money is not who we are.

And it never will be.

"No," my father agrees, rubbing his brow. "But we're different in that. As you learned this week."

"And that is why I knew I could love you always," my mother says to him. "I never wanted to be my parents. Hateful and money driven while being outwardly charitable."

They peck on the lips, and I swear, in my whole life, I've only seen that like ten times. They love each other, but now it seems they're learning that love is beautiful. Not contemptuous or something to be shadowed or scorned.

"Ugh," I bellow. "Okay. I get it. You love each other. Stop making out and help me clean this crap up."

"Naturally," my father chides sardonically. "Because we haven't had to watch all your lovers in the news at least a dozen times over?" Another laugh. "Once you took over the foundation, the Van Der Heusens started pressing even harder."

"And you went along with it?" I counter.

My mother shrugs. "Not exactly. I had us meet for lunch to see if there was any chemistry. No harm in that, I figured. You and Millie tolerated each other well enough as children, and I figured if there was something between you two as adults, all the better. There wasn't. You didn't smile at her once. You could hardly stand to sit through lunch and talk to her. Then I saw you and Bianca exchange glances and texts through the window of the foundation when we returned to the building, and I knew I was right about her. Honestly, I only attempted with Millie because we were concerned about what would come your way once you took over and we weren't wrong. We did assume marrying Millie would make your life easier."

"But you were hoping things would develop between Bianca and me first," I surmise.

A smile crosses her face as she leans her head on my father's shoulder. Since her latest scare over Thanksgiving, they've been much more physically affectionate with each other than they were when we were children. "Yes. That was our hope. We never wanted an arranged marriage for you, Kaplan. We wanted you to find love, but you were so antagonistic to it. I knew you'd never get there without the right sort of..."

"Interference," I finish for her.

"That's one word for it." My father laughs, kissing my mother's cheek. "We never said anything to the Van Der Heusens about any sort of arrangement. They took that initial lunch as a yes to their requests and ran wild with it, despite your mother telling Catherine that she didn't think it was the right match for you."

I take a sip of my bourbon and let all of this marinate in my brain. I should have known all along the reason my mother hired Bianca was for me. I mean, yes, she's got the degrees, but she had no experience.

"I'm crazy about Bianca. I love her. She's everything. Regardless of that, I wouldn't have married Millie." I point at the fucking contract sitting like a loaded weapon on the table.

"I received this contract last night," my father says. "Before they made the announcement of the engagement. It comes with a dowry of five million dollars, plus a trust fund from her grandparents for another five."

"What?" I choke. "A dowry? Is that a joke? Do we suddenly live back in the eighteen hundreds?"

"I hadn't heard of something like that either. Typically these contracts are more about preserving wealth on each side in the event of any issues between the couple. So I had Fairchild look into it."

"And?"

"And we're going to make a statement tonight through our PR people that you have no relationship with Millie Van Der Heusen and that any claims of an engagement or marriage or relationship are just. Claims. All false."

I cross my legs at the knee and level my father with a look. "What am I missing?"

"Senator Van Der Heusen is going to be charged with the sexual harassment and assault of two of his former interns. The Van Der Heusens are in the process of trying to pay them off to keep their silence, but they're hoping Millie being engaged to you—"

"Would take the spotlight off that," I finish for him. "Jesus. These fucking people."

"I won't even argue your language," my mother pipes in, setting her glass down on the table. "They are something else. So with your permission, we'd like to make that statement as soon as possible prior to any of that breaking."

"Yes. Go for it. The sooner, the better. If you want, I'll make the statement myself."

"If that's what you'd like, you're welcome to it," my dad agrees. "But we have people who can do it for you if you wish not to."

"I'll do it. I'll be ever the Abbot-Fritz," I tell my mother when she throws me a wary eyebrow. "I promise. But I can't let that stand."

"Well," she says, lifting her glass and taking a sip. "Now that all that ugliness is settled, I'm assuming you were away with Bianca this weekend?"

"Yes."

"And when do I get to meet her as yours?"

I tumble forward, finishing off my drink as I go. "You're honestly fine with me being with her? I know she has money, but please tell me—"

"Kaplan, I don't give a damn about her money," she cuts in and my eyes go round at her use of the word damn. Octavia Abbot-Fritz doesn't swear even in the minor sense. "I've never been worried about money. I've been worried about you. About your happiness and your life. If you tell me she's the woman you want to be with and she's right for you, then I think you already know how your father and I feel about it."

I blow out a breath. Then another. "But you said—"

"Of course I said all that. And to a certain extent, that would have been nice. But ultimately, all we ever wanted was for you to find the one who is right for *you*. Not us. Honestly, Kaplan, after all your brothers and sister have been through, I was sure you would have picked up on all of that."

I shake my head, a smile I can't contain on my lips. "Mom, you're seriously fucking crafty. Like scary crafty. You could have just told me."

"No, darling. I couldn't have. As a mother of six, I learned very early on that if I told you I wanted you to do something, you always went and did the opposite. A little reverse psychology and subterfuge have been my best parenting weapons to date."

Jesus.

I laugh because at this point, there is nothing else to do. Wait till I tell B. She'll die. "Can I bring her for dinner this week?" I ask.

"That would be lovely." My parents stand and I do the same. "Now, let's go clear your name."

32

If Kaplan Fritz thought I was going to be waiting at home for him to sort out his crazy love life, he had another thing coming. I'm far too itchy and jumpy to sit still, so I came out here to my studio so I could work. I need to work. I need to occupy my mind with something other than what's going on.

When we got off the plane, and I turned my phone back on, it was loaded with texts from Charlie and Greta. It was a lot of, oh, we knew it when we saw them together on the street, and wow, they make such a beautiful couple.

Barf.

I didn't contribute much.

I'm feeling a bit sour and it's not Kaplan's fault necessarily. It's that he can go and say whatever he wants, but the world—and his parents —want him with someone like Millie. Not someone like me. And I have a feeling it's going to get ugly before it gets better.

He says he's in this with me, and I have to have faith in that. I have no reason to doubt him and that's what I'm clinging to. So until then, it's fire and metal and water. It's listening to some loud kick-ass, girl-empowering music. It's shaking my ass while I pour the melted liquid gold into the ring cast I made. I'm so excited about this piece. I have to find the right stone for it, but I wanted to recreate the Horcrux ring from Harry Potter. The one with that cool stone and antique-looking gold, but I'm going to add my own flair and style to it.

Just as I'm done pouring the gold, my phone chimes with a text.

Kaplan: I've got a surprise for you.

That's all it says, only for another text to come in, but this one is a link to a news network. Setting everything down and taking off my gloves and goggles, I find a stool and sit down. With a tremulous hand and a nervous heart, I tap my screen that had gone dark, unlock it, and click on the link in the text.

Immediately it takes me to the website of the news network, but it feeds directly to a recording. I hit play and watch the screen and it brings up the evening news broadcast with two broadcasters talking.

"Reports of the engagement between Dr. Kaplan Abbot-Fritz and Millie Van Der Heusen broke early this morning and quickly took social media by storm."

"That's right, Bill, but in a shocking new development, news networks across the Boston area as well as several national entertainment agencies received a prerecorded interview between Kaplan Fritz and a local anchor from our station. We have the entire video for you tonight. Take a look."

The screen changes to what appears like a formal living room of sorts where Kaplan is sitting in a chair with a man sitting across from him. The anchor starts first.

"Good evening, I'm Peter White. For years now, Boston has been obsessed with their favorite Abbot-Fritz family. They're followed like the British Royal family. Their love lives the stuff of front-page news and viral Twitter posts. This past year especially has given Bostonians and the world enough Fritz love-life gossip to write a romance book series. But I'm here tonight with Dr. Kaplan Abbot-Fritz, whose engagement to Millie Van Der Heusen was just announced this morning. Thank you for taking the time to meet with me, Dr. Fritz."

The camera changes over to Kaplan. "It's my pleasure. I'm delighted to be here speaking with you about this."

"Excellent. So let's get down to it. You had said you wanted to make a public statement. Not exactly something you're known for in your family."

Kaplan chuckles, leaning back in his chair and crossing his legs. "No. Discussing my personal life in public is not something I've ever been comfortable with, but given what happened this morning, my family and I felt it was essential to set the record straight."

"Then, by all means, the floor is yours."

"Thank you. While away on a brief weekend trip, it came to my attention that there were reports of an engagement between me and Millie Van Der Heusen. I'm here tonight to tell you those reports are completely false."

"False?" the anchor repeats, his voice bathed in amazement as he jerks forward on his chair.

"That's correct. Millie Van Der Heusen and I are not engaged. We're not involved in any way. I've been acquainted with Millie for most of my life as our mothers were friends, but that is the extent of things. There is no relationship between us. There is no engagement. And there never will be."

"But what about the pictures of the two of you that were taken?"

"They were nothing. Harmless and completely innocent. I met Millie in the restaurant, where we briefly caught up before I had to return to the hospital. Those photographs were taken as I was walking her to her car in the rain since she didn't have an umbrella. Millie is a terrific person, and I wish her the best, but she and I are acquaintances and nothing more."

The reporter leans back in his chair, eyes wide, utterly flabbergasted. "I have to admit, I'm stunned by this as I'm sure the rest of our viewers and the world will be. The reports of the engagement came directly from her family this very morning. They claimed the two of you were madly in love."

Kaplan shrugs but appears as cool and unruffled as one can be. "I'm not sure what to say about that other than all of that is completely false. I am *not* in love with Millie Van Der Heusen, and we are *not* engaged. Myself, I learned of the claims the way everyone else did. By watching it on television this morning. The truth is, I have been dating an incredible woman for a while now and out of love and respect for her, I could not allow false claims about me and Millie to perpetuate."

The reporter picks up on this juicy bit, shifting so he's closer to Kaplan once more, ready to pounce. My heart starts to pound. "So you're telling us you're romantically involved with someone else? Someone who is not Millie Van Der Heusen."

Kaplan smirks into the camera. "That is correct. This woman and I briefly knew each other years ago and have recently reconnected. In fact, we were together this morning when we heard the news of the engagement."

"That must have come as quite a shock to you both."

He chuckles humorlessly, running a hand through his hair. "It did indeed."

"And is this relationship serious?"

"Yes. Bianca and I are extremely happy together and very much in love."

The phone slips from my hand, landing hard on the concrete and shutting off the rest of the interview. Holy crapballs. He said my name. On the news. On national freaking news, Kaplan Fritz announced that he and I are in a relationship and that we're in love.

My phone starts vibrating on the ground, the screen lighting up with notification after notification. I can only imagine what all of that is. What was a secret relationship with a famous billionaire just went prime time. Yikes. The press will be all over us. All over me. And while the idea of that makes me want to throw myself into the forge, Kaplan is worth it.

Eventually they'll grow bored and move on to the next thing.

Bending down to retrieve my phone, someone is already there, beating me to it.

"Hey," he says, his green eyes all over me.

I stagger off the stool. "Have you been here the whole time?"

"Does it make me weird or a creeper if I say yes?"

"Did you watch me watch you?"

A slow nod and now my face is flaming hotter than the fire two feet from me. "Did I freak out? Gasp? What?" I don't even remember how I reacted.

"You stared at your phone like it was about to give you a juicy piece of celebrity gossip and you didn't like what was said."

Is he crazy? How could I not like what was said?

Without hesitation, I throw my arms around his neck and jump up onto him so he has to catch me. "I love what was said." My lips land on his in a bruising kiss. "I love everything you said. I can't believe you did that. Told them about me like that."

"B, you're mine. And I want the world to know it so that there's no more confusion."

God, this man. This man who is just so absolutely perfect for me.

"Tomorrow is going to be one nutty day," I murmur against his lips.

"I know. We'll go into the hospital together along with Axl and Slash and then on Tuesday, I'll bring you into the foundation because I'm your boss, and well, that's probably a problem."

"Gee, why didn't I think of that sooner?"

He pinches my butt and sets me down. "I'm not worried about it. I'll speak with HR and get it sorted out, but we're not breaking any laws and I haven't shown you a lot of favoritism."

"You did fire Jenny."

"Kelly had it coming from the second I stepped foot in that office."

I snicker at how he refuses to call her Jenny.

"Are you done here? Can we go home?"

"I don't have any of my stuff."

A kiss to my lips. Hands in my hair. "We'll get it in the morning. But I'm thinking you should start keeping some things at my place. A toothbrush. A hairbrush for your long, long hair. Clothes. Shoes."

"You want me to keep a bag of stuff at your house?"

He smiles against my lips. "Or all of your stuff. I'm sure I could manage to make room in my closet for your shoe collection."

"Doubtful, but I'm not moving in with you. I just moved into my place."

"Which I already know is a six-month rental."

I gasp into him only for his mouth to start working its way down my neck in a very distracting way that makes it nearly impossible for me to hold on to my ire. "You looked into my rental?"

"Absolutely," he says unrepentantly, licking along my pulse point. "So for now, we'll start with that bag and we can keep adding to it."

"Kaplan, we haven't been doing this very long. Not even a month since we started sleeping together."

He pulls back, his forehead dropping to mine. "Worried we won't last? That we'll burn out?"

"Maybe a little?" I laugh. "I haven't had the best luck with love or relationships."

"That's because it wasn't right. As a man who is much older than you, I can tell you with assurance, you're stuck with me. Quite possibly for life." He presses me against him. "Bianca, I've waited my whole life for you. No way am I letting you go now. Come on. I have a surprise for you at home."

"Another surprise?"

"Yep. Only I'm not sure how much you'll love this one."

A half an hour later, we walk through the back door of his place, and I feel ambushed. Again. Only this is in a really great way. Kaplan stands behind me, his mouth by my ear, before anyone realizes we're standing here.

"They didn't want to wait to meet you, though I held my parents off until dinner some night this week."

"They wanted to meet me?" I don't know why I'm so affected by this, but I am. I'm practically choked up.

"They're here on a Sunday night, aren't they?" Kaplan takes my hand and leads me into the kitchen and great room area of his house. "Remember what I said," he yells just as a stunning woman with black hair and blue-green eyes squeals in excitement.

She rolls her eyes at him before cutting her gaze to me. "Are you a hugger?"

"I'm a huge hugger."

"See. Release Bianca, Kaplan Fritz. She is safe with us," she says in a booming, theatrical voice. "I'm Raven, Luca's much better half.

You've met him already, so I'm sure you'll agree." She points to a guy wearing a blue sweater and jeans with dark hair and green eyes like Kaplan's.

"We've all been rooting for you since day one he mentioned you," a man who I already know to be Oliver Fritz tells me. "And for Kaplan to mention a woman at all..." he trails off, doing a mind-blown gesture with his hands.

"Straight talk," a pretty blonde who I know is their sister Rina agrees. "Counting. The. Seconds here."

"You'll never get rid of them now," a beautiful redhead tells me. I think she's engaged to Oliver.

"But you won't want to either," another blonde informs me. This is obviously Grace and the man beside her with the dark eyes and dark hair holding the tiny baby has to be Carter.

"It's true," a woman with slightly darker blonde hair, hazel eyes, and a Southern twang informs me. "I'm the newest to this crew and you can't help but love them. Even when they're broody and intolerable." She winks at me and the guy who is obviously Landon, Luca's identical twin, just stands there, half shrugging as if to say, yeah. Not much of a talker, from what Kaplan has told me about him.

"Well, now that I know you're a hugger, I get first dibs," Luca announces and launches himself across the room, racing Raven, who gets in on it a second too late. A laugh bursts from my chest as he reaches me first and steals me from Kaplan's grip. He lifts me in the air, giving me a squeeze. "Glad to see you managed to thaw old baby face's ugly, untouchable heart. Incidentally, I won the pool because of it, so thanks for that."

"What was the pool?" I ask when he sets me down.

"That Kap would drop the L-word in under a month after you two started doing the deed. Ten grand, pretty lady. High-fives to that."

"Ten grand?" I choke on my saliva. And tongue. It's a wonder I'm able to breathe.

Luca gives me a devilish grin and wow. Who the hell bets ten grand on something like that other than billionaires?

"My turn." Raven hip checks Luca out of the way and then she's all over me, hugging me fiercely like we've known each other forever. "Kaplan's like my best friend and older brother rolled into one so I'm going to love you just as hard as I love him, but if you fuck with him, I'll break all your bones the same way."

I laugh because how can you not? "Noted. Promise you won't have to break anything."

"Good stuff."

Then the rest of them descend. I meet everyone. Including Stella and Layla and Baby Owen. All are absolutely adorable. Everyone is hugging me and smiling and telling me they're so happy I'm with him. I can't help but be overwhelmed. In the best possible way. Having Kaplan's family like and accept me without question or judgment is everything my heart needed.

They don't linger, the hour already late and after the last hug and promise of dinners and drinks and girl shopping trips—I can already tell Rina and I will be besties with that—Kaplan locks everything up, sets the alarm, and then it's just us. Showering together. Falling into bed. Making love. Kissing. Talking. Holding. Laughing. Touching.

Swearing a love to each other that will never end.

A love that knows no bounds or limits.

A perfect love that can only exist between two imperfect souls.

EPILOGUE

Bianca

"I might throw up. Like for real this time."

"Amelia, you've said that like ten times since you woke up this morning," Layla chirps, adjusting the crimson sash on her black dress.

"I know, but I'm totally serious now. I think it's food poisoning. The sushi from the rehearsal dinner, perhaps?"

"She does look a little green," Elle whispers to me out of the corner of her mouth as we stare at Amelia in the three-way mirror in all her wedding dress gorgeousness. And wow, let's just talk about gorgeous. Red hair and sleek white gown. I might be having some wedding dress jealousy as I remember the monstrosity my mother forced me into. This is *nothing* like that.

"Totally agree," I murmur back, so my voice doesn't carry. "Could it be the sushi? I had three pieces."

"It's not the sushi," Raven promises. "I had six pieces, and I'm fine. This is just Amelia, and if Amelia isn't overthinking or freaking out about something, then Amelia isn't breathing."

Good point. Hard to argue about that because, well, that is Amelia.

"How's Oliver? Does anyone know?" Rina asks, her eyes on her phone as she types into what is likely her sibling chat.

"Grace texted a few minutes ago to say Oliver is Oliver," Elle jumps in. "Calm, excited, adorable."

"So how do we get Amelia on the same page? The ceremony starts in like…"—Rina glances down at her diamond Tiffany watch—"twenty minutes. Shots? I could go grab a bottle of something. Tequila, I'm thinking. That's what got me down the aisle."

All of us exchange nervous glances. Especially as Amelia doubles over, splinting her stomach.

"Tequila," Raven and I agree.

"So, while you're already freaking out, I might have something to tell you."

"What?" Amelia groans at her younger sister, Layla, cutting her a sharp gaze that clearly says she's not in the mood.

"I sucked my first penis last night."

And that's it. Because all of us practically collapse with loud gasps and horrified expressions.

"Holy shit!" Rina sputters. "Tequila! I'm going to find the biggest bottle of tequila I can." And then she races out of the room like her hair is on fire and she's seeking water.

Except Layla is fifteen and I think I was similar in age the first time I did that deed. But still, it's different because well, it just is.

"You did not," Amelia snaps, righting her body and spinning on her tall, willowy sister who has at least five inches on her. "Who? Who was the little prick? I'll kill him."

Layla twirls a piece of her long, expertly curled hair with an impish grin that only riles her sister up more. "I wouldn't call his prick little."

Another round of gasps, and it's like watching live-action soap operas.

"Layla Jean Atkins, you tell me who put his penis in your mouth right this instant." She slams her heeled foot down, the furious thud heard around the room even though it is hitting the Oriental rug.

Layla folds her arms defiantly, tapping her strappy heeled foot.

"And what if I don't?"

"Layla, I cannot do this with you now. We have not had the BJ convo. We've had the sex and the masturbation and the oh my God, why didn't I have the BJ convo with you? I'm the worst guardian big sister in the history of guardian big sisters. Are you okay? Were you happy? Do you like the guy? Did he reciprocate? Who the fuck is he?! If you don't tell me, Oliver will find out and kill him. Like for real, kill him. He's a Fritz. He'll make it look like an accident, but the boy will be dead."

Layla starts laughing, doing some crazy arm-and-hip-swinging dance. "Told ya you weren't going to barf."

"Layla!"

"Amelia, chill yourself before you pop a bead or a stitch. I just had to get you out of your head for a second."

Oh boy. The ladies and I exchange looks.

"By telling me you gave a boy a blow job?"

"Well, can't help a girl if she's curious about it now, can you? You're the one who lets me read romances."

"Tequila!" Rina pants as she shoots through the door, a clear bottle held victoriously up in her hand. "I have tequila. Here." She shoves it at Amelia and uncorks it for her. Amelia wastes no time taking a hearty sip.

"You're telling me you've been reading romance books with BJs in them? That is so not approved." She takes another swig from the bottle and then hands it back to Rina as she continues to square off with Layla.

Rina starts drinking from the bottle too before rejoining us and handing it to me. I stare at it for a second and then shrug. When in Rome, and yeah, I think we all need it to get through this. The alcohol burns a warm path down my throat, and I cover my cough with my arm as I pass it on to Raven.

"That might be my bad," Raven whispers guiltily in my ear as she takes her own large gulp. "I didn't realize the last book I gifted her had that scene. But in my defense, the freaking thing said young adult online."

"I've read some seriously steamy books that call themselves young adult," Elle tells her. "Young adult simply means age nowadays. Not necessarily sexual content."

"Fuck," Raven hisses, snatching the bottle back from Rina and tossing back another shot. "Well, at least she didn't actually do the deed, right? That's something."

"She didn't?" Rina asks since she was out of the room for that revelation. "Thank God. Otherwise my brothers would have gone teenage boy hunting at the reception."

"Alright. That's it," I yell into the room, taking a step forward because someone has to get this party going before we head out into the garden of the Fritz Martha's Vineyard home. "Layla, no more BJ talk or unnecessarily raising your sister's blood pressure, though I will give you props for the initial... blow."

Everyone starts laughing, including Amelia, whose color is improving by the second.

"Amelia, you look stunning. So much better than I did as a bride my first go-around."

"Thank you. I just—"

"We know," all the ladies grouse. "You're nervous."

"Do you love Oliver?" Rina asks solemnly.

"More than anything in the world," Amelia replies instantly, turning back to the mirror and taking in each of our faces before returning to the dress.

"Do you want to be his wife?" Elle continues, rubbing at a spot on the side of her dress over her bump. She, Landon, and Stella just moved into their brand-new dream house, but Elle is a tiny little thing. A tiny little thing who is sporting a tiny little bump with two heartbeats inside it.

"Of course."

"Then vagina up, Aunt Amelia," Stella chimes in from the corner where she's been reading on her Kindle all this time. "Uncle Oliver loves you. You love him. I think sometimes you adults make love so much more complicated than it needs to be."

And no truer words have ever been spoken.

"Stella, you don't deal in men. Men are such drama."

"Layla, legit, I think it's us who are the drama. Or maybe you, in this instance, since I don't think I could ever tell Elle I went down on a chick to get her mind off marrying my dad."

"You better not." Elle covers her face with her hands. "God, Stella. How do I have that convo with you? I've never done that."

"Neither have I," Stella tells her. "Relax. We'll cross that vagina when we get to it. For now, Amelia, you've got twelve minutes and a slew of people waiting to watch you say 'I do' to Uncle Oliver. If you love him and he loves you, then I don't understand why you're nervous."

"Now you sound like me." Layla jumps over to her phone, picks it up, and starts playing "Confident" by Demi Lovato. And we all start getting into it. Singing along and rocking our rock star poses and drinking tequila straight from the bottle and by the time we leave the room, we're ready.

More importantly, Amelia is ready to marry Oliver.

Which she does. With a sobbing Grace by his side and a sobbing Layla by hers.

The ceremony is small. But the party is in full swing between the Fritz ballroom and the beach where there is a bonfire and s'mores and a separate band, this one more reggaeish. That's the spot where Kaplan and I find ourselves as the summer sun dips into the western sky and the stars start to come out, kissing the deep-blue sky.

We sailed his catamaran here, and I'd be foolish to believe the man doesn't have plans for us this week—since we both took it off— beyond the wedding and the island.

It's been a crazy several months, all things considered.

Kaplan went in and made an announcement to the entire office that we were together and that it wasn't planned or thought out, but that it was real and not going anywhere and that everyone needed to adjust to it. He vowed not to show me any favoritism. A point he's proven multiple times as we've fought over many foundation things.

The spring gala happened, and it was an absolute raging success for everyone. All told, we raked in close to a million dollars, by far their highest total even divided by three. We have one we're already planning for the fall, and I can't wait to see how this one does since we're mixing things up a bit by hosting it on the Fritz mega yacht.

But at this point, I'm practically running the foundation and it feels good. Other than some minor CEO oversight, Kaplan has his trust placed in me, knowing how much this foundation means to my heart and soul. His mother and I have bonded over it several times, and on occasion, I call her for backup.

The media and the world had a slightly harder time adjusting to our relationship.

They followed us around relentlessly for weeks. Not to mention a few not-so-nice things were posted. Some people thought it was a lie. A publicity stunt. Women threw themselves at him harder than ever, thinking they'd be the ones to lure him away, because how could a man like Kaplan Fritz ever love a girl like me? But once Senator Van Der Heusen was charged with sexual harassment and assault, the world moved on to that. Then it was discovered that Millie had a secret love affair with her mother's assistant and all hell broke loose for that family.

"All my siblings are getting engaged, or married, or having kids," Kaplan murmurs in my ear as we slow dance, our bare feet playing with the sand.

My head falls to his shoulder. "That's what people do when they get to a certain age."

Luca is proposing to Raven tonight in the garden. She has no clue. Evidently, this is where they first got together. Where they fell in love. Even if it ended in heartbreak the first time. And now that Elle is pregnant, I'm guessing she and Landon won't be far off. I think he was planning on doing that anyway. Grace and Carter got married shortly after Owen was born in a tiny ceremony that was only family. Kaplan was the best man.

We're the last ones.

But I don't think either of us is in any particular rush to change that.

"Is that what you want?" he croons, whispering into my ear. "To get married and have babies?"

Or maybe I'm wrong?

Pulling back, I play with some of the hair tickling the top of his collar, trying to read his expression. He's giving me nothing to work with. "Not this minute, no."

"I'm turning thirty-seven in September."

"Oh, I'm not saying it's a bad idea for you. You're old and should probably get on that. I'm saying for me, I'm not ready for kids yet."

He pinches my nipple through the chiffon of my dress until I squeal. I smack his hand away. "There are people here," I hiss, looking around and rubbing discreetly at my smarting nipple.

His lips layer with mine as he stares into my eyes. The warm ocean breeze whips across us, kicking up the fire and causing sparks to shoot up into the night sky. "No one is paying us any attention. So, you're saying not this minute, but what about finally agreeing to move in with me? Your lease is up next month."

"That I can do." Especially when I practically live with him already. Most of my clothes and shoes already have a home in the second master closet.

"So, if I gave you a pretty diamond, told you I loved you and asked you to be mine forever?"

I pause, tilting my head because this is the first time we've ever discussed anything like that. "I thought you never wanted to get married?"

"I didn't say I did. Just curious about your thoughts on it. Can't blame me for having them tonight." He's smiling the smile that makes my insides mush as he glances back up at the house where the main party is happening.

I think about this for a moment, staring into his emerald-green eyes. I have no real response that I can give him because I haven't allowed my mind to go in that direction. Though I'd be lying if I said the idea of being his forever didn't set off a fleet of drunk, giddy butterflies in my stomach.

"I don't know if I'm a diamond kind of girl." Been there once already and that didn't go so well.

"Then it's a really good thing I didn't get you one."

Only now, he's lowering himself onto one knee, staring up into my eyes like I'm his reason for breathing and existing. Like without me, he'd perish, and his world would end. The amount of love shining up at me from this man makes my breath catch and tears sting my eyes.

"What are you doing?"

"Tying my shoes."

I laugh, the first tear hitting my cheek. "You're barefoot."

"Oh right. So maybe I'm showing you something instead."

And then he's opening up a jewelry box that has... "My ring!" I gasp, and immediately more tears start falling. "I sold that. How did you—"

"You sold it to me. You just didn't know it."

My hands cover my mouth as my body shakes uncontrollably.

I started selling some of my jewelry a few months ago and this was the one piece I was most reluctant to let go of. I loved it so much. But I had no practical reason to keep a gold ring with a huge floating emerald.

He bought it. For me. I can't believe he did that.

He reaches for my hand, prying one of them from my trembling lips. "Bianca Bunny Barlow, I love you. From the moment you walked back into my life, everything has changed in the best imaginable way. My mother likes to tell me I'm smiling now, but it's more than that. I'm happy. You make me so fucking happy. And that's all I want to do for you. Make you happy forever. I was going to do this tonight on the boat but looking at how beautiful you are by the fire... I couldn't wait another second. Will you marry me? Be my wife? My partner? The mate to my soul?"

"Yes," I cry, nodding vigorously. "Yes. I can't believe you. Of course, I'll marry you."

A breathtaking smile lights up his face and he stands, sliding the ring, *my* ring on my finger. In my next breath, he's lifting me in the air, kissing me like it's what he was put on this earth to do. I cling to him, wrapping my legs around his waist and kissing him back with everything I have.

The way I'll kiss him forever.

With all the wild love and passion and happiness I have swirling through me every time I look or think about him. Every time I'm near him. This man. This layered, complicated, sweet, incredible man owns my heart just as I own his.

"You really want this? To get married?" I breathe against his lips. "No more Dr. Untouchable who swore himself to a life of being alone?"

"Only with you, B. Being alone is miserable without you. It's dark and vacuous. You brought color and texture and light into my life. You're the only one. Ever. It's always only been you. I even asked your stepfathers and mother for permission."

"You did? You asked them if you could marry me?"

"They said no, but I decided to say fuck it and do it anyway."

I laugh as he twirls us around in a dizzying circle.

"They said yes," he whispers into me, holding me impossibly close. "But even if they had said no, I would have begged you anyway. You are my heart. You are my ocean. You fill my soul."

THE END.

THANK you SO much for reading the Doctor Untouchable. I hope you loved Kaplan and Bianca as much as I do. If you're new to the Fritz family or to me, thank you for taking a chance on me and this book and keep reading to the end for the first chapter of Doctor Scandalous, the first book in the Boston's Billionaire Bachelors series.

*If you've read this whole series and are sad to see them go, I can promise you'll see more of them in the next series! Speaking of... Coming soon! A brand-new five book series about best friends whose lives were torn apart by tragedy and the irresistible women they fall for.

END OF BOOK NOTE

Hello lovely readers! Anyone else in tears right now? Just me? I can't believe this series is done. I need to thank you. This series, these amazing doctors, changed my life. I cannot tell you what your continued support of not only me, but these characters means. I am floored and honored and so very grateful!!

I loved writing this book. After Luca's book, I honestly needed something like Kaplan's. It was so much fun to write and I just fell so hard for both Bianca and Kaplan. Kaplan has a heart unlike others I've written and I think he might have climbed into the lead as my favorite book boyfriend ever. For now at least. But for real, I could have written him forever.

Bianca to me was a breath of fresh air. She's strong and confident, but like all of us, struggles with parts of herself that others might not view as beautiful or perfect. Learning to love yourself for who you are is not an easy battle. It's fucking impossible some days. Maybe that's why I admire her so much. She fought and didn't allow others opinions of her to derail who she knew she was. If that makes sense, lol.

Though this is the end of the series, the Fritz boys and possibly Rina will pop up in my next series that will release in early 2023 and I will continue to write in that Boston world for it. As the song says, Boston you're my home.

I want to thank my incredible betas, Danielle, Patricia, and Kelly for their efforts with this book. I'd be lost without them! That goes same for my lovely editors Ellie and Emily. Rock stars, all of you.

I also need to thank for my family. My husband and three beautiful girls. I'd be nothing without their continued love and support and hugs and laughter. They give each day meaning and fill my heart and soul with more joy than I ever imagined possible.

So this is it. The end, but also the beginning. I promise you'll love my next crew. They're amazing and I've already started working on them.

Much love!!!

XO,

Julie (J. Saman)

ALSO BY J. SAMAN

Wild Love Series:

Reckless to Love You

Love to Hate Her

Crazy to Love You

Love to Tempt You

Promise to Love You

The Edge Series:

The Edge of Temptation

The Edge of Forever

The Edge of Reason

The Edge of Chaos

Boston's Billionaire Bachelors:

Doctor Scandalous

Doctor Mistake

Doctor Heartless

Doctor Playboy

Doctor Untouchable

Start Again Series:

Start Again

Start Over

Start With Me

Las Vegas Sin Series:

Touching Sin

Catching Sin

Darkest Sin

Standalones:

Just One Kiss

Love Rewritten

Beautiful Potential

Forward - FREE

DOCTOR SCANDALOUS

OLIVER

I'm walking toward the gates of hell. And they charge for admission.

"Oh, Oliver..." Christa Foreman greets me with a slow once-over, her pastel-pink lips curling up into an impish grin. She's aptly named, because our senior class president was no joke when it came to strong-arming and manipulating her fellow classmates into getting what she wanted. "It's so good to see you. Wow. I mean, I see your pictures in magazines and on social media every now and then because I follow you, but you're way better looking in person than I remember from high school."

"Um. Thank you?" It comes out as a question, my head tilting in her direction.

"Sure. No problem." She licks her lips, her long, fake eyelashes batting faster than a butterfly's wings at me. "Are you here alone tonight?" She giggles as a flush creeps up her cheeks. She's married. Can we just say that? "I'm only asking because I need to know how much to charge you. I got stuck collecting money until the event coordinator can get her shit together." She huffs out a flustered breath, rolling her eyes derisively. "Anyway, it's a hundred per person. Should I put you down for one or two?"

And this is where I hesitate. Not over the money. The money is not an issue.

"Just give me a second."

Christa stares longingly at me, licking her lips. "Sure. I'll give you all night."

"Right." Because I have no idea what else to say to that. I don't remember Christa being so overtly interested in me when we were in high school. Then again, that was ten years ago, and I was most definitely taken. Which is both the main reason I don't want to be here and the main reason I came. But now I'm starting to reconsider everything.

I have nothing to prove by being here.

Not to *her*, her douchebag husband—my former friend—or anyone else.

I should just go. Maybe meet up with Carter, who I already know is going to our favorite bar, and get lost in a night of fun. Nothing about this hellhole will be fun. And in truth, I could really use a drink. A quiet one. It's been a shitful week. Too many patients. Not enough time. Oh, and finding out that your mom's cancer is back is always a winner.

I slip my phone from my pocket and shoot off a text to my best friend, Grace.

Me: Sorry, babe. Not gonna be able to make it.

The message bubble instantly dances along my screen. **Grace: It's not a choice, honey pie. Everyone is already asking when you're going to get here. Everyone.**

And instantly I'm tempted to ask if *she's* asking. In fact, my thumbs, who seem to have a mind of their own, start to type that very question until I tamp them down and rein them under control. Of course, she's asking. That's what she does. She continues to hunt me down with terrorist-level determination, even all these years later.

She's likely giddy at the prospect of rubbing her picture-perfect life in my face without even caring that she's the last person on the planet I want to see tonight or any other night. Hence why now is the perfect time to leave.

Me: Don't care.

Grace: Yes, you do. Come on. I know you're already dressed for tonight. Carter sent me a text.

Carter. My traitorous brother.

Grace: Just come inside the hotel. Come up to the reunion. Have a drink with me. See the people you haven't seen since high school who will fall at your feet the way they did back in the day. Oh wait, they still do.

Me: You're doing a shitty job of selling it there, sweetums.

Grace: Everyone will think you're a pussy if you don't come.

Me: Nice gauntlet drop.

Grace: I thought so. Now get your ass over here!

I growl out a slew of curses under my breath, still seriously contemplating fleeing for the sake of my sanity, when I catch sight of a short, curvy redhead in a tight, backless black dress, higher than high heels, and fuck-me red lips that match her hair walking up to Christa. She's as late as I am, and before I know what I'm doing, a smile cracks clear across my face.

I know her instantly.

Even if it's been ten years since I've seen her. A guy never forgets the girl who gave him his first boner. A first-ever boner in class, I might add. We were twelve and she bent over to retrieve her fallen pencil when a flash of her training bra caught my eye. Instant erection.

I was pretty smitten after that moment, as you might imagine.

"Amelia," Christa greets her, her face now lacking any of the warmth it had when she was talking to me. "I had no idea you were coming."

What the fuck? You'd think in the ten years since we graduated from our annoyingly prestigious prep school that the rich girls would get over the self-created, mean-girl bullshit they had with the scholarship kids.

Amelia turns redder than her hair, and she takes a small step back before straightening her frame and squaring her shoulders. "Well, I'm here. Graduated same year as you. I even received the invitation in the mail. Must have been an error on your part," she finishes sarcastically.

"Uh-huh. It's a hundred-dollar entrance fee," Christa snaps, taking far too much pleasure in announcing that sum as she purses her lips off to the side, giving Amelia a nasty-girl slow once-over.

"A hundred dollars?" Amelia asks, though it comes out in a deflated, breathy whisper.

"Yup. Sorry," Christa sneers with a sorry-not-sorry saccharine sweet voice. "No exceptions. Not even for the kids who were on scholarship."

And that's it. Before Christa can say anything else that will make me want to throttle her, I walk over to Amelia, wrapping my hand around her waist. "Sweetheart," I exclaim. "You made it. I was starting to get worried."

Amelia jolts in my arms, her breath catching high in her throat as she twists to face me. Then she looks up and up a bit more because she's about a foot shorter than I am even in her heels. Suddenly, two sparkling gray eyes blink rapidly at me, and my heart starts to pound in time with the flutter of her lashes, my mouth dry like I've been eating sand all night.

"I'm sorry," she says, confused, her parted lips hanging just a bit too open for us to be selling this. "I think you must—"

I lean in, my nose brushing against her silky red hair that smells like honeysuckle or something sweet and I breathe into her ear, "Just go with it."

She swallows audibly as I pull back, staring into her eyes and wondering how a color like that is even possible when she smiles and robs me of my breath. *Whoa.* That's unexpected.

"I didn't mean to worry you..." She trips up, biting into her lip like she's searching for a suitable term of endearment. Or maybe my name? I guess it is possible she has no idea who I am. We didn't exactly run in the same circles, and I just came up to her and wrapped my arm around her. "Oli," she finishes with, and I blow out the breath I didn't even realize I was holding.

"It's fine. I just didn't want to go in without the most beautiful woman in the world on my arm."

Amelia gives me that stunning smile again, this time with a blush staining her cheeks, and I marvel at how it makes her eyes glow to a smoky charcoal. Goddamn, she's fucking sexy.

"Wait," Christa interrupts. "You're with her?" She points at Amelia.

"I sure am," I declare without removing my eyes from Amelia's because those eyes, man. They're just too pretty not to stare at. "I'm a lucky bastard, right?"

"You're with him?" She turns that finger on me.

"So it seems," Amelia replies, her tone a bit bewildered, though there is a hint of amusement in there, too.

"But. You're. You. No. You're Oliver Fritz," Christa sputters incredulously. "And she's Amelia—" Her words cut off when I throw her my most menacing glare, already knowing the exact nasty nickname she's about to throw out. Why certain women feel the need to degrade and belittle other women, I'll never understand.

I slip two one-hundred-dollar bills from my wallet and toss them at Christa. "Have a good night," I say instead of what I'm really thinking. My fingers intertwine with Amelia's, and then I'm dragging her past Christa, down the long corridor with the paisley rug and gold walls, toward the ballroom.

I guess I'm going to my high school reunion after all.

The second we're out of sight of Christa, Amelia yanks her hand from mine, stopping in the middle of the hall and turning to stare up at me. "You remember me?" she asks and then shakes her head like that's not what she meant to say.

"Amelia Atkins. You were in most of my classes from the time we were in sixth grade or so, on."

"Right. What I meant to say is, thank you for stepping in back there, but it really wasn't necessary."

"Maybe not. I'm sure you can handle yourself with women like Christa. But it felt wrong to stand there and watch that go down, doing nothing. I can't stand women who feel the need to hurt others just to make themselves look and feel better."

She folds her arms over her chest, giving me a raised eyebrow. "And yet you dated a woman who did exactly that all through high school."

Touché. A bark of a laugh slips out my lungs. "Can't argue with that. Hell, I dated that same vicious woman through college too. Adolescent mistake. What can I say?"

Still, at the mention of that particular woman, an old flair hits me straight in the chest. My fingers find my pocket, toying with the large diamond solitaire set in a diamond and platinum band I stuck in there tonight. It's *the* ring. The one I nearly gave to said woman who was screwing around on me with my friend, Rob. A lesson in betrayal I've never forgotten. It's why on certain occasions, I carry it with me.

A reminder to never get too close again.

"Sorry," Amelia says, withering before my eyes. "That was insanely rude of me. I don't even know why I said that. Christa got my hackles all fired up, and I just took them out on you instead of her, like I should have. Damn, some women seriously suck, right?" I can't stop my chuckle, though I think she was being serious. She stares down at the rug, shifting her stance until she's leaning back against the wall opposite the closed doors where the reunion is taking place. "Look, I wish you hadn't paid for me. Money and I aren't exactly on speaking terms at the moment. It's going to take me a while to pay you back. But I *will* pay you back. I just don't have that kind of—"

My fingers latch on to her chin, tilting her head back up until our eyes meet. "I don't care about the money. And I don't want you to pay me back." She opens her mouth as if to argue with me, and I shake my head, cutting her off again. "I mean it."

She huffs out a breath. "Well, thank you. That's very generous. But if this is how this night is already starting off, I'm thinking maybe I should just go. Hell, I shouldn't even have come here in the first place. I don't know what I was thinking. My sister talked me into it, and I thought..." She shakes her head. "Never mind. It's stupid."

I prop my shoulder against the wall so I'm facing her, folding my arms while I stare at her because I can't seem to help myself. "Why is it stupid?"

"You really want to know?"

"I really want to know."

Those big eyes slay through me, slightly glassy with emotion. "Because no one in there wants me there. You heard Christa. I was fooling myself into thinking that I could waltz in here ten years later and everyone who treated me like garbage growing up would finally see me for me. That they'd finally realize we're all on an even playing field now that high school is over. It was going to be like putting all my old bully nightmares to rest once and for all. Only, nothing has changed. I'm still the girl wearing thrift store digs who couldn't even afford to pay the entrance fee."

Wow. That's...

"Can I tell you something?" I ask.

Her hands meet her hips. "You mean something to rival the way too personal verbal diarrhea I just spouted at a man I haven't seen in a decade?"

She's trying for brave and strong, and even sarcastic. But she's sad. I can see it in her eyes that bounce around my face, almost as if she's not sure she wants to know what I'm about to say. No one wants to be slammed back into their high school nightmare. She wanted to walk in there and make all those assholes eat their words.

I want that for her too.

I like Amelia. I always have. There was something about her that just got to me on a weird level I never quite understood. She was sweet and nerdy and quiet and reserved. So understatedly beautiful. Her hair was all wild with red curls. Her glasses a touch too big for her face. Her body small with her ample curves hidden beneath her ill-fitting prep school uniform.

And looking at her now, after hearing what Christa was saying to her...

In truth, I do remember people being that nasty. Though now I'm positive it was a lot worse than I knew about if Christa's reaction to her tonight is anything to go by. I only heard comments here and there that I didn't pay much attention to, nor did anything to stop. Even if I never directly contributed to it, by not stopping it, I was part of the problem.

That's on me. And it's not okay. I should have done more to protect her. I should have said something.

"Something like that. You told me yours. Now I'll tell you mine."

"Alright."

I step into her, bending down like I'm about to tell her a secret when really, I just want to be closer to her. Smell her shampoo that makes my cock jump in my slacks. Feel the heat of her body as she starts to blush from my proximity.

"I don't want to be here either. I got talked into it by my friend, Grace, and now here I am."

Her eyebrows knit together. "Why wouldn't you want to be here? You're a doctor. You were the most popular guy in our class. Captain of the football team. Everyone loved you. Still do, if the tabloids are anything to go by."

I suck in a deep breath, ready to tell her something only my family and Grace know. "My ex is not only in there with her husband, my former friend, but she's pregnant. Likely going to be delivered by either my brother or my best friend since she sought them out to be her OB. How's that for irony?" I roll my eyes. "The only saving grace I have when it comes to Nora is that she never knew I was about to propose. I had the ring in my pocket, ready to drop down onto one knee, but before I could do anything, she told me she was in love with Rob and that we were over."

Amelia sucks in a rush of air, her eyes flashing. Her hand shoots up, covering her parted lips as she stares at me with a combination of shock and sympathy. "God. That's awful."

"The real kicker of all that is I had made a lot of sacrifices for her. A lot. Nearly everything I wanted I had given up for her with the exception of medicine. But I chose NYU to be with her instead of playing ball at Michigan. I finished college in three years instead of four because she said the sooner I can complete med school and residency, the better. Then, on the fucking day I got into Columbia for med school and was set to propose, she informed me she had been cheating on me for the better half of six months."

Six. Fucking. Months!

"Jesus, Oliver. I'm so sorry. I never heard anything about that."

"That's because no one knows, so if you wouldn't mind keeping that to yourself, I'd appreciate it. The last thing I want is for that to hit the press next."

She reaches out her hand, touching my arm and giving me a squeeze. "Of course. I'll never tell anyone. I don't blame you for not wanting to go in there. It seems we both felt like we had something to prove by showing up tonight."

That's not the reason I came tonight. But Nora is the main reason I didn't want to go in. I've successfully avoided seeing her for years. In truth, I've been over her for a long time, just not over what she did to me. Most of my bitterness and resentment is on me. I should never have made those sacrifices for her.

I gave up pieces of myself I can never get back.

But Amelia deserves more. She always has, and she never got it. She deserves to have people look at her and treat her with the respect they never did. They owe it to her. Hell, I owe it to her. I don't want her to leave tonight the way she is now.

"I only wish it had turned out better for us," she continues. "But I think my carriage has officially turned back into a pumpkin and I should just cut my losses and head home. Tonight can't possibly end the way I had envisioned it."

Like a bolt of electricity flowing through me, suddenly I'm giddy with an idea that is quite possibly the most ridiculous idea in the history of ideas. Christa nearly swallowed her tongue when she thought Amelia was my date. So maybe everyone else will react the same way if that's what they see. Bonus for me—I'll have a hot as hell woman on my arm and maybe Nora will leave me alone.

More than that, I *want* to go in there with Amelia. I want to spend more time with her tonight. And if they don't like it or think less of me for it, well, I don't give a shit.

But Amelia being my date isn't enough. Not with my reputation.

They'll just assume I'm using her, because ever since Nora and I split up... I've been somewhat of a player. A fact the media loves to report on. Hell, my face is splashed across the internet every other week, showing me with a different woman each time. Not in the last few months or so, but it's been the standard of my life since Nora. It's the way I keep from getting hurt again.

And the media reporting on it all? Well, that's the standard of all my brothers' lives. It comes with being a Fritz and living in Boston. We own this city. We're royalty. For better or worse, that's how it is.

But if Amelia and I really want to make an impact tonight... if I really want to make all those assholes who hurt Amelia choke, and Nora—who still calls me to tell me *all* her 'happy' news—realize that I've finally and officially moved on from her... it needs to be more than just people thinking I'm dating Amelia.

They need to know she's something special. Believe she's something special *to me*.

My fingers dig back into my pocket, locating that ring. Looking at her... plotting this insane idea... I'm hit with the fact that I know it will change everything. Both for her and for me.

A deviously crooked smile curls up at the corner of my lips.

Yeah. I have an idea, alright. And I think I can get Amelia to go for it. It's only for a few hours anyway. What could go wrong?

Want to know what happens next? Pick up your copy of Doctor Scandalous to find out!

CPSIA information can be obtained
at www.ICGtesting.com
Printed in the USA
BVHW051207060922
646311BV00006B/382